WHAT'S A PARENT TO DO?

WHAT'S A PARENT TO DO?

by

C. S. LOVETT, M.A., B.D., D.D.

Author of

SOUL-WINNING MADE EASY
DEALING WITH THE DEVIL
THE 100% CHRISTIAN

published by
PERSONAL CHRISTIANITY
Baldwin Park, California

CONTENTS

100,000 Prodigal Parents 9

It's tough to be a Teen 10

CHAPTER ONE
Rebellious Parents—Rebellious Children 17

CHAPTER TWO
What Makes a Teen-ager Tick? 27

CHAPTER THREE
The Parent's Second Chance 38

CHAPTER FOUR
The Home—Seminary of Heaven 50

CHAPTER FIVE
Godly Fear—Christian Motivation 63

CHAPTER SIX
Punishment that Penetrates 82

CHAPTER SEVEN
The First Squeeze 98

CHAPTER EIGHT
Increasing the Pressure 118

CHAPTER NINE
Places and Pressure 142

CHAPTER TEN
People and Pressure 163

CHAPTER ELEVEN
The Warning Technique 184

CHAPTER TWELVE
Teens Need Excitement 196

APPENDIX

Two Urgent Questions 217

Your Teen-ager Unsaved? 248

THE MAGIC WORD

(If you've got the courage to use it—and back it up)

In a permissive society it is easier for parents to say, "YES," than handle the guff they get when they say, "NO!" Yet, handling those squawks is vital for Christian guidance. Young people are healthier and happier if they do not get their own way, but learn to handle disappointment. What you do and say in the first FIVE SECONDS after your child asks . . . "WHY NOT?" . . . measures your ability as a Christian parent.

100,000 PRODIGAL PARENTS . . . !

Before I wrote **What's a Parent to Do,** I mailed out 100,000 PC bulletins* to Christian parents and leaders around the country. I invited them to respond to some of my ideas on Christian discipline, with a view to doing a book on rearing children. The Holy Spirit led many to send in their reactions. As you would imagine, some were critical, others were enthusiastic. All were helpful. The Holy Spirit used those letters to shape my approach in this book.

A startling consensus filtered through those letters. Here's what mothers and dads told me:

- A number of fine books for rearing children are already on the market. I didn't need to write another.

- Many confessed to knowing what God expected of them as parents, but since their children hadn't really caused them much trouble, they didn't take any pains to coach them in spiritual matters. They let their kids grow up pretty much by themselves. (Christians, seemingly, confess things in a letter, they won't admit in person.)

- Some admitted substituting love for discipline. They said they knew God demanded discipline, but somehow they couldn't bring themselves to do it, and used reason instead of a stick.

- Most wanted help in knowing what to do with their teens after they had failed to raise them in the discipline of the Lord. With alarming signs now appearing in their lives, they wanted to know what could be done to turn them from worldliness to the way of the Lord.

- Many said they had led their children to Christ, raising them in church and Sunday school. Now they were shocked to see them rebelling against the things of the Lord.

This consensus overruled my original intention. Consequently this is not a manual on how to raise kids in Christ. It deals specifically with teens. It shows how to salvage them for the Lord after parents have goofed. Those with the courage to try the Bible's method of dealing with self-willed teens, will be delighted with the way the Holy Spirit backs their actions.

---

*PC bulletins are monthly newsletters mailed to more than 100,000 key evangelicals across the United States each month.

Introduction

IT'S TOUGH TO BE A TEEN

 A mother and father wanted to go out for the evening. They took their thirteen year old boy to Grandpa's house. As they dropped him off, Grandpa asked . . . "When do you want him back?"

"When he's 19!" replied the father.

Now that father was beginning to feel the pangs of rearing a child through those "terrible teens."

What comes to mind when I say . . . "teen-ager?"

- Strange creatures with a language and music of their own who live on the other side of the generation gap?

- Boys and girls with bewildering ideas about hair, clothes, the value of money and what makes for a good time?

- Insolent youngsters defying authorities, insulting police and vandalizing campuses?

- Hippie types indulging in sex orgies, dope, crime and vigorously protesting every action and tradition of the establishment?

Look Magazine* wanted to know what America thought of its teen-agers. Fletcher Knebel was commissioned to travel the nation sampling the country's mood. His report told what Americans think of "the kids:"

> "The kids, it would seem, have become a symbol of almost everything that alarms and irritates their elders. To hear it from the lips of older America, the kids rob, riot, drop out, seize, mock, utter obscenities, goof off, grow beards, wear long hair, and scorn the noble work on which their parents have built their lives. . . ."

---

*November 18th, 1969

BUT IT'S NOT EASY TO BE A TEEN TODAY.

America's opinion of the "kids," may be justified. But adolescent life is tough. Modern teens grow up in a world very different from that of their father's. Certainly it is different from their grandfather's. It's harder to be a teen now than it was a generation ago. Those born during the atomic age live under the shadow of annihilation. Even worse, instant communication exposes them to the "new morality" which is fast creating a totally permissive society. The world in which young people are now rising has more **influence** on them, makes greater **demands** and is more **competitive** than anything we have known before.

The most difficult time for youngsters is NOT between one and twelve, but between 13 and 19. It is an interval during which they are neither children nor adults. They are "in-betweeners," neither fish nor fowl. It is during this time that they awaken one morning to discover, "Hey! I'm me! I'm growing up into a person!" They are staggered to find themselves blossoming as individuals. Somehow it doesn't seem right for people not to notice. So inexperience leads them to employ outrageous methods for attracting attention to themselves. When that happens, both the teen and his parents suffer "growing pains."

As if discovering himself an individual were not enough, certain other changes take place too:

1 Tremendous PHYSICAL changes occur in the adolescent. One prominent doctor says the changes of the "in-between-years" are as remarkable as birth itself. A lot happens within a person's body when he is acquiring the capacities to be a father or mother. It produces a befuddling gap during which he doesn't know whether to act like a child or an adult. He hangs on to his childish ways with one hand while reaching for maturity with the other. Much of the strange behavior we see in early teens is over-compensation for the awkward feelings they suffer during this time.

2 Some remarkable MENTAL changes are occurring too. With the intellectual capacities developing, they reach

11

a place where they can make their own decisions. It is quite a discovery to find you can think for yourself and act independently of your parents. As soon as youngsters get a taste of this independence, they begin to question the rules and habits of their folks. One way of asserting this new independence is to defy the established order of the home.

Picture the span of years like this:

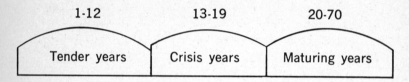

1-12	13-19	20-70
Tender years	Crisis years	Maturing years

During the pre-teen years, 1 to 12, youngsters submit to the authority of their parents almost without question. These are the TENDER YEARS. A parent can do practically anything with a young life during that interval. Then comes the time of explosive change, the years 13 to 19. These are the CRISIS YEARS. During this time personalities mushroom into reality. That is when guidance and Christian counsel is needed most. Finally the young people leave home to enter the years of MATURITY. From 20 to 70 their lives expand according to the truths and principles built into them while under the authority of their parents. The maturing years tell the story of one's success or failure as a Christian parent.

> **NOTE:** This book focuses on the teen-ager. It has little to do with his first twelve years, except as these principles can be applied to pre-teens. Much of the counsel needed to escort a teen-age Christian through his crisis years, can be adapted to younger children. Since little children require little attention in the tender years, they are usually left to grow up by themselves. Few parents bother with any special training for them. If they are not particularly troublesome, they blend into the background of the family's way of life. It is not until they begin to create problems that parents take a hard look at them. The time of serious problems comes when they enter their teens. That's when most parents WANT help. Therefore this book focuses on the crisis years.

Our subject then, is the Christian teen-ager. The target is the crisis years.

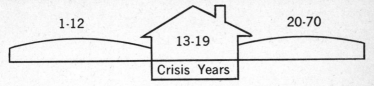

Consider all those adjustments he must make. He doesn't even understand himself. He's not really a child, nor yet is he a man. He's as eager to fly a kite with the kids as he is to drive the family automobile. You'd think his hands would be full trying to cope with all those wild, surging feelings within himself. Oh, if only that were all. He has still more facing him. Even while struggling to know himself, enormous pressures are being exerted from **outside his home.** As if growing up were not enough, today's teen-ager has to endure fantastic external forces. That is why he is often referred to as . . . "something else."

The outside pressures.

● The use of drugs by people under 18 has reached emergency status. Narcotics among teens has jumped 778% in the last two years. **Life Magazine** reports that more than 12 million people have now tried Marijuana, with most of them juveniles.

● The number of arrests of juveniles in this country is frightening. F.B.I. director, J. Edgar Hoover, in commenting on the teen-age crime explosion, said:

> **"A tragic and terrifying consequence of our society is the spiraling waves of youthful lawlessness. Youth crimes have not only increased in number, but also in viciousness. Kids today are showing a total disregard for life and property."**

● The number of arrests of drunken girls has increased by 90.7% in the last two years. Along with dope, alcohol is now a young people's problem.

● But the greatest pressure, by far, is the "new morality," —our country's obsession with sex. Can anyone disagree that our nation is descending into filth? With the Supreme Court opening the doors to pornography and sex acts on the stage, theaters and movies are becoming cesspools. Not only does nudity abound, says **Time Magazine,** but every kind of sexual perversion is now being carried on in plays.*

Sex has become the dividing point between the generations. Thanks to modern birth control methods, the volume of sexual intimacy overshadows anything known a few years ago. Recent demonstrations on the Berkeley campus saw placards reading, "Sleep with a stranger tonight!" Boys at the last Easter blowout at Ft. Lauderdale, Florida, wore tee shirts emblazoned, "Help stamp out virginity!" No wonder Mr. Knebel summed his article in **Look** with these words:

> **"One thing is sure. The boy-girl sexual revolution is deep and wide, and puritan America is gone forever!"**

"No nation in history," says Billy Graham, "has been able to go in this direction and survive for very long. I think the great threat to our democracy is moral decadence."

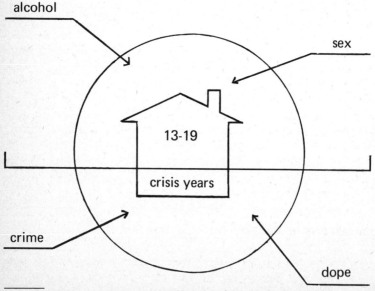

*July 11th, 1969

IS THE CHRISTIAN YOUNGSTER IMMUNE?

"Accepting a date to a drive-in movie is like accepting an invitation to sexual relations."

That was the answer a young girl gave an interviewer taking a survey on teen morals. Sexual promiscuity is already the norm for a huge segment of our society. Today's young people enjoy a privacy unavailable a few decades ago. Many own their own cars at 16. They are stimulated in these drive-in theaters. Wierd sensual music surrounds them. All kinds of pornography can be had at the local drug store. With sex the obsession of their culture, how can they remain immune? To believe that Christian young people can live in a land saturated with filth, dope, crime, and sex—and that it would have no effect on them—is ridiculous.

Young people spend more time **in the world** than they do at home. They find more things which appeal to them away from home, than they do at home. Do they not go to schools for their education, play in the parks or on the streets, eat in snack bars or coffee houses, find their friends on campuses or in clubs, get their books at libraries, and have good times at theaters, amusement centers, and sports arenas—all away from home? Sure they do. Is it really possible for them to spend all of that time in the world and not be affected by it? Hardly.

● Then—as if these mighty forces outside the home were not enough—the teen-ager also has an instinct to CONFORM.

You have a girl 13. At her school other 13 year olds are going steady. Even if she doesn't understand what it is all about, she begs you to let her go steady. Her yearning persists, no matter what you say. She longs to be one of the gang. She'd "rather be dead than different," from other kids. She is more concerned with what those kids at school think than what you think. That is the worst kind of pressure for an emerging adolescent.

SO WHAT'S A PARENT TO DO?

"I feel the control of my boys slipping out of my hands. I don't like it. It frightens me, but what can I do? I don't understand my children and they don't understand me."

A godly mother sobbed that plea to me the other day. She was keenly aware of the world's influence on her teen-age boys. It was greater than anything they got at home or at church. She was frustrated. She felt guilty. She knew God would hold her responsible. She was burdened with fears of failing Him and her boys.

But God has a remedy for every heartache, an answer for every problem. Unknown to her, there was a lot she could do. The simplest answer to the evil forces bearing on young-sters from outside the home, is a return to the principle of **God's authority** within the home. Those external pressures on young people must be met with **greater** pressures as parents dare to act in accordance with God's Word. Spiritual pressures can be awesome if Christian mothers and fathers will make use of their resources and discipline their youngsters as God intends.

In the chapters ahead we will be talking about techniques, methods and mechanics for applying GREATER pressures in the home. There is a lot of know-how to be brought to bear on this matter. No teen can withstand the overwhelming might of the Lord administered by God-fearing parents. But you may have to change, too. If you failed to exercise God's authority for the first 12 years of your child's life, that has to stop. If you want to salvage your boy or girl for Christ, it will be necessary to take an entirely new stand on Christian discipline.

You have resources in Christ that are more than adequate for handling ANY disappointing or rebellious situation in your home. Learning how to USE them **in love** is the secret of get-ting teen-agers through those crisis years safely. This book was written to show you . . . HOW!

Chapter One

REBELLIOUS PARENTS—REBELLIOUS CHILDREN

A 17 year old youth stood before a judge in a Midwestern courtroom. He heard himself sentenced to a stiff prison term for breaking into a house and making off with $6000 in furs and jewelry. After sentencing the boy, the judge asked the lad's father to step into his chambers. They were next door neighbors. The judge wanted to explain.

The father slumped into a chair, his face buried in his hands. He moaned his consternation:

"I don't understand it. His mother and I have given him everything. That boy knows how much we love him. He didn't need the money. Why did he have to steal?"

"That's why I asked you in here, Henry," said the judge. "We've known each other long enough for me to speak freely. I'm sorry to say this, but I've seen this coming for a long time. You hit the nail on the head when you said you've given your boy everything. That's the trouble. You've given him too much. You should have been more selfish with that boy!"

MORE SELFISH . . . !

Any psychologist would tell that father his boy's criminal behavior was due to over-generosity and over-protection. His mother and father did so much for him, he was unable to do anything for himself. Feelings of inadequacy began to develop within him. As the years went by, those feelings became stronger. They finally erupted in the rebellious act of stealing.

That boy **wanted** to be punished. When those who loved him refused to discipline him, he turned to someone who would —**the law.** Of course, he wasn't aware of these feelings. They brewed in his unconscious. As far as he knew consciously, he was miserable and restless. If you asked why he was so out of sorts, he wouldn't be able to tell you. He just ached inside. Everything felt wrong. Without realizing it, the boy longed to lash out at his folks for turning him into a dependent.

17

No teen consciously seeks to avenge himself on his parents by getting into trouble with the law. He is moved by an **unconscious** drive. He doesn't say to himself, "My parents have deprived me of confidence by overprotecting me, so that now I'm afraid to meet the world on my own." What he suffers is unreasoned. It takes place down deep where there is no reasoning or understanding. The strange thing about it is, he still thinks he loves his parents. Inwardly those feelings of love he once had, have since turned to bitterness. No matter how things appeared on the surface, hatred was building within him. Parents who refuse to punish their youngsters in love, earn their hatred regardless of superficial appearances to the contrary.

IT'S HARD FOR PARENTS TO ACCEPT THAT.

Johnny's father was no exception. He didn't like hearing he had been overprotective. Worst of all, he hated to think he had damaged his boy by refusing to discipline him:

> **"Maybe he's seen too much television. You know how much crime there is on TV now. Couldn't that be the reason?"**

But the judge wouldn't let the blame be shifted:

> "Henry, we've been neighbors for years. I've watched that boy grow up. It wasn't easy for me to sentence him today. I'd rather another judge handled the case. But now I must be blunt.
>
> As your neighbor, I know as well as anyone how much you have given your boy. I know you have been devoted to him. But you have withheld from him the one thing he needed for security and development —DISCIPLINE. I know it hurts to have me say that, but it's true. You have deprived your boy of discipline."

Then the distraught father came out with a confession:

> **"We never believed in spankings. We always felt we could convince Johnny with love and reason. I don't really see how you can say this happened because we didn't spank him."**

Poor Johnny

His father and mother had withheld from him the most urgent ingredient for personal development—discipline. Parental discipline is the bedrock of any young person's security. Without it he feels deserted. Apart from it he cannot learn to discipline himself. The goal of all external discipline is, of course, self-discipline. Everyone must be disciplined by others before he can learn to discipline himself.

 Ann Landers, one of the nation's syndicated columnists, often makes this comment about teens:

"Parents do their kids no favor when they let them run wild. Youngsters need to have set limits. It gives them a feeling of security. I feel sorry for teens who can do as they please. They feel, deep down, that nobody loves them enough to insist they behave themselves. Discipline is a special kind of love. Kids know it and want it."

Johnny's soul was starved for discipline. When he performed an evil or belligerent act, he hoped against hope his dad would punish him. He wanted to feel the pain of punishment which would wipe out his guilty feelings. When it was not forthcoming, he became sick in his spirit. A belt applied to his bottom would have brought welcome relief. As it was, his parents tore him apart. Finally, he broke the law hoping it would punish him. As wild as it may seem, Johnny was relieved when the judge pronounced sentence on him. At last someone cared enough to punish him.

YOUNGSTERS WANT PUNISHMENT.

Even toddlers long for discipline. Haven't you watched a little fellow become cranky and out of sorts? He fusses and fumes. You try offering him toys, but he throws them down. Nothing seems to please him. Then you give him a few swats on the bottom and what happens? He settles right down. In moments he is at peace.

Does the toddler reason out such things? Of course not. He is not even conscious of them. Yet, he has a passion for punishment. INTUITIVELY he senses his need for discipline. He doesn't have the ability to reason it. It's an unconscious process. It occurs in that part of a person where there is no reasoning. All a toddler can do is whine, but he is whining for a whipping.

The undisciplined teen gets just as cranky. But he doesn't whine for a whipping. At least not in the same way. His whining is more adult, more consistent with his age. He drops out of school, gets into trouble with the law, lies and steals. Some with this inner ache, refuse to eat. Others dabble in dope and drink. The passion for punishment leads some to keep bad company, stay out till all hours, goof off on wild escapades or join a gang of rebels. There's no pat formula. Your teen may get sassy, sulk, or slam doors. Again he might leave his room in a mess, lose his books at school, or claim to be sick much of the time. He might let his hair grow long or insult you, thinking to force you to discipline him.

WHAT'S AT THE BOTTOM OF IT?

The Holy Spirit. It is the Spirit's job to convict people of sin:

> **"When He is come, He will convict the world concerning sin, and righteousness, and judgment"** (John 16:8).

That applies to everyone, sinner and saint alike. Christians HAVE the Holy Spirit. They receive Him at salvation (Rom. 8:9). But the unsaved are also subject to His convicting power. Without this conviction, no one would ever be saved. His ministry is universal. Whenever ANYONE does wrong, he knows it. Consequently, when a teen disobeys his folks or violates the rules of his home, he is convicted of sin by the Spirit. The moment he does anything he shouldn't, down deep inside him the Spirit says . . . "You deserve to be punished."

> NOTE: While the Holy Spirit convicts ALL men of unrighteousness, His working is more powerful in the Christian. The believer, with his knowledge of spiritual things, has an understanding of what he OUGHT to be in Christ. Hence, the Christian teen is bothered more by the Spirit's witness. By virtue of what he has learned about God's will, he is more alert to what displeases God. The saved teen finds himself convicted of the evil in many things, which might not bother a pagan teen at all. The Holy Spirit's operation in the unsaved person is called, "Pre-salvation illumination." It is treated fully in the author's book, "Soul-Building Made Easy."

No sooner does a boy disobey his parents, than he is convicted by the Spirit. He knows he has sinned and feels guilty. At the same time he senses he should be punished. Like the toddler, he is intuitively aware that punishment will remove his guilt feelings. And it does, as we will see.

But that's not all he feels. He knows his parents should punish him. Why? They are the ones he has sinned against. They represent God's authority in the home. They are the ones to administer punishment. Spiritual instinct tells the Christian lad his mother and father are the PHYSICAL ARM of the Lord. They are the ones who should deal out physical punishment in accordance with the inner witness. Therefore, he EXPECTS them to chasten him.

Look again at the three steps:

1. The Holy Spirit convicts the boy he has sinned. This makes him feel guilty. Those guilt feelings are uncomfortable.
2. He is intuitively aware that punishment will remove those guilty feelings. He yearns for the ache to be taken away.
3. He expects his parents, as God's agents in the home, to punish him and relieve those feelings.

It looks like this:

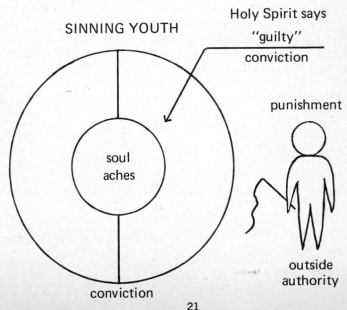

SINNING YOUTH

Holy Spirit says "guilty"

conviction

punishment

soul aches

conviction

outside authority

21

The drawing

See how the Spirit witnesses to the youth's soul? He knows he has sinned. He is convicted. He knows he's guilty and should be punished. He wants to be disciplined.

Then see the parent, whip in hand. He is God's agent to minister punishment. He is the one who can remove those guilt feelings. Thus the youth is aware of two great authorities. There is the Spirit's authority INSIDE him, certifying God's truth to his soul. His parents are God's authority OUTSIDE him to teach and discipline him for the Lord.

Now we see **why** a boy wants his parents to discipline him. He wants them to AGREE with the Holy Spirit. He wants his parents to provide the punishment the Spirit says he deserves. It seems only natural that the OUTWARD authority of God should agree with the INWARD testimony of God. The boy longs for that agreement. It confuses him when the working of God outside of him disagrees with the witness of God inside him. That disagreement produces the ache in his soul.

When parents won't punish.

Parents who REFUSE to discipline their children WAR against the Spirit. The disagreement triggers an alarm in the youngster's soul. At once he feels sick. The contradiction between his parents and the Holy Spirit tears him apart. It shows up in his eyes. He isn't physically sick, though that can come in time. He is emotionally sick. It cannot continue long without taking its toll. When the inner authority of God is at war with the outer authority, it tears at the foundation of a teen's existence. Here's what's happening:

The Spirit says:

>"You have sinned. You deserve to be punished. Your parents, My agents, will now punish you."

The parents say (by their actions):

>"Not so, you don't deserve to be punished. You are a good boy. You haven't really sinned. The Spirit LIES!"

22

Imagine Christian parents calling the Holy Spirit a Liar! But that's what happens.

REBELLIOUS PARENTS PRODUCE REBELLIOUS CHILDREN

It can be a shock for Christians to discover themselves at war against the Holy Spirit. Most love the Word of God and like to think of themselves as submissive to it. However, when it comes to raising their children "as unto the Lord" many are stubborn and resistant. They just won't yield. Some might blush as they read these lines, realizing they are as rebellious against God as their children are against them. The basic cause of rebellion in young people today is the rebellion of fathers and mothers against the Holy Spirit.

Parents cannot defy God in the matter of discipline and get away with it. Punishment of children is a big thing with God. As far as the Lord is concerned, it is urgent. If mothers and fathers defy Him and withhold discipline, they can expect their kids to defy them. Rebellious parents produce rebellious children. How can we be sure? There's no other way to produce them.

> **NOTE:** A harvest of rebellious youngsters is only one of the consequences of parental rebellion against God. God does not wink at disobedience, but "chastens those He loves." Though parents allow their children to be wayward and disobedient, God does not. His hand can be felt in a man's body, his job, and even his family life. More than one Christian father has lost a son or wife through his failure to be the man of God he should. Others have found themselves reduced to desperate circumstances because of this. Many more suffer the anguish of broken hearts.

You can see the ache in kids today.

Undisciplined kids hurt inside. It affects their behavior. Many in our land are absolutely wild. They go about saying, "Peace, brother," because their souls know no peace. They are peace conscious, because their spirits burn so badly. They are mixed up, hungry, almost insane with a craving for kicks and thrills. They are trying to silence the alarm ringing in their souls. They are fleeing an ache which can't be cut out.

Some try to drown the alarm with loud, sensuous music. Surely you've noticed how young people are absorbing weird sounds. Watch the face of a rock singer. See the twisted agony there. See him contort and writhe and shriek forth the pain in his own spirit. He gyrates and screams, reflecting the sickness of his soul. Those gushing emotions come from a pit of despair boiling below the surface. He is himself a tempest. His inner turmoil inspires his style. Young viewers love it. Why? They identify with it. They have the same sickness.

This is why they turn to drugs. They want to numb the pain in the secret place. Take a good look into the eyes of an undisciplined teen. You'll see his agony. Poor miserable creature, he doesn't even know what is driving him to such desperate ends. Neither do his parents. Spoiled youths all have one thing in common—a restless spirit.

My wife just walked in the room and handed me a timely clipping. Listen to what this pitiful young girl wrote to Ann Landers:

"My parents spoiled me rotten. They let me do anything and everything. They let me go any place with anybody. Any kid who thinks life like that is fun, is crazy. I practically raised myself and my life is a mess."

Now there's one youngster who tasted the bitterness of an undisciplined life and says so. Apparently she was trying to sound a warning through Miss Lander's column.

When parents do punish.

When mothers and fathers are faithful to apply discipline as needed, there is instant harmony between their actions and the Spirit's witness inside the boy. It actually feels good to a teen to be punished when he deserves it. His soul enjoys immediate relief. Like the toddler I mentioned earlier, he is at peace. Of course, he doesn't exactly thrill to the spanking, that hurts. Even so, **harmony at the root of his existence** gives him a feeling of security. And that is a great feeling for a teen.

24

Parents who cooperate with the Spirit to punish as directed by the Lord, can produce a youth whose soul is like a rock. When discipline is applied in a way that demonstrates God's love, it has a miraculous effect on one's stability and behavior. A settled assurance comes over that boy. That's why children never turn from parents who discipline them in love. They are themselves the foundation of joy and spiritual health to their children. They are the HEALERS of their souls.

SO GRAB A STICK.

Is that what you are expecting me to say? It does seem to be in order. But we're not ready to talk about sticks, yet. We've only begun to learn what makes teen-agers tick. Until we get the complete picture, we shouldn't speak of punishment. Just whipping a boy won't bring peace to his soul. There's more to it than that—a lot more. We'll come to the matter of discipline soon enough. First, we must dig deeper into what makes a teen tick. That's next.

This book was written for Christian parents raising Christian teens. It assumes all parties to be safe in Christ. However, it is possible a non-Christian parent could be reading these lines. If so, I should caution you that the principles and techniques found in the pages ahead, require close cooperation with the Holy Spirit. This book was designed for those who are ready to trust the Lord to back their actions with the witness of His Spirit.

Therefore, if you are one who has not yet received Christ as your personal Savior, you will NOT be able to use this book. If you are honestly concerned for the way your son or daughter is turning out, you should consider God's free offer to save you—right now. It is as simple as opening a door. Get alone in a place where you can speak out to Him directly. He'll hear you. Pray like this:

> **"Dear Lord, I can see that my kids are on the road to ruin and I don't want them to end up in hell—eternally. I don't want to go there either. So if you really are willing to save me, I here and now open my heart to You and ask You to come into my life. Amen."**

If you can do that, and mean it, Jesus will come in—**instantly!** You'll feel the peace He gives and it is fantastic! After that, you can ask Him for the wisdom and backing you need to salvage your teens from the terror ahead of them. He'll give that, too. You can check the back of the book for the way to bring your children to Christ. It will be more meaningful however after you learn of the great authority God has given you as a parent.

Chapter Two

WHAT MAKES TEEN-AGERS TICK?

On a midwestern farm, a young lad turned a rifle on his mother and father and older brother. Though he was not yet a teen, he deliberately shot them to death. Do you suppose those parents dreamed their "little angel" would one day hate them enough to kill them? Did they suspect that the little bundle which once cooed in his crib, would also stare in hatred at them over a rifle barrel?

You've held a new baby in your arms. Did it seem possible a devilish nature resided in that infant? When you consider how cuddly he was, it seemed unthinkable he was already equipped to do evil. Just below that innocent surface lurked a nature dominated by Satan, just waiting to manifest itself. Did not the mothers of Adolf Hitler, Joseph Stalin, and Al Capone, peer lovingly into the faces of their infants? How they would have laughed had someone told them the devil was at home in those little darlings.

Every child is born with an evil nature.* Adam saw to that. His fall gave the devil dominion over human nature. We have only to consider that all murderers, sex fiends, embezzlers and hardened criminals were little babies once. There is no way to hide the fact that the nature of every child is subject to Satan. It emerges almost instantly after birth. Unless held in check by the parents, it surfaces with increasing devilishness.

Let's track the emergence of a child's nature.

- When he's brand new, he doesn't care what time he gets you up. All he knows is he's hungry. He wants you to wait on him. All babies are selfish by nature. They want only for themselves. They start off that way. They stay that way. Increasingly they fuss for what they want, and insist you get it for them.

---

*See the author's book, SOUL-BUILDING MADE EASY, for a complete discussion on human depravity through the fall of Adam and how the human spirit is under control of Satan. The book also shows how God's remedy is a new nature imparted to those who receive Christ as Savior. A knowledge of the Christian's two natures is absolutely essential to understanding God's working in man, as well as offering the key to many critical passages in the Word of God.

- At eighteen months he goes in the opposite direction when you call him. Ask him to put something in your hand and he is apt to throw it on the floor or put it behind him. By that, he is saying, "You can't have it, it's mine." When he starts talking, "No" becomes one of his chief words.

- At 2½ he wants exactly **what** he wants, **when** he wants it. He won't give in. He refuses to budge from his demand. You can't get him to change his mind. Everything has to be done his way. He can be domineering, even demanding. He tries to order his parents about. If he wants mother to do something, he won't let father do it instead. He finds the tantrum a swell device for getting his own way.

- By the time he's four, he's biting, throwing rocks, breaking toys, and running away. He shows anger and resentment when you stop him at play in order to get dressed or go to the bathroom.

- Six year olds display their natures with such words as "I hate you," or, "I'll kill you." It should be no surprise when a child of 11 or 12 actually does it. He has the capacity and will power. An undisciplined child can be seriously neurotic by five or six.

        . . . and so on.

The "Spock" generation behaviorists say it is normal for kids to do such things, that they are merely letting off steam. They call it a "phase" which will be outgrown in time. DON'T YOU BELIEVE IT. We are now reaping the harvest of that kind of thinking on our streets and campuses. This is what the devil wants parents to think. He authored the notion that punishing and disciplining youngsters scar their little personalities. It's stupid to think a Satan-dominated nature can be allowed to go unchecked. No, it's **dangerous.**

God's Word demands children be disciplined. Experience reveals they become "sick" when they are not. Why? Satanic pressure is exerted upon them to yield to their evil natures. Since that fallen nature is under the dominion of the devil, submitting to it is the same as yielding to the devil himself. Satanic control leads to all forms of sickness. The Bible uses pretty strong words when speaking of those with one nature, that old nature which is opposed to God:

A captive of Satan (Eph. 2:2)
Cannot receive the truth (1 Cor. 2:14)
Cannot believe in the Lord (John 12:39)
Cannot please God (Rom. 8:8)
Cannot come to Christ without the Spirit's help (John 6:44)
A slave to sin (Titus 3:3).

One could go on and on about the awfulness of the old nature. Because of it, people do terrible things. The nicest boy (or girl) you know has this nature which could lead him into the worst crimes of history. So thoroughly evil is it, the devil leads susceptible youths into actions which break their parent's hearts. Outwardly it seems a child is rebelling. Actually, though, he is being led by Satan through his own nature. More frightening, is the fact that Satan can lead young people to adopt his own attitude toward God.

> **NOTE:** It is easy for Satan to lead self-willed boys and girls into evil. Why? The self-centered life is the same as a Satan-centered life. This truth is developed in the author's book, DEALING WITH THE DEVIL, which shows how the spirit of Satan operates under the guise of SELF. Every Christian should be equipped to detect Satan's working through the spirit of self and ready to deal with him defensively. God's Word promises, "Resist the devil and he will flee from you" (James 4:7). Teen-agers desperately need to be equipped with the anti-satan skill. DEALING WITH THE DEVIL offers a 4-step plan for detecting the devil's presence and putting him to flight.

EVIL NATURE—EVIL CHILD?

 A non-Christian mother had two sons. One became an outstanding citizen, the other a criminal who had to be put away from society.

How could two men with the same parents turn out so differently? The difference was NOT due to their natures, for they both had IDENTICAL natures. The old nature is the same in every person—fully corrupt. Why then the great difference in people?

Herein lies a useful truth.

There is a big difference between HAVING a depraved nature and SUBMITTING to it.

It is one thing to possess the fallen, adamic nature, quite another to yield to it. Thus, we distinguish between a person's WILL and his NATURE. They are not the same. God does not send children into this world with natures which control their personalities. That would be awful. Such a thing would guarantee that each person would be 100% controlled by Satan. Such is not the case. God has given each person a WILL, and the will is sovereign in all things. God Himself will not violate it. Therefore, Satan has no power over anyone's will. He can only APPEAL to it. But he is able to present enticing appeals to the will because of his control of the old nature.

The difference in human personality is due to the way the children learn to HANDLE and control their natures. The degree to which a child is taught to discipline himself, so as NOT to obey the promptings of his old nature, to that SAME DEGREE he is an orderly child. Those who learn self-discipline, end up as nice children. Those who don't, become delinquent. Therefore, observe this:

The degree to which a person submits to his Satan-dominated nature— to that degree will his behavior be directed by the devil.

It can be shown like this:

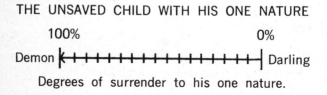

THE UNSAVED CHILD WITH HIS ONE NATURE

Degrees of surrender to his one nature.

See the differences in degree of surrender? The unsaved child, because of his free will does NOT have to submit to the devil's coaxing **if he doesn't want to.** The more a child is taught to resist the evil impulses rising within him, the nicer he is. On the other hand, the child who yields to those impulses (satanic compulsions), can be cruel and selfish. One who is very self-controlled is a darling child, whereas one who is utterly undisciplined, is a little demon. Depending on how a lad is raised, he will resist or submit to the suggestions coming from his Satan-dominated nature. Again, this is the unsaved child, who has only the fallen, adamic nature.

NOTE: Discipline must be TAUGHT. There is no way for a child to teach himself to be good. The impulses of his nature are evil ONLY. This is why Billy Graham's quote is true . . . "You don't have to teach a child to be bad!" The tendency to do good is NOT present within the child. It has to be PUT THERE from the outside. Self-discipline, therefore, comes as the result of EXTERNAL discipline. Discipline must first be IMPOSED on a child before he can learn how to discipline himself. How a youngster turns out depends on the way he is taught to resist the evil surging within him. Children left to their own, grow up like weeds. The evil seed is there. Given the opportunity, it will appear and blossom.

● Do we not see young people who are upright and honorable even though they are not born again? Indeed. There are many wonderful men and women in our country who do not know Christ. Some unsaved parents are wonderful disciplinarians. They are careful to raise their children in such a way they learn how to discipline themselves. Yet, these are NOT HOLY people. They are not at all godly. Until a child receives Christ, there is no way for him to be holy, for it takes a **godly nature** to be a godly person. There is no way to acquire that nature apart from receiving Christ, the Holy One of God.

THE GODLY CHILD.

 A child evangelism teacher has just finished her lesson. It's time for the invitation:

"May I see the hands of those who want to receive the Lord Jesus? Lift them up, I'll see them."

Hands go up. All other students are dismissed. The teacher gathers her little respondents around her. As far as anyone can tell, they are genuinely sincere. Some 10 year olds bow their heads and ask Jesus to come into their hearts.

When the experience is genuine, the children receive the Holy Spirit. At once they are equipped with a NEW nature. God does not perform any repair work on the old nature. He gives Christians a brand new one instead. Then the Christian has **two** natures. He retains his old Satan-dominated nature, even though he receives a new one dominated by the Holy Spirit. The apostle Paul labels the Christian's two natures "old man" and "new man" (Eph. 4:22, 24).

The new nature is Christ's own nature, produced by Him during His sinless life on earth. As surely as those born of Adam (the human race) receive the old nature by physical birth, those born of Christ receive the new nature by spiritual birth. That's why the Bible describes it as:

Born of the Spirit (John 3:8)
It cannot sin (I John 3:9)
Created in righteousness and true holiness (Eph. 4:24)
As righteous as Christ Himself (I John 3:7)
Those receiving it become partakers of the divine nature (II Peter 1:4).

● At once a new dimension of behavior opens to the child. He now has a nature which PROMPTS him to please God. Holy impulses stir within him. The degree to which he submits himself to the appeals of his new nature, to that same degree he will manifest the personality of Christ. Whereas before salvation his behavior could range from DARLING to DEMON, now he can go in the Godward direction ranging from DARLING to DIVINE. The total range of his behavior now looks like this:

THE PERSON WITH TWO NATURES

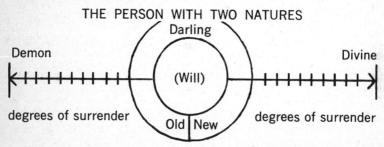

Once a child acquires the new nature, the Holy Spirit has access to His will. That is, HE can make APPEALS to the will through **the new man,** just as Satan appeals through **the old man.** This child now has a built-in TENDENCY to do what is right in God's sight. Please note it is a **tendency only.** There is nothing about the new nature which overrides the human will, any more than there is about the old nature. A person's will remains sovereign regardless of his two natures. God's program is based on man's FREEDOM OF CHOICE.

NOTE: Having the new nature no more guarantees a boy will be holy, than having the old guarantees he will be bad. Put another way, having the new nature no more makes a person completely holy, than having the old nature makes him fully evil. Neither nature is allowed to dominate the will. A man is holy or evil ONLY to the degree to which he submits to either nature. A Christian 100% yielded to his old nature would still manifest the personality of the devil, whereas one surrendered 100% to the new nature would manifest the personality of the Lord.

 Here's a new baby in a bassinette. See how feeble he is, how helpless? He has scarcely any strength at all. A new Christian is like that. The moment he opens his heart to Jesus, he begins a new life. He starts out as a spiritual infant. Though his new nature has come from God, it is weak and must grow. His old nature had to develop when he arrived in the world. Now it's the new nature's turn.

The older a person is BEFORE he comes to Christ, the bigger head start the old nature enjoys. If a boy comes to Jesus when he is twelve, the old nature has a 12 year advantage. That, of course, gives Satan more to use in appealing to the boy's will. On the other hand, there is NOTHING in the Christian's new nature, until someone PUTS it there. It is urgent that parents get as much spiritual material as they can into the new nature fast. The more that is on deposit, the more the Holy Spirit has to use in presenting suggestions to the child's will. There is no way around it, those earlier years without Christ give Satan a whopping advantage.

NOTE: Children should hear exciting stories from God's Word and those stories should be filled with as much drama and emotion as possible. Their imaginations are so vivid, they should be made to burn with the Christian adventure. Little ones are capable of wonderment as they hear about Jesus. Therefore, they should soak up all possible experiences connected with the Gospel. They should bow their heads at mealtime; hear praise and thanksgiving on their parent's lips; Christian music should ring in their hearts. A great deal of godly material can be stored in them which the Spirit will use later on. Godly training in the early years reduces the devil's advantage.

THE DEVIL'S ADVANTAGE

Usually a child can make a good decision for Christ by the time he is ten. You know some who were saved earlier than that. So do I. Then there are those who can't make a good decision until twelve or so. But ten years seems a fair point for the early decision. Even so, 10 years is a big head start for Satan. A lot of selfishness and wilfulness can accumulate in the old nature during that time.

 Consider the boy who is saved at twelve. Think of all the TV he has seen. His imagination is loaded with lust, violence, crime, and lawless adventure. Think of all the things he has heard at school, the whispered evil that flowed in "behind the barn" conversations. What of the LIES in advertising, corruption in politics, the sexy ads in newspapers, and the lurid pictures at the newsstands. Imagine all the wicked material that has passed before his eyes and ears filling his old nature with inflammables for Satan to use.

The more a boy watches TV, hangs around with that certain crowd, browses the magazine rack at the drug store, the bigger his "old man" becomes. His old nature is full of passions and feelings which the devil can use to fire suggestions into his mind. With the ideas so exciting, there is no way for a teen to resist them. What is there on the new nature's side that is EQUALLY EXCITING? Nothing—unless you put it there. Chances are you haven't. Likely all your boy or girl has is some Bible theory. Sure, he has some vague ideas about salvation. He believes heaven exists and one day he will end up there. He might even have a few Bible doctrines stored. But how does that material compare with the explosive, flesh satisfying stuff in his old nature? It doesn't—and you know it.

This may not seem so urgent as long as a child is a preteen. Parents are fooled by the fact that pre-teens accept their authority so readily. They think the child is coming along nicely in the Lord. So the follow-up is neglected. Then, when the kids enter their crisis years — pow! The devil's advantage shows up in one explosion after another. When that sex drive awakens and new energies rage within their personalities, Satan's appeals to those kids are many times greater than that of the Holy Spirit. Then the parents wonder what went wrong.

THE NEW NATURE NEEDS THAT AMMUNITION

Let's say you have a daughter. She made her decision for Christ when she was 11. Now she's a sophomore in high school. At one time she enjoyed Sunday school, but lately her interest has shifted to a circle of friends at school. She doesn't even know whether they are Christians or not. They don't discuss such things in that crowd. It bothers you that she prefers these worldly friends to the Christian young people at church. This new trend in her life is obviously away from the things of the Lord. It has you concerned.

Then your church announces a special meeting for teens. A gifted youth worker is scheduled to speak. This would be terrific for your daughter, you think. Perhaps he might be able to reach her. Maybe he will say something that would change her direction back to the Lord. Down deep you know that is wishful thinking. But you don't really know what else to do.

Unfortunately, there's a school function scheduled that same night. All of her gang will be there, especially the boys.

Yes, she's noticed them. So far you haven't put much into your daughter's life spiritually. Oh, she's heard a few Bible stories and memorized some Scripture verses in the past. But she's never really been involved in the excitement of the Holy Spirit or the thrill of witnessing for Jesus. You've sort of left it up to her and the church to take care of that. In fact, you've left so much up to her, it appears getting her to this special meeting will also have to be left up to her. You'd like her to go, but it's now beyond you to insist:

> "Darling, there's a special youth program at the church this Friday night. They're going to have a terrific youth speaker, a man who specializes in teen problems. I'm sure it would put something vital into your life, and I would like for you to go. I know you have something going on at school that same night, but I believe this would be better for you."

What do you think she'll do? There's little doubt about that. She will attend the school affair. Why? Satan has more going for his suggestion than the Holy Spirit has with your appeal to go to church. The same would be true of your boy, if the choice were between a church affair and a trip to the lake. What is there in the new nature for the Spirit to use in combating the devil's appeals? What does the Spirit have to use in overruling the desires of the flesh? Nothing—unless you put it there. But that's the problem, you haven't done that.

The strength of the new nature, you see, is no greater than the SPIRITUAL EXCITEMENT built into the new Christian. Just as the "weakness of the flesh" is the strength of Satan, so is the "fire" of the new man, the strength of God in a teen's life. The more godly enthusiasm that is kindled in a lad, the more thrilling appeal the Holy Spirit can make to his will. Young people have to be "turned on" for Christ. If not, they will be "turned on" by the devil. Parents should think about that.

What is there in the new nature of the Christian teen to match the excitement of hot rods and way out clothing styles? What can compete with being "IN" with the crowd at school? I could go further and ask, what is there on deposit in the new nature for the Spirit to use in competing against LSD, sex-orgies, and criminal escapades? Christian teens run into these things. Unless mothers and fathers kindle a spiritual bonfire in the new nature, a teen has very little chance of spiritual survival today. We'll talk more about that in a later chapter.

WAIT A MINUTE . . . !

"Hey! How come your telling me what I should have done! I can't go back and correct the mistakes I made. I need help with my kids now. I'm worried about the present situation."

Really? Do you honestly want help in dealing with the trends showing up in your teens? If God gave you a second chance would you take it? All right, let's see if you mean business. Your second chance is coming up—next.

Chapter Three

THE PARENT'S SECOND CHANCE

 I was raised in the San Joaquin Valley where great irrigation ditches scar the countryside. My brother and I would roam those brush covered gulleys in the dry season. On one occasion we stopped where two tiny trees had just begun to grow. They were close to each other. For a lark, we tied them together. Twenty years later, I had an opportunity to return to that same spot. There they were—just as we had left them. Only now their huge trunks were entwined. Every time I hear the expression—"as the twig is bent, so grows the tree"—I think of those twisted trunks.

Human lives can be shaped in the same way. The early training of a youngster stays with him all of his life—and into eternity. It was this fact which inspired the noted missionary, Francis Xavier. He became inflamed with the idea of shaping children and it brought him great success in India. Today he is most famous for his words which memorialize his passion for settling youngsters in the faith . . .

"Give me the children until they are seven and anyone can have them afterwards."

Xavier had a package. That's the only reason I mention him here. He developed a complete catechism designed to capture young lives. Then he aggressively installed it in the children on his mission field. Before long a multitude of seasoned Catholics were found all over India. His method was so successful, the Roman Church adopted it to spread its mantle over the Far East. Masses of heathen were brought into Catholicism as the result of Xavier's system. His work is an outstanding example of what can be done by installing a package of spiritual truth in a child.

WHEN SHOULD PARENTS START?

 A young Christian mother asked her pastor when she should begin serious spiritual training for her young son.

"How old is he?" asked the pastor.

"He's just turned five," she said.

"Then you are already five years too late," was his reply.

Those familiar with God's Word know He insists we train our offspring from the cradle. The reason is obvious. You can move slowly with small children, taking your time. Almost no pressure is needed. Tender little minds bend to influence. They are happy to receive spiritual truths from their fathers and mothers. Love and respect make them WANT to **believe every word.**

Some children receive Christ when they are six years old. Certainly any child can experience Him by the time he is nine. Even if it doesn't occur until a child is ten, that still leaves two good years, two tender years in which to instruct him. Until kids reach the age of rebellion, you can plant all the godly truths you want. There is no challenge or opposition, and you can take your time. The truths can be installed one by one. Since there is no hurry, you can wait for the results to appear. By the time a youngster is twelve, quite a package of truth should be in operation.

When a boy is twelve, he should be **spiritually equipped** to meet the forces due to awaken within him. If the right truths have been installed, he will also be ready to handle the **external** pressures of sex, crime, dope, alcohol—as well as the worldly suggestions of the kids at school. By this time, he should desire God's approval so much, it can offset the natural desire to want the approval of the other youngsters at school. The father who equips his boy with a spiritual anchor (package of godly truth) can look forward to an exciting time with him as he enters those "terrible teens." It can be thrilling to watch the seed you sowed during his pre-teen years, burst forth as he reaches for manhood.

But alas . . .

This year many Mid-western schools were closed due to an extremely heavy blizzard. The children were forced to stay home. It caused near panic among the mothers. They didn't know what to do with them. It upsets their routine. They definitely didn't regard it as a wonderful time to put the things of the Lord into their lives. To the contrary, the school board was deluged with complaints. Irate mothers demanded the city find some way to keep the kids at school, even though no classes were in session.

Are Christian parents an exception? Sadly, no. They don't prize those pre-teen years any more than the unsaved. Oh sure, they want their children to learn about the world they live in. They would even like for them to BE SOMEBODY in that world. But it doesn't occur to them they are throwing away the child's chance to be somebody in the NEXT world. They let the easiest time for installing God's truth pass without a second thought. It is a rare Christian who devotes himself to putting a complete package of spiritual knowledge into his youngster's life.

Why is this? Most parents adopt the "furniture" philosophy, "Little children should be seen and not heard." That reduces them to the level of chairs. They are wanted only when needed. Because their hearts are so tender and submissive, it is easy to force them into the family routine and make them stay there, unnoticed. Like the rest of the furniture, they blend into the background.

In the average Christian home, if a child doesn't make a nuisance of himself or disturb the routine in some way, he is allowed to grow up pretty much by himself. Not infrequently does one hear . . . "Mother's busy now, you go outside and play." Or a busy dad replies, "Later son, later." Christians are so busy doing their own thing, they scarcely give thought to "twig bending." Some are relieved when their kids reach school age. Then the city becomes the "baby-sitter."

And if that were not enough . . .

Many Christians consider their job done when the child is saved. They feel almost no responsibility after that. "The Lord can take it from there," they say. So they relax. If anything more is needed, the Sunday school can give it to them. They have no burden to forward them in the Christ-life or get them ready for the judgment. They may have all kinds of worldly ambitions for their children, but they lack any **spiritual ambition** to see them get ahead in the next life.

But parental responsibility CANNOT be shifted to the church. Few Sunday schools are geared to transplanting a godly package in young lives. Those that are, don't have the time. A few minutes a week, filled with interruptions, announcements and nice stories, can't make a dent in the task. This isn't to say they shouldn't go to Sunday school. Of course they should. Children need all the inspiration they can get. But the young person whose spiritual coaching is limited to Sunday school teachers is to be pitied. They can't give him nearly enough. The HOME is the place for bending twigs, not the Sunday school.

● How careful we are to see that our youngsters get a good education. We want them to get ahead **in the world.** We think it only right they learn how to handle themselves properly and get along socially. We're particularly happy if they can enjoy the things we missed when we were kids. On the surface, at least, it appears we want the best for our kids. But we mean the best of THIS life only. When it comes to seeing that they get ahead in Christ, we fail them utterly. We carefully install good manners for this life, but ignore the graces needed in the next. We don't bother to install any spiritual ambition in them. Then — when they hit those bewildering teens — we reap the consequences of our folly.

THE CONSEQUENCES . . . ?

All at once your boy is 13. His body strengthens rapidly. He takes pride in that. He finds he can think for himself. He can make up his own mind about things. He now thinks his way of doing things is better than yours. He's ready to argue about it. If you disagree, resentment shows on his face. A 13 year old doesn't mask his feelings.

Then he starts taking an interest in the world about him. It may begin with sports or activities at school. He receives different opinions from others. No longer is he sure you are right about everything, even if your way is God's way. When your ideas don't coincide with those of his teachers or the kids at school, he doesn't hesitate to challenge them. He begins to question your position on matters that really count. That wouldn't be so bad, except he seems to prefer the opinions of others. **He'd rather conform to his own generation.** The approval of the "crowd" means more to him now.

At first the rebellion is confined to little things. It may even seem cute at first. He tests your tolerance more and more. Within a short time, he is no longer interested in your counsel, the more so when it is spiritual counsel. He has his own "philosophy," as he calls it. His ambition now is to be with the other kids, have a good time, and do his own thing. Then it hits you—**"He's headed away from the Lord!"** When you take a hard look at the symptoms appearing in his life, it's rather frightening. What you are seeing is nothing more than the harvest of your own disobedience.

Harvest? Of course. There is a Law of the Harvest. What a man sows, he also reaps. It's God's inexorable law that we get back, in MULTIPLIED form, precisely what we plant. This applies, not only to what we sow in the ground, but also in the lives of our children. If we sow neglect, we end up watching their misspent lives. If we sow a healthy package of spiritual truth, we reap the glorious fruit of dedicated lives. We always get back what we plant. You know how one watermelon seed produces a whole vine of melons.

That's my point. If we fail to train our children as God demands, we will behold the consequences in their lives. We won't see it while they are still in their pre-teens. But as soon as they pass over the 12 year barrier, the harvest of neglect will appear. It is not hard to recognize the seed we have planted. The crop that blossoms betrays our failure as a Christian parent. I'll list some of the harvest of parental failure. Maybe you can guess which seed was sown.

THE HARVEST OF DISOBEDIENCE

1. Your child now questions your instructions. He challenges your right to insist on his obedience. He demands an explanation every time he can't do what he wants to do. If your explanation doesn't hold water in his eyes, he doesn't see why he should go along with you.

2. He complains it is no FUN to go to church. It doesn't seem fair, he says, for you to make him go when he doesn't want to. He'd much rather attend some sporting event, putter with his hobby, or mess around with the kids. Anything is better than going to church, even staring at a TV set. Christ is not one of his major interests.

3. You are not happy with his choice of friends. They are not the kind he should take up with. You are sure they are not Christians, at least

42

there is nothing about them to indicate otherwise. You wonder about their talk and the suggestive ways in which they kid around. What's worse, these non-spiritual friends seem more important to him than any of God's people—or the Lord Himself.

4. There's an occasional defiance of your authority. There is hostility and rebellion when you announce what the Lord wants from his life. He resents it. You can see it. He seems determined to go his own way, whether you like it or not. Only his dependence on you for financial support keeps him in tow. If he had his own money, you probably couldn't deter him from doing as he pleased. Your influence is getting weaker all the time.

5. That which saddens you most, is his unabashed preference for the ways of the world. He admits his passion for worldly things. As he moves further and further from spiritual things, the direction of his life becomes clearer. That frightens you. You wonder about the salvation decision he made earlier. His future with Christ doesn't look so bright at this point. If he really is born-again, and things keep on as they are, he is likely to enter heaven a "second-class citizen." And it is the next life that counts.

● Of course, you never dreamed things would turn out like this. Had you known what was coming, you might have acted differently. But that's the way every harvest works. You can't see what you've planted until it bursts from underground. You don't suspect the consequences of your parental neglect while it is germinating. It cooks just below the surface, waiting for your boy to enter his teens. When the crisis years come, the harvest of your neglect begins to appear. Your failure to **plant a spiritual package** during his pre-teens produced the frightening crop of worldliness you now see.

Don't blame the boy. He had nothing to do with it. You are the one who disobeyed. You shunned the task God gave you. You forgot he was God's child and not yours. There was plenty of time for you to get a package working in his life, but you simply didn't bother. Now you're faced with the sickening consequences of your own disobedience. It's not a pretty sight, is it?

The telephone rings. The sheriff's office is calling. They have your 14 year old son at the station. They want you to come and pick him up. He was in a car with some other teens when it was stopped by officers.

There was alcohol in the car. Your boy wasn't drinking, but he was in the company of those who were. Since he is so young and an "innocent" member of the party, they don't want to book him.

An innocent victim? You certainly would like to think so. You're ready with excuses for him. You're ready to defend him. But he was there. He knew the kind of people he was with. He preferred that crowd or he wouldn't have been there. Why did he think it was OK to be with this bunch? There was no SPIRITUAL ALARM within him to WARN him he was in danger. Any boy who is truly headed for heaven, has no business with such an alien gang. Had a godly package been installed in him, he never would have been in that car. His fear of God would have warned him away.

● Many a mother has sobbed out a broken heart as she met disappointment in her teen-age son or daughter. Godly parents are pierced with sorrows when their youngsters turn from Jesus to worldliness. A sick feeling comes when you realize your children are NOT going to live for Christ. Again, that's the harvest of **your** disobedience, not theirs. When you fail to **train them up** in the way they should go, there is nothing to keep them from going their own way. You know how deadly that can be:

> "There is a way which seemeth right unto a man, but the end therefore are the ways of death" (Prov. 14:12).

To avoid such pain, one must install biblical truths when his children are tender. Molding them according to God's Word is EASY when they are little. Your methods can be ever so gentle. But you didn't do that. Now you are reaping the consequences. Your children have entered their teens. Now you must watch their spirituality fade as the evil of this world creeps in and takes over.

BUT CHEER UP—you have a second chance!

The very fact that this book is in your hands is evidence God is giving you a second chance. If your children are still under your roof, there's a lot you can do. You can still make a penetration with the truth. It's not too late. But I won't deceive you—**it won't be easy.** If you're looking for an easy answer, you won't find it here. There is no painless way to cope with the teen-age harvest you have sown. A look at the chart below shows that. The painless period is behind you. If you are going to salvage your teens, it will have to be during the CRISIS years.

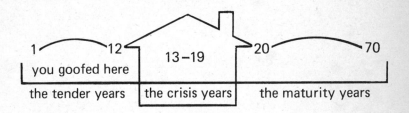

See what you're up against. When you have to do in the CRISIS YEARS what you should have done during the TENDER YEARS, it's bound to be rough. You can't check the mounting forces in your child with a few polite words. You don't reverse rebellion and resentment with scoldings and light taps. When teens suffer the explosion of drives INSIDE them and carnal pressures OUTSIDE, it has to be met with the POWER OF GOD . . . **in your hands!** To revamp a dissident teen-ager is like trying to reverse the Colorado River.

Even so, it has to be done. Instead of the gentle persuasions you could have used earlier, you must now employ shocking methods. Now that you have waited until the "terrible teens" to begin your obedience, events are going to be abrupt and startling. Yet, if you really care—if you earnestly wish to salvage that boy or girl for Jesus, you'll do what you have to.

So take heart. There's a lot you can do. The techniques you are going to read may seem revolutionary, but I assure you they are as old as God's Word. The strangeness will be because we don't see God's Word obeyed today. I want you to face this matter as squarely as you can. You know it will take drastic measures to instill life changing truths in youngsters already challenging your authority. So get ready to use greater pressures and stricter measures to counter the ungodly tendencies showing up in their lives.

You will have to be firm.

Inasmuch as you are dealing with rebellious wills, you can see how the gentler, softer methods of dealing with little children cannot apply. It might be distressing to hear that. You may shrink from the stern measures I am going to suggest, thinking it would cause you too much pain to use them. Ah, but is it any less painful to see those precious lives going to waste? Are you not already suffering as they turn away from the Lord Jesus? That isn't easy to bear, is it?

Though you may be a little shocked at the disciplines I will propose, I asure you doing things God's way is FAR LESS painful in the long run. The Holy Spirit wonderfully soothes your suffering when you are in God's will. He will be your "Comforter," from the first moment you determine to do what He expects of you. You'll never be sorry for taking the action needed to salvage your boy or girl for Christ.

● Now then, isn't it comforting to know it's not too late, that God has a plan for dealing with teens. Sure it is. Even if your son has his bags packed and is ready to move out, you can still put some truth in his life—if you know how. But should your boy or girl be only 16 or 17, you could have as much as a year or two in which to install an entire package. All it takes is the courage to do what you must do. When we come to the PLAN for installing the truths, you'll see how a year or two can be a long time. Now that this book has reached your hands, you have a second chance.

> **CAUTION:** Your boy might enter his teens with no problems other than a lack of interest in spiritual things. Beware! The temptation will be to handle him as you did when he was younger and keep on ignoring God's requirement to TRAIN him up in the way of the Lord. It would be the easiest thing to let him go on through his teens as a "good boy," forgetting he is also GOD'S BOY. You might be proud of him because he does well at school, attends church regularly, and causes no trouble. If, on top of that, he is diligent, courteous, and obedient, you could mistake his **respectability** for **spirituality.** The temptation to neglect the spiritual development of a "good boy" is very great. It would be awful for you to feel satisfied as a parent and let him face the rest of his life without the truth package he needs.

46

SO GRAB YOUR SECOND CHANCE.

There won't be a third. Once that boy (or girl) leaves home, there will not be another thing you can do to salvage him for Christ. You will be all through as a parent. When he goes out that front door, it will close on your last opportunity to do what God requires. Picture yourself at the Judgment Seat of Christ trying to explain why you allowed your boy to leave without the Christian basics at work in his life? Perhaps that thought doesn't move you at all. But I assure you, when it happens, you'll be moved—to tears.

But what about your boy? If you have no fear of judgment as a parent, think what is going to happen to your boy. He is going to reap the consequences of YOUR disobedience. If he departs from your home without spiritual truths working in his life, those next 50 years will be wasted—**as far as God is concerned.** Oh, he may marry a nice girl and enjoy a decent life, as men measure things, but he will come to the end of his days with no treasure laid up in heaven and a spiritual infant besides. Instead of maturing during those 50 years, he will enter heaven a pauper in the sight of God. See it like this:

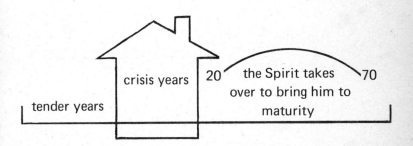

See that 20 to 70 year interval? That's when God takes over to finish the job you start in the home. He counts on you to get certain truths working. Then, when your boy leaves home, He will use the rest of the years to bring him to maturity—if those truths are operating in him. If not, he will go through the rest of his life simply existing. He will come to the end of his days completely unprepared to live with Jesus. He will not be equipped for heaven. Instead, he will be a casualty. He will come before the Lord empty-handed. He will enter eternity "flat broke." There is no way for him to reap a spiritual harvest if you refuse to sow the spiritual seed in his life.

But—when God has a "truth package" to use during the 20-70 span, it is a different story. He can then send testings and trials into a young life and they will do some good. The boy will react to them according to the way he has been taught. God can then use situations and circumstances to mold him after the likeness of Christ. The Christian who is equipped with the basics of the faith life, is brought closer and closer to Jesus as the years go by. He learns to accept every testing as from the hand of God. And it refines him. The package makes it possible for God to get a man ready for eternity.

When parents fail to give the Holy Spirit those basics to use during the 20-70 year interval, it is unlikely a man will discover them for himself. It is a rare person who does. Therefore, they must be installed before a youth leaves home. But you say, "Are there not cases where people have become interested in the Word and equipped themselves with the truths later on?" Yes, but they are rare. I'm one of them, perhaps you are too. But that's an awful chance to take. If your son or daughter is not taught the basics which God INSISTS should be in young lives, it is 98% certain they will not discover them for themselves after they leave home. The casualty rate is almost 100%. Are you ready to gamble on those odds? I hope not.

NOTE: Just how God brings Christians to His likeness through the testings and trials of this life has been fully covered in the author's book WHY DIE AS YOU ARE! It will shock you to discover how each day must be squeezed for its opportunities. Failure to do so, means great loss at the Judgment Seat of Christ. Every believer will be evaluated on the basis of what he has done with his one life on earth. And he will be awarded a PERMANENT place in Christ's kingdom on the basis of it. There will be no chance to return to earth to improve one's status with the Lord. It remains fixed and irrevocable after the judgment. Those who want their children to prosper in the NEXT life, must do all they can to see they know how to extract the most out of this one **for Christ.** Read WHY DIE AS YOU ARE and see why that

20-70 year interval is the one which really determines your child's standing in eternity.

So much for the future. Right now you are confronted with those frightening trends in your teen. Can they be checked? Can they be reversed? You're wondering **"What kind of a plan is powerful enough to transform a rebellious youngster?"** At this point, you'll have to take my word for it, God has such a plan. We'll be coming to it shortly. But first we need to talk about that package of Christian basics. When you see what God expects us to install in our youngsters, you'll agree that powerful techniques are needed to make those truths operative in teen-agers. The package is next.

Chapter Four

THE HOME—SEMINARY OF HEAVEN!

Samuel Coleridge, the 19th Century philosopher, was chatting with a man who didn't believe in giving spiritual instruction to children. It was his theory that a child's mind should not be prejudiced in any direction until he reached an age where he could choose his own religious opinion. The wise Coleridge let the remark pass for a time. Then he asked his visitor if he would like to see his garden. The man said he would.

So Coleridge took him to a place in the backyard where only weeds were growing. The man looked at him in surprise:

"Why this is not a garden! There is nothing here but weeds!"

"Well you see," said the wiley Coleridge, "I didn't want to infringe upon the liberty of the garden in any way. I wanted to give it a chance to express itself and choose its own production."

God, keenly aware of man's depravity, does not want children raised on the neglected-garden basis. The weeds of sin appear altogether too early in lives to permit such a thing. Put three toddlers in a crib. Place a toy in their midst. How long is it before the fussing and grabbing and hitting starts? When parents employ the neglected-garden technique, there is nothing to check the depravity which the fall of man brings to every child.

Not a few Christians have forgotten or just don't care that God holds them responsible for the rearing of children unto Him. Many parents are content to govern their offspring solely for their own luxury and convenience. Just because a child joins a family via the birth process, doesn't mean he is the exclusive property of a mother and father.

CHILDREN BELONG TO GOD

With God's part in childbirth unseen, we tend to regard new arrivals as the fruit of our bodies—**and nothing more.** But that is not the case. Children are more than a product of the mating instinct. They belong to God. They are His BE-FORE they arrive in our homes. They are His before they are ours. They are merely LOANED to us. Though a baby is seemingly produced by our bodies, it is nonetheless the property of God. The Bible is certain about that:

"Lo, children are an heritage from the Lord . . ." (Psa. 127:3).

Two facts are announced here:

1. **Children come from God. They are His before they are ours.**
2. **God entrusts them to us for sacred care. We are to raise them for Him and unto Him.**

When God was ready to bring forth His image into the world, He did not ordain that infants should rise from the soil like flowers, and then fade away. Neither did He have them arrive in some Santa-like fashion as mysterious gifts under a tree. Instead He conceived an ingenious plan. He harnessed the birth process of the animal kingdom and used it as a device for bringing His images into the world one at a time.

Every 6th grader knows human bodies are a part of the animal kingdom. "Homo Sapiens," is the impressive word they learn at school. Yet, bodies can only produce bodies, they cannot produce people. **People are more than bodies.** Modern psychology is fast concluding man is not a body after all. He merely WEARS one. This truth is as old as the Bible itself. Job knew his body was simply an earthly shell:

"I know that my Redeemer lives . . . and after my skin, even this body, has been destroyed, then from my flesh or without it, I shall see God" (Job 19:25, 26 Amp. Bible).

The body—an "earth-suit."

The human body is an "earth-suit" which allows God's image to operate within space and time. Inside every body is an invisible image of God. Psychology's best techniques are aimed at getting the man inside that body to reveal himself. Once clinicians gather all the clues they can about that unseen man, they construct what they call a "personality profile." That profile is what has been projected by the person inside that body.

The production of children by parents is God's ingenious way of bringing His images into this world. Don't you think that using human bodies as vehicles for His images is a remarkable plan? By natural birth, He can populate the world with His own children, yet mothers and fathers feel as though their babies really belong to them.

God's part is unseen, unfelt.

Does the average person sense he is cooperating with God by furnishing a human body for one of His images? To most minds, births take place with no thought for God whatsoever. Seldom is He connected with the process. That's because His part is unfelt, unseen. If He operated in any other fashion, it would violate the faith method. If His working in the affairs of men could be detected, faith would no longer be necessary.

 Parents can plan to have a child, but with that, their option ends. They have nothing to say about the **identification** of the person coming to live with them. That is, they have no part in determining WHO will be in that body when it arrives. They must wait and see WHO it is. They can furnish the body, but they cannot produce the person who will live in it. Our heavenly Father retains to Himself the privilege of deciding just WHO goes into each body arriving in the world.

It is up to God precisely WHEN a person enters the human stream. It has to be that way. People can have no choice about that. Certainly parents have none. They don't even know whether they are going to have a boy or girl, let alone WHO is coming to live with them. Consequently, the color of our skin, our family name, and when we enter history are all in the hands of our heavenly Father. That's His part in the process. It's all decided BEFORE we leave His hand. First thing we know, we are in the bosom of a loving mother and father. Ingenious, isn't it?

Does that diminish the thrill of parenthood?

Is the joy of parenthood lessened because we furnish bodies for people? No. With God's part undetected, it is as though we bring forth these infants ourselves. A child arrives in our home per our timetable. Yet, if we're people of faith, we understand it is also God's timetable. **Outwardly** we have brought forth a child, **secretly** God has brought forth His image. Because His part is undetected, there is nothing about the event to dilute a parent's joy.

One might ask, "Just when does God place His image inside a developing body?" No one knows for sure. Science hasn't answered that question yet. It is still being debated as to when the developing fetus suddenly becomes a **person.** The majority opinion holds it is when the mother first feels life. Others say it is when the infant emerges into the world. A third opinion holds the soul is added at the instant of conception. We can see how this might pose a problem for the abortionists, but it won't make any difference as far as this book is concerned. The point is: we proceed with parenthood because a living person emerges from within us. We treat a child as though we had given it life. The truth is, we do give **physical life** to the body, while God presents us with a **living soul.**

IT'S NATURAL TO LOVE YOUR OWN

 I was trimming the palm in front of our house. I didn't see a mother dove on her nest. She sat there motionless. Her young were under her wings. As I chopped at one branch after another. I got closer and closer to that nest. Finally, I was too close. The mother bird flew out and dropped to the ground. She flopped around as if wounded. She wasn't though. It was a trick to draw me away from her nest. Birds often do this. When my dog took after her she came perilously close to letting herself be caught. She took flight only in the nick of time.

That dove risked her life for the sake of her little ones. We've all heard stories of animals protecting their young. A powerful instinct operates in higher animals to protect and provide for their own. God means for His images to enjoy an environment of sacrifice and devotion. Why? That is the climate of heaven. That is the way He feels about His own. He sacrificed Himself to preserve His children. What is better, then, than having them arrive in the arms of fathers and mothers who would be devoted to them?

1. When children are nurtured and cared for by devoted parents, they apprehend **by experience** what it is to **be loved.** This makes it easy for them to understand God's love for them later on. Having experienced a parent's sacrificial love, the truth of our heavenly Father's is easier to comprehend.

2. After the child becomes an adult, he takes his turn as a parent. Then he learns about **another kind of love.** He thrills to holding "his own" in his arms. He learns **by experience** what it is to love your own more than life itself. In that way, he samples something of what God feels.

My mother was a school teacher. When I was a teen-ager, I did my homework and went to bed. But my dear mother had to stay up and grade papers. Long after my brother and I were comfortable in our beds, she burned the midnight oil. Why? Just to provide for us. I used to ask myself, "Why does mother work so hard?" Now that I have raised my own children, I know. She was sacrificing herself for her young. I grew up knowing what it was for someone to care for me. That experience helps me comprehend my Savior's devotion to me. I am able to understand that kind of love for I beheld it in my own mother.

HOME—THE SEMINARY OF HEAVEN

The home is the dynamic center of development where children learn WHO they are, WHY they are in the world, and WHERE they are headed. It is the place of earliest and most lasting instruction. It is the seminary of eternity. Parents have the solemn duty to bring their children into intimacy with the Lord and prepare them to live with Him forever. The years they spend at home are the most critical of their lives.

During that time they are neither toys for our amusement, nor slaves to do our errands. Neither are they to be the targets of our irritability and impatience. God considers the raising of HIS children a sacred stewardship. Once they leave our shelter, we will have done all we're going to in meeting God's requirements as mothers or fathers. But until that time, the Bible insists we are responsible for the spiritual upbringing of our offspring. We are strictly charged to see that certain truths are taught them:

> **"And thou shalt teach them diligently to thy children, and thou shalt talk of them when thou sittest in thine house, and when thou walkest by the way, and when thou liest down and when thou risest up"** (Deut. 6:7).

Again the Word tells how God . . .

> **". . . appointed a Law in Israel, which He commanded our fathers that they should make them known to their children; that the generations to come might know them, even the children which should be born; who should arise and declare them to their children . . ."** (Psa. 78:5, 6).

We should all know, therefore, the specific items God expects a father or mother to transmit to his children. It's quite a package.

THE PARENT'S PACKAGE

There is an order to be observed in those things which Christians should pass on to their sons and daughters. Each child should be equipped with these Christian basics:

1.   A personal knowledge of the Lord Jesus. Naturally that has to be first. Youngsters should experience Christ in salvation as soon as possible. Spiritual progress is based on that experience. After that, they must learn to beware of His presence so as to enjoy Him intimately. Upon that foundation they should next learn:

2.   That they are God's children as well as yours, that you are raising them for Him. Whereas they will live with you but a few short years, they will spend eternity with Him. Consequently, He is their true parent. Your parenthood ends when this life is over. As long as they are in your care, they must honor you and obey you, for you stand in God's place. It helps

them to accept your discipline, when they understand you in turn must account to God for the way they turn out.

3. That they will not only be disciplined by you, but also by God. "Whom the Lord loves, He disciplines as often as necessary" (Heb. 12:6). God's disciplinary measures can be very rough. Christians should fear them. Because of this, your children must learn "the fear of the Lord." This does not mean they should be afraid of God, but afraid of being out of His will. The "fear of the Lord," is a precious device which warns the soul of danger. No Christian teen-ager is safe without it.

4. That every Christian has two natures. No Christian, young or old, can understand himself and why he does certain things, until he learns that his will is caught between two gods. The Holy Spirit, animating his new nature, prompts him to live godly. The devil, animating his old nature, stirs his emotions and passions, prompting him to fulfill the desires of the flesh and live for himself. As soon as boys and girls are old enough to learn about Christ and heaven, they are old enough to learn about Satan and hell. It is vital for them to know how to deal personally with both gods. It is almost impossible to go far in the Christian life minus this knowledge. Without some instruction in the warfare of the Christian life, teen-agers are an easy prey for Satan. They will be led off into the world as soon as the sex drive awakens.

5. That this world is a TEMPORARY training ground for God's image, a place of PREPARATION for eternity. Young Christians should have it fixed in their minds that they are "strangers and pilgrims" passing through this life, headed for the real one (1 Peter 2:11). Once this truth becomes working knowledge in them, certain auxiliary truths flow from it:

> a. Inasmuch as this world and all it offers must be left behind when one dies, it is foolish to set one's hopes or ambitions on anything in it. To squander time or talent in accumulating a fortune, fame, or family is an awful waste. True wealth is that which can be EXTRACTED from this life for Christ. God does not view riches as the world does, i.e., wealth, health, and leisure to enjoy both. True wealth consists of godliness and investing in others to bring glory to Christ. That is the nature of things in heaven. Since that's where they are going to spend eternity, that's the wealth they should seek.

b. When viewed against eternity, life on earth is but a puff of smoke. It is over in a flash. The Christian's most valuable possession is time. He will never be this way again. Youngsters should be taught to set their eyes on the next life, and compete against other Christians for the best jobs of heaven. As men of this world compete for a good place in this life, so must God's people invest themselves to earn the higher places in Christ's kingdom. There will be differences in rank and capacity in heaven, even though each Christian is brought to perfection in Christ.

6. That this world is ruled by Satan who hates God. Consequently, Christians will not fare too well in this world if they live out and out for Christ. Youngsters should be taught that "all who live godly in Christ Jesus shall suffer persecution" (2 Tim. 3:12). The ugly alternative is to soften one's stand for Christ and get along with the world. Being a Christian does not automatically entitle a person to the best of this world. Instead, he can expect a hard life full of testing. However, nothing temporary is unbearable. The Christian can rejoice that he is God's child and bear his title and affliction proudly. He can take anything this world throws against him. Christians will not always be a persecuted minority, but for the time being, persecution brings out the best that is in them.

7. That he will appear before the Judgment Seat of Christ (2 Cor. 5:10). There, his PERSON and WORKS will be evaluated and his future position determined. Since this judgment is eternal, no changes can be made in one's heavenly status afterwards. Parents who love their children will make sure they have every opportunity to prepare themselves for the judgment. Young people should be taught: (1) how to work on their personalities so as to become more like Christ, (2) how to invest both their time and money in the things of the Lord. The rewards for this are fantastic (Matt. 19:29). The only treasure they will have in heaven is that which they lay up for themselves (Matt. 6:20). Those who are not taught to prepare for the judgment, are **defrauded by their parents** of life's greatest opportunity.

That's some package, isn't it?

We don't hear much about those things today, let alone teach them to our children. Yet, they are as basic as they can be. Each of these truths has to be at work in the Christian if he hopes to succeed in Christ. Our responsibility is clear: God wants us to raise our boys and girls in these truths. Let me restate them in briefer terms:

1. A genuine salvation experience as they receive the Lord into their hearts and learn to enjoy His presence.

2. Coming to appreciate God as their real Father and looking forward to spending eternity with Him.

3. Learning the "fear of the Lord" with its power to restrain them from wandering away from His will.

4. The contest of the believer's two natures and Satan's power to manipulate a Christian through the old nature.

5. The temporary nature of this life and the brief opportunity to get ready for heaven.

> a. The things of this world have no value in heaven except as they are used to glorify Christ. The Christian's only treasure in heaven is that which he lays up for himself.
>
> b. With the next life the important one, they should be taught to discount this one and enter the competition for getting ahead in the next life.

6. This world is hostile to Christians, who are a persecuted minority. Since the program of God is one of suffering first and then glory, those bearing Christ's reproach here can expect to share in His glory there.

7. The finality of this one life is determined by the Judgment Seat of Christ where one's person and works are evaluated to determine his reward (eternal status).

> **NOTE:** I want you to become familiar with that list. Go over it several times. Not that you are expected to memorize all the items, but you should fix the general scheme in your mind. As we continue through the book, I will be referring to the **parent's package** from time to time. It will be a useful device if we both understand what is meant by "the package."

PARENT'S PACKAGE

Now let me ask, "How would you like to have that package installed and working in the life of your boy or girl?" What fantastic Christians they could be as the Holy Spirit used those truths to guide their young feet. This is what God wants. He expects Christian fathers and mothers to devote themselves to seeing that these truths function within every child. He will hold them accountable for the way they discharge this responsibility. That is not meant as a threat, for there is a promise attached to it which God has put in writing:

> **"Train up a child in the way he should go, and when he is old, he will not depart from it"** (Prov. 22:6).

ISN'T THAT PRECIOUS?

Please note God does not say . . . '"EDUCATE" the child, nor does He say advise the child, nor yet to inform or instruct the child. Parents are to TRAIN UP a child. To educate a person is merely to tell him WHAT to do. To TRAIN him is to see that he does it—and stay with it until it becomes a part of him.

A distraught mother stood weeping beside the ambulance while the drivers lifted the lifeless form of her little boy onto a litter. He had been run over by a passing motorist who couldn't stop in time to avoid hitting him. The youngster had dashed off the curb directly into the path of the oncoming car. In her anguish the mother sought to fix the blame:

"I told him a thousand times not to go into that street!"

That, of course, was the problem. She merely TOLD him, that's all. She did not train him to the place where it was HABIT for him to stay out of the street. Now he was dead and the fault was hers. Had she used a switch so severely that his little body bore the scars, it would have been better than this. Having her boy alive, though marked up a bit, would have been better than finding his body mangled and dead. Had she dealt (disciplined) with her boy until it was **part of him** NOT to go into the street, she would have saved his life.

Parents are not off the hook when they TELL their kids what to do. They must TRAIN them as God asks. Training is the rubbing of education into one's spirit. If you merely tell a lad what to do, though you say it a thousand times, it is not guaranteed that he will follow your counsel. But if you train him, so that it becomes habit, he can no more depart from it than he can run from himself. That's what God means by . . . "Train up a child . . . and he will not depart from it."

BUT MOST PARENTS JUST TALK

"You're going to have to speak to that boy, dear."

You've heard that before. People get alarmed over their teen-ager's behavior and feel it is time to do something. But what? Sit down with him for a little chat? Should they quote him a few Bible verses and tell him he's headed for trouble? That won't work. Time for talk has long since passed. It would have been great when he was little and soaked up your advice like a sponge. In those days he believed every word you said.

Now it's too late for talk. Rebelling teens don't dig it. Besides they challenge what you say now. Talk is fine in the tender years, but in the crisis years—forget it. No "little chat" is going to counter the powerful feelings Satan turns loose in kids. Mothers can plead, fathers can growl, but teens will do as they please. It's folly to appeal to a youngster's INTELLECT while Satan is arousing his EMOTIONS. You might as well shout at the wind. In order to counter the devil's work in teen-agers, parents must use . . .

COUNTERING EMOTIONS

If I were to ask, "Which emotion should fathers and mothers use to counter Satan's appeals?" you'd come back with the sweet reply—"LOVE." That sounds very nice and proper, doesn't it? Well, I'm sorry—that's NOT the emotion. We need something more powerful than parental love. There's only one emotion that is greater—FEAR. I know that startles you. But mama-love and papa-love do not have the same effect on them it used to.

Why not? They've discovered a new kind of love—EROS! That's the Greek word from which we get our modern word "erotic." It is sex love. It encompasses all the powerful feelings that surge when boy meets girl. With the awakening of the sex drive, an exciting new love-emotion stirs within young people. It's so overwhelming and compelling, parental love can't compete with it. Therefore, we need an emotion which is even more powerful than EROS. That emotion is fear.

FEAR—the countering emotion.

When young people enter their teens and those mighty drives awaken, Satan enjoys fantastic leverage. He cannot override their wills, but his appeals are almost irresistible. Parents, seeking to compete with Satan, must answer with the countering emotion of fear. Fear is the one great emotion to which everyone responds. Fear alone can check the awesome forces unleashed in teens.

Consider how fear checks the military powers of this world. Were it not for the fear of atomic retaliation, the Red Star of Russia would be waving over every nation by now. Russia fears an atomic encounter with the U.S. As long as she does, an all out war is delayed. God is using FEAR to hold the world's greatest forces at bay. It is the greatest deterrent to evil we know. Ah, but fear also moves people to do what is right.

Do you drive a car? You obey the traffic laws, don't you? Why? Is it because you are eager for a safety award? Is it because you thrill to law-keeping? Hardly. Fear makes you drive carefully. You are afraid of getting killed or caught. Why even the sight of a police car makes most people slow down. That car represents a punishing authority. Riding in that car are professionals. They are hired to punish you if you make a driving slip. And you know it. It is your fear of them that makes you slow down and drive as you should.

Similarly, godly fear can motivate a teen to do what is right as well as deter him from evil. His fallen nature makes the use of fear necessary. If he didn't have that old nature, then parental love would be sufficient. But he does have that nature and it is filled with violent, flaming emotions. If equally passionate emotions were on deposit in the NEW NATURE, then it would be a different story. The Holy Spirit could use them to counter Satan's suggestions. But those emotions are NOT there. You failed to put them there. So now FEAR has to be the countering force in your home, as well as the prime tool of the Holy Spirit.

When teens are beyond the "talk" stage, when they are in rebellion against both their parent's and God's authority, fear is the precious answer. It can end the heartache and suffering in many a mother and father. But how to use it is another matter. It requires wisdom, and can only be used with LOVE. Parental love, you see, is fine—**when it is accompanied by fear.** Right away, you say . . . "But perfect love casts out all fear." I agree. Unfortunately your children don't love you with a perfect love. If they did, they would obey you perfectly and there would be no need to use fear.

Don't shudder at the word "fear." The greatest men of any age have been God-fearing. The finest children this world has ever seen, have feared to disobey their parents. The next time you are present at a wedding, listen to the preacher's words. He will say . . . "Marriage is not to be entered into lightly, but reverently, discreetly, and IN THE FEAR OF GOD." Heard that before? Sure. Now here's my question: if people should marry in the fear of God, should they not raise their children in that same fear? God expects it . . . as we see next.

Chapter Five

GODLY FEAR—CHRISTIAN MOTIVATION

Back into a hot stove! OUCH! There is pain. Instinctively you jump away. Now that is marvelous. If you didn't feel pain, you would have remained against that stove to damage your body. Pain made you move. Think of the charred hands and feet we'd have if it were not for pain. No one likes it, but we are thankful for its warning. Without it our bodies wouldn't last long.

The soul of man has a similar device—**FEAR.**

WHAT PAIN IS TO THE BODY, FEAR IS TO THE SOUL.

There are countless human fears, as you know. Man dreads everything from financial ruin to fear of the dark. We're not interested in the long list of human fears. We're concerned with the kind which warns a person of SPIRITUAL DANGER. That kind is the **fear of God.** Not only is it a powerful deterrent, it is a motivator. The fear of God is a device for warning and moving men.

GODLY FEAR

Of our American pioneers it has been said:

THEY FEARED NOTHING BUT GOD!

Today the reverse is true. **People fear everything but God.** That applies to Christians and non-Christians alike. It wasn't like that years ago. Our country was founded by people who feared God. In the early days, people used to talk about fearing God. The pious person was spoken of as a God-fearing man. He is hardly mentioned anymore.

Fear is a necessary part of God's plan. It is the most compelling emotion at His disposal. He uses it to counter self-will in man. It offsets the lusts of the flesh which stir in the old nature. The Holy Spirit uses it to quicken His appeals to the Christian's will. Fear is the one emotion which can move Christians to obedience. To protect us from wasting our lives and squandering them in disobedience, God gave us the capacity to FEAR Him.

The fear of God moved the heroes of faith. Consider Abraham, the greatest of them all. Recall how God told him to take his only son to the mount and there slay him as an offering. That dear man feared God so much he dared not disobey. It wasn't until he was ready to plunge the knife into his boy, that God spoke to him:

> **"Lay not thine hand upon the lad . . . for now I know thou FEAR-EST GOD, seeing thou hast not withheld thine only son from Me!"** (Gen. 22:12).

That is God's testimony to this truth. Abraham FEARED God. And because He feared, he dared not to disobey. God said FEAR moved Abraham to faithful obedience.

Now hear the apostle Peter: "FEAR GOD," he says, advising Christians to live out their entire lives in fear of Him! Listen. These are his words, not mine:

> **"And if you address as Father, the One Who impartially judges each man's work, conduct yourselves IN FEAR during the time of your stay on earth"** (1 Peter 1:17).

In teaching the fear of God, do I invent a new doctrine? Indeed not. That we should fear God is a truth as old as the Book itself. The apostle Paul agrees. It is the fear of God, he says, that moves men to holy living:

> **"Therefore having these precious promises, dearly beloved, let us cleanse ourselves from all defilements of the flesh and spirit, perfecting holiness in the FEAR OF GOD!"** (2 Cor. 7:1).

● What is it that moves you, dear reader, to live a holy life? What is it that stirs you to obey the Lord's commands? Isn't it the fear of God? I hope so. If you have not yet come to appreciate this precious device built into your soul, you could easily squander your life in self-living. Love may make you **desire** to obey the Lord, but it is FEAR that **prods** you to do it.

GODLY FEAR MOVED PAUL

Why did the great apostle burn himself out carrying the Gospel to the Gentiles? Was it because he loved to travel? Was it for personal satisfaction that he endured beatings and imprisonment? Was it a passion for punishment that finally led him to martyrdom? Of course not. He was motivated by the fear of God. There was a secret terror in his soul. He said so:

> **"For we must all appear before the Judgment Seat of Christ that each one may be recompensed for his deeds in the body, according to what he has done, whether good or bad"** (2 Cor. 5:10).

Now hear his astonishing conclusion:

> **"Knowing therefore the TERROR of the Lord, we persuade men . . ."** (2 Cor. 5:11).

See? That's what motivated the Apostle Paul—**FEAR!**

GODLY FEAR SHOULD MOTIVATE US ALL

Do you tend to discount the seriousness of the Judgment Seat of Christ? I can understand that. It seems so far off. It is human to be more concerned with what is at hand. But the Judgment isn't the only time God deals with us. His chastening hand can fall upon us—NOW!

> **"For whom the Lord loveth He chasteneth (now) and scourgeth (now) every son who He receives"** (Heb. 12:6).

Our heavenly Father keeps His Word. He doesn't "spare the rod." He deals severely with His children in this life. He deals with disobedience now. Many a saint lying on a hospital bed can testify to that.

When God tells parents to raise their children AS UNTO HIM, He means it. He won't tolerate disobedience. We might wink at disobedience in our young people, but we are foolish if we think God lets our disobedience pass unnoticed. Some of the sicknesses and sorrows in Christian homes are due to the parents' refusal to bring their children up in the fear of the Lord. Delinquent parents often find themselves in God's "woodshed," though few are willing to admit their failure to discipline their children has put them there.

If the fear of God functions in our lives as it should, it will affect the way we raise our sons and daughters. God has made it perfectly clear what He expects. Ignoring His will is folly. If we refuse to raise them as He instructs, we can expect His chastening. It is inescapable. When God spanks, it hurts. The fear of divine discipline should move all of us to raise our children as unto Him.

But someone protests. Love should be the prime mover, he says. We should obey God because we love Him. Oh, that love would move us. But alas, it isn't the powerful stuff people think it is. It moves very few of us. If love were the real motivator, we'd all be a lot busier for Christ than we are. Why, we don't do for our mothers as we ought, yet we love them. We don't do for our husbands and wives as we should, yet we love them. We might as well face it. In spite of our love for Christ, we ignore Him most of the time, paying little attention to His orders. But let Him lay His hand on our bodies and we get interested right away.

> **NOTE:** I am NOT saying we should live in fear of God as a person, neither am I teaching that we should live in a state of perpetual fear. I speak only of the fear to disobey Him and be out of His will. A life of constant fear of God would be horrible. The fear of God is a device ONLY. When we are in His will, there is no fear. But in those times when we trifle with Him and ignore His orders, we have every reason to fear what can happen to our spirits and bodies. Our souls, of course, are safe. The safety of one's soul depends on the obedience of Christ, not on the Christian. While the Lord loves us enough to die for us, He also loves us enough to discipline us. Many have discovered to their regret that He is a strict disciplinarian. His chastening hand is greatly to be feared. God can play rough.

CHILDREN SHOULD LEARN THIS FEAR OF THE LORD

"THE FEAR OF THE LORD IS THE BEGINNING OF WISDOM."*

---

*Psalm 111:10

Our children haven't begun to "wise up," until they learn the fear of the Lord. If mothers and fathers need to walk in the fear of the Lord, then their children should fear Him also. God wants parents to install godly fear in their youngsters as soon as possible. But not with words only. They must learn it by **experience.** It must be taught to them. Beyond that they should be able to see the fear of the Lord in their parent's lives. It is impossible to instill godly fear in young people unless mothers and dads manifest it themselves.

A teen-ager should be able to say:

"My mother's life is directed by the fear of God. I can see it. I know it affects the way she is raising me."

The same should be true of a father. A lad should be able to say, "My dad is afraid to disobey God. I know he fears to be out of the Lord's will." But children will not recognize the fear of God unless they are first TOLD about it. It is not recognized without instruction. Children do not grow up to fear the Lord automatically, neither does it rub off. It has to be taught, and the best time for teaching it is when they are being disciplined.

When I was little, my grandparents bought me a new suit. I was to wear it to Sunday school only, and change my clothes the moment I got home. Grandpa promised me a good spanking if I played in that new suit. Sometime afterwards I procrastinated and played for a time. I tore the trousers. Oh, oh, I knew what was coming. I was afraid to go into the house. So I skulked about outside until dark. I thought Grandpa might forget the spanking if enough time went by.

Then I became hungry. The hunger was worse than a whipping, so I went in. Sure enough, Grandpa was ready and waiting. I got my "lickin." When he asked me why I didn't come in the house after I tore my suit, I answered,

"I thought if I stayed outside long enough, you'd forget about it. How come you didn't, Grandpa?"

"God doesn't forget to spank me when I need it," he replied, **"and that helps me to remember to spank you when you need it."**

At that time my grandfather was suffering from diabetes. The Lord was dealing with him about something. The chastening hand of God was hurting him. I'm sure that's why he didn't forget to spank me. It's amazing how pain prods us to do what is right.

Let's say your daughter has not been buckling down at school. The academic side of her high school life is suffering because the social side receives most of her attention. She thrills to her friends at school, but she is not applying herself to her studies. You've decided to clamp down on her social activities until her grades are raised. Here she comes asking if it would be all right to have her girl friend stay over night. This time your answer is going to be, no.

"But mom, why not? I don't see why I can't. Please Mom."

"No dear. And that's the end of it. Don't ask me again."

"Jerry has his friends over all the time, I don't see why I can't."

"SLAP." That was the back of your hand as it struck her full across the mouth. There wasn't much force behind it. It didn't need force. You were not trying to produce pain. Shock works as well. That's why you acted so swiftly. She looks at you in amazement, not knowing whether to speak or cry.

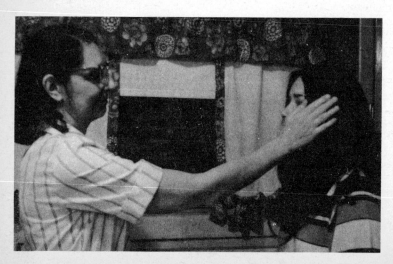

"Go to your room dear."

You say that sweetly without the slightest elevation of your voice. You have done this coolly. There is no anger.

"Mother will be along in a few minutes to explain why she slapped you."

The startled girl complies without a word. A few tears might come to her eyes. You may have to hold back your own.

What next? Go to your place of prayer. Spend a few minutes with the Lord. This is to prepare you spiritually for the interview with your daughter. Five minutes should be long enough. In the meantime, your girl is having thoughts of her own. She is apprehensive. She doesn't know what is coming. Her emotions are stirred. Good. You need that. There's little use trying to install any part of the parent's package without an accompanying emotion.

> **NOTE:** Man is an emotional creature. He responds to emotion more quickly than to reason. Yet, reason is supposed to govern his emotions. However, the fall changed that so now man does what he feels like, rather than what he should. This gives Satan the advantage. He uses emotions to lead young people. He stirs up their old natures which are full of emotional material. Therefore, your leadership must be emotional too. That's why discipline is necessary—it is an emotional time. There is no way, you see, for **rational** conclusions to offset Satan's **emotional** suggestions. Therefore, your finest teaching will be done via emotional scenes with your youngsters. Since emotions are hard to handle, you go first to be with the Lord. Only in His strength can you get the most out of an emotional scene with your son or daughter.

● You're ready to go to your daughter's room. She's on the bed. She may try to conceal her feelings by pretending to be reading a magazine. Again, she may be crying. The tenderhearted ones cry. You sit down beside her. Your arm goes around her.

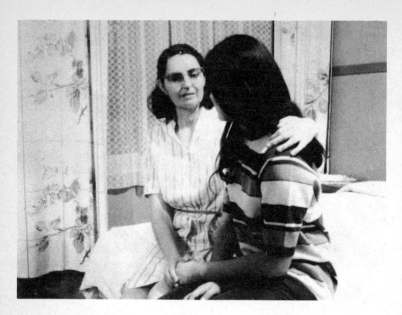

"Mother's sorry she had to slap you, dear. Now I will explain why it was necessary. When I told you that you couldn't have Betty over tonight, I gave you a clear, direct answer. It's important that you learn to respect my decisions, even more important that you obey me. Normally, I might have given you an explanation for my no. But this time I decided to use my parent's prerogative and give the explanation five minutes later.

"Mother loves you very much. You know that. And because I love you, I must teach you to obey me. Do you know why? (Don't wait for an answer.) God requires it of me. He holds me responsible for the way you turn out. The Bible instructs me, dear, to raise you in the discipline of the Lord. And I must, for I am afraid to disobey God. He requires me to teach you to obey without question, so that you will learn to obey Him that way too. If you won't obey me whom you can see, you won't obey Him Whom you cannot see.

"I don't want to stand before God in the Judgment trying to explain why I ignored His orders and didn't teach my girl to obey. I know today's experience has shocked you. But it is because I fear to disobey the Lord, that I must teach you to obey me. You can be sure mother did what she did, because she loves you. Some day I hope you'll teach the same thing to your children. I trust you will love them enough to deal with them as I have dealt with you. One of the most important things any parent can teach her child is the fear of the Lord."

70

● That scene gives you an idea how such teachings can be accomplished in an emotional situation. Once a mother takes her stand, she cannot retreat from it when a similar situation arises in the future. By her example, her child will come to see that she does fear the Lord. That example is worth more than hundreds of clever lectures. When this technique is used, a child will start fearing to disobey her mother . . . and God.

> **NOTE:** The fear of the Lord is listed in the parent's package. In the scene just described, the matter of the Christian's judgment was also a part of the teaching. So in this case, two features received emotional stimulation. The fear of the Lord and the idea of Christian accountability will both go into that girl's new nature where the Spirit will have them for future use. Those ideas now have emotional content and will be available to the Holy Spirit for countering Satan's suggestions. They are no longer theory only.

THAT GIRL WAS AFRAID

What did the girl feel as she waited for her mother? Apprehension and fear. She didn't know what was coming. That always produces uneasiness. If nothing else, she suffered the fear of the unknown, that dread which accompanies the unexpected. Emotion was definitely present when that mother spoke of her own fear of God. The girl was in a position to identify with those feelings. Talk of fearing God when the girl was **already fearing** her mother, made it an ideal teaching situation.

Ah, but did she stay afraid of her mother? No. As soon as she received her mother's explanation, the fears subsided. She understood her mother did what she did for two reasons: (1) she feared to disobey God, (2) she loved her daughter. Once a child is reassured of her mother's love, fear **vanishes.** Why? "There is no fear in love, but perfect love casts out all fear" (1st John 4:18). It was a perfect love the mother showed toward her daughter. She was willing to do what was necessary IN LOVE, and the daughter's fear disappeared. It was cast out.

> **NOTE:** See how that mother's love was a PERFECT love? What made it perfect? It was based on God's Word. She truly loved her daughter for she disciplined her according to the revealed

will of God. She acted in obedience to God's Word. That's what made it perfect. Only love based on obedience to God can be called perfect love. That was the kind the Lord Jesus showed toward us. He died in obedience to the will of God. Feelings of affection or fondness for a child, yes, even sacrificial devotion, are NOT perfect love. Why? They are based on the animal instinct to cherish YOUR OWN. Even dogs do that. While it is parental love, it is not perfect love. Only perfect love casts out ALL fear.

YOUR CHILDREN MUST FEAR YOU

 A recent newspaper column published a mother's question:

"If I insist on strict obedience, won't I lose my child's devotion in time?"

The columnist replied from her personal experience:

"I marvel at the way my husband handles our children. He'll say, 'If you do that once more, you'll go to your room and have no allowance for two weeks.' My kids mind him, because they know he will do exactly as he says. And they think he's great. They show a perfect combination of love and fear for him. They love him because he is good to them, and they fear him because they know he doesn't lie to them about discipline."

You are a "god" to your children, especially when they are little. At first, you are the supreme authority in their lives. In giving them birth, you are their life-giver. They know no other authority. As far as they can see, you are their only provider and protector. You are the only law they know, therefore, you are their ruler. They hold this opinion of you for a number of years, and it doesn't change much as they grow older. Unless you teach them otherwise, you are the only "god" they know.

Of course, it is your ambition to shift the control of their lives from yourself to the true God. But that is a gradual process. Even when they are pressing toward adulthood, you still represent God to them. They are under your control as long as they are under your roof. That is the way God wants it. As long as your children continue to live with you, they should look on you as representing God's authority in the home.

Therefore, they must fear you. To what extent? Just as you fear God. If you want them to grow up as God-fearing children, they must learn to fear you FIRST. Then that fear should be transferred from you to God. That is the goal of Christian parenthood. However, it is not you, as an individual, they fear, but your power to punish them.

We do not fear God as a Person, but we do fear His faithfulness to discipline us if we disobey Him. It is the Lord's chastening hand we fear, not the kind of a Person He is. He is a good Father and provider. We are not to stand in dread of Him for any reason, except as we disobey Him. So should it be with us and our children. They are not to fear us as parents and providers, but they should fear to disobey us. We stand in God's place to administer discipline in His Name, and that they must fear. If we are as faithful to deal with their disobedience as God deals with ours, they will fear us.

FEAR IN OPERATION

Let's see how fear serves as Christian motivation in your 16 year old boy. He's been invited to go to the beach with a gang from school. But it is Sunday and you want him in church with you. You know that beach parties are fun—for the flesh. Satan's appeal to his will has a great deal of power. Going to the beach with friends has far more emotional attraction than sitting in church.

Since your boy is a Christian, let's picture his two natures and see how the forces line up. By referring to the visual, we can see how Satan's suggestion is more appealing to his will, than that of the Holy Spirit.

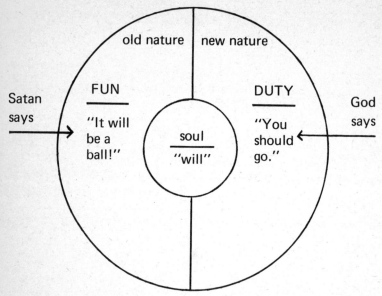

You are going to even up the competition by using FEAR as Christian motivation.

"Son, I want you in church today. I know you would like to go to the beach with your friends, but our family must be in church together. So, plan on going with us."

"Awh Dad, I can go to church anytime. But I don't get invited to the beach every week. They always do the same old thing at church. It's nowhere near as much fun as going to the beach. How about it? Can't I go. Please?"

"No son, I want you to go with us."

"What if I decide to stay home, then?" (A slight hint of rebellion is showing. Your firmness brought it out. Of course, it's been there all along. That's what you are really dealing with!)

"I told you what I want you to do. Now I expect you to do it. You obey me son, or I'll have to discipline you. I don't want to, you're a pretty good boy. I'd rather think you are willing to do as Dad asks."

"But Dad, you just don't understand. I plain don't want to go. (His feelings are rising.) I'm sixteen now. I ought to have some say in whether I have to go or not."

"No more argument son. You are going with us. If you disobey me, you will not be allowed to take driver's education when your turn comes up. You'll have to wait until they can fit you into the program later on. Now don't mention it again or you'll force me to get even more strict with you."

> **NOTE:** See the teeth in your command. A new element has been introduced—the FEAR to disobey you. Now the Holy Spirit has some emotion to work with. Until now, there was no contest. Until you threatened to defer his Driver's Ed., your boy had little to fear in defying you. He faced no real risk. Your boy's choice is no longer between FUN and DUTY—he must now decide between FUN and FEAR. Both are emotions. Satan's appeal is not so one-sided now. Until some FEAR is set against Satan's offer of FUN, the contest remained unfair. Satan usually wins unless the Spirit has a countering emotion at His disposal.

"OKAY, I'LL GO."

The Holy Spirit wins this round! The FEAR of punishment won out over the promise of FUN. That was the real battle. As long as your boy's choice was between FUN and DUTY, it was hardly a contest. But with the threat of consequences added to the conversation, he was faced with a more serious choice. He chose to obey. The issue shaped up like this:

See how the introduction of FEAR gave the Spirit a more even chance in competing for your boy's will? It added emotional content to His appeal and He won. True, it was a reluctant . . . "Okay, I'll go," but it was still a victory. And there's more. You're not through, yet. An ideal teaching situation is at hand. You will be able to install something from the parent's package.

● It's early. There's plenty of time before church.

You go to your place of prayer. You prepare your heart before the Lord. You have had a skirmish with your boy and you must remove every vestige of hostility before you speak to him. Your heart should swell with love for him and a desire to put the best into his life.

Then you go to him. You put your arm around him. You will be able to talk to him like a man of God, because you have first talked to Jesus.

"You made the right decision son. I want to thank you for that."

"What else could I do?" (His shoulders rise and fall in a hopeless shrug.) "You know how badly I want to drive. You didn't leave me much choice, Dad."

"I know son. But there are two sides to every story. I didn't have any choice either. I'm in the same boat you are. God has ordered me to raise you to obey me. I have to insist on what I think is best for your life spiritually. If you think you were in a tough place, your Dad was in one too."

"Yeah? How?"

"I am as afraid to disobey God as you were to disobey me. You were faced with losing your driving privilege, but I could lose my job, my health—why I could even lose your mother. God doesn't fool around when it comes to discipline. So you see, we were both stuck. (Note how this identifies with your boy's feelings.) You have to obey me, or get punished. I have to obey God or get punished. The power to punish you is in my hands, the power to punish me is in God's hands. Because He loves me, He WILL discipline me. And because I love you, I MUST discipline you."

76

● Does a teen-ager savvy that kind of talk? You bet. And he also FEELS it. That's the way to bridge the generation gap. He feels his dad is in the same spot he's in. That softens his hostility and resentment. He says to himself,

"My dad makes me do these things, because God makes him do things. He's just as afraid to disobey God as I am to disobey him."

When that truth goes into your boy's mind and spirit (un-conscious) with emotion, you have accomplished a remarkable teaching. The truth of the fear of God is planted within him. A new bond is created between a boy and his father when a lad says to himself, "My Dad's in the same boat I'm in."

> **NOTE:** Many parents have wondered why certain sicknesses and tragedies strike their homes. You are finding out why, right now. When mothers and fathers refuse to raise their children as unto Him, He must discipline them. "It is a fearful thing to fall into the hands of the living God" (Heb. 10:31). Those hands are rough when it comes to discipline. He hits hard, and it hurts. He knows where a man is tender. We spank kids on the bottom, but God hits people in their bodies, their spirits, and their pocket books— wherever they are the tenderest. He disciplines us for our own good, that we may "share in His holiness" (Heb. 12:10).

Does it matter if your boy goes to church feeling sorry for himself? Not at all. You have sown a fantastic seed in his heart. Any further feelings or grumblings that are stirred as he sits there, will only add steam to the truths you planted in him. He will not be able to shake the fact that you dealt with him on exactly the same basis God deals with you. No matter how upset he gets, it will merely add useful emotion. When a lot of emotion is added to a truth as big as that one, the Holy Spirit will be able to use it again and again. You have just accomplished a masterful bit of teaching.

NEVER LEAVE VITAL CHOICES TO A TEEN.

 Dr. John Baillie, the noted theologian testified this was the kind of training he received. It began with the earliest days of his life:

"There never was a time when it seemed my life was my own to do with as I pleased. From the beginning, the center of living was NOT inside me, but outside of me. I knew my parents had the right to ask of me what they did and I had no right to refuse. I also knew that what they desired of me was right. I understood that my parents were under the SAME CONSTRAINT that they were so diligently transmitting to me; that the ultimate source of their authority was God."

But someone says:

"What's wrong with leaving the decision up to the boy? Why not simply give him your reasons for wanting him to go to church with you and let him decide for himself. Should you be telling a sixteen year old what to do? Doesn't it make for a stronger Christian to put a lad on his own?"

Rarely does that work. Almost never, in fact. Why? It's like placing the boy in the devil's hands. The lad hasn't a chance. Satan will win every time. There's no way for the Spirit to win a decision when the choice remains between what he'd LIKE TO DO as against what he OUGHT TO DO . . . **with no consequences attached.** As long as a youth lives under your roof, you are responsible to compel—yes, that's the word— compel him to do what you think is best for him. Either that or answer to God.

Our government requires youngsters to go to school. The law says they must. If your children came to you asking whether they could go to the beach instead of school, there'd be no question about it. To school they'd go, like it or not. If you are lax about this, authorities are soon at your house inquiring why your child isn't in school. The government feels it is in the child's best interest to have an education. The Law makes him go whether he wants to or not.

How strangely parents behave when it comes to spiritual matters. They seldom give thought to a child's best interest spiritually. They are inclined to be easy on them. Going to school seems necessary, because the law says so. But participating in Christian fellowship, because God says so, doesn't seem important somehow. These parents compel their youngsters to attend to their social duty, but they are lax when it

78

comes to their spiritual duty. It would seem that Christian parents who fear to disobey the truancy laws, would fear even more to disobey God.

God holds you responsible for seeing that what is best for your children spiritually, goes into their lives. You cannot escape that responsibility by passing the decision on to them.

But what if a boy refuses to go?

Suppose Satan wins after all? Suppose, in spite of your threats, your boy decides to stay home? What then? You must do exactly as you said. You cannot be like those parents who promise punishment and never deliver. You know the kind I mean. You hear them all the time:

"If you do that again, you're going to get a lickin."

Then what? The child does it again. Does he get his "lickin?" No. The parent LIED. A promise to spank is as important as any other made to a child. It should be no surprise when children raised like that, begin to lie to their parents at an early age.

● So you call the school. Your boy is dropped from the driver education roster. It's a bitter pill for him, but there's nothing he can do. He has to accept the disappointment. You can't lie. You promised it. But as we saw earlier, this is what your boy hopes you'll do. It's an unconscious hope, of course. But his security is based on your cooperation with the witness of the Spirit within him. God's Spirit says he deserves to be punished. You cannot act any other way without warring against the Holy Spirit.

Your boy respects your stand. Don't think he doesn't. And he'll love you for it. He sees in you the kind of a parent he is going to be. As long as he is assured you love him, the discipline can only make him richer. He may groan a little outwardly, but there is immediate relief in his soul. This is the kind of firmness it takes to install the parent's package.

NOW WE CAN GRAB THE STICK

At the end of chapter one, I said it was too early to talk about punishment. But we have since learned what makes a teen tick and what is needed to counter Satan's appeals. We're ready to discuss discipline.

 Have you ever trained tender plants? You used a stick didn't you? You stuck it in the ground beside the flimsy stalk and tied the weak stem to it. You left it there until the stalk was strong enough to stand by itself. Once you TRAINED it to grow as you wanted it, you took the stick away.

In that same fashion God wants His children TRAINED in the truths of the parent's package. The stick is the quickest and best way to make their paths straight. Once they have the habit of regulating their lives by those Christian basics, you can take the stick away. External discipline is no longer necessary when teens learn how to discipline themselves. That's the purpose behind all parental discipline. God guarantees they will not depart from HIS ways if the truths are implanted with a stick.

Consider the boy who learns to think of heaven as his real home. He is inclined to shun this world and regard himself a stranger in it. Or take the girl who views Jesus as her MASTER as well as her Savior. She is ever looking for ways to please

Him. And how about those teens who can handle Satan's attacks? They are not overcome by evil, but live in the victory of Christ. That's what the package can do when correctly planted in a young life. To implant means to penetrate. The only way we can salvage rebellious teens today is with punishment that penetrates. That's next.

> **NOTE:** The purpose of this chapter was to introduce the subject of godly fear and show that it can be installed in teen lives. It did not teach HOW to implant fear, only that it can be done. I have said it must be done in an emotional situation. Do not, however, conclude that I am leading up to a life of bondage and fear. Again I ask you to think of fear as a warning device. It warns people when they are in danger of being disciplined by God. Since His discipline is painful, don't you find it precious that we are warned? Of course. Think, then, how cruel it would be to let your children venture forth into the world without this protective device built into their souls. It is one of the finest gifts you can give them, for it can spare them a great deal of pain and protect them from wasting their lives.

Chapter Six

PUNISHMENT THAT PENETRATES

 The mother of George Washington was seated next to a distinguished French general at a formal banquet, when the officer turned and asked:

"How did you ever manage to raise such a noble son?"

"I taught him to obey," was her instant reply.

Mrs. Washington reared her son according to the Word of God. The "Father of our Country," was the product of his mother's obedience to the revealed will of God.

GOD WANTS YOUNG PEOPLE DISCIPLINED

In chapter one we saw how the Spirit convicts the youth who disobeys his parents. By that same witness he knows he should be punished. To this agrees the Word of God. Here are some observations from wise old Solomon in the book of Proverbs:

 "For whom the Lord loves He corrects, even as a father corrects the son in whom he delights" (3:12).

"Foolishness is bound in the heart of a child, but the rod of correction will drive it far from him" (22:15).

"Withhold not correction from the child, for if thou beatest him with the rod, he shall not die. Thou SHALT beat him with the rod and shall deliver his soul from hell!" (23:13, 14).

"The rod and reproof give wisdom, but a child left to himself brings shame upon his mother" (29:15).

"He that spares his rod hates his son: but he that loves him is diligent to chasten him as needed" (13:24).

"Discipline your son while there is hope, but do not (indulge your angry resentments by undue chastisement and) set yourself to his ruin" (19:18 Amp. Bible).

NOTE: As long as a boy is under your roof, his situation is not hopeless, his ruin is not inevitable. As long as he depends on you for support, it is within your power to install those truths which God can use to direct his steps after he leaves home. However, it does require discipline. There is no way to salvage a teen-ager apart from discipline.

"Blows that wound, cleanse away evil; and strokes that reach the innermost parts (keep one's steps from going astray)" (20:30).

Shocking as it may seem, the LAW demanded the death penalty for a stubborn and rebellious son. Listen: "For rebellion is as the sin of witchcraft, and stubbornness is as iniquity and idolatry" (1 Sam. 15:23). A child's stubbornness and rebellion finally lead him to idolatry and revolt against God. Knowing that, hear what God told Moses to say to the leaders of Israel:

"If a man has a stubborn and rebellious son who will NOT OBEY the voice of his father and mother, and though they chasten him, will not listen to them; then shall his father and mother bring him out to the elders of the city at the gate of the place where he lives, and . . . then shall all the men of this city STONE HIM TO DEATH; so shall ye cleanse out the evil from your midst, and all Israel shall hear and fear" (Deut. 21:18, 19, 21).

"Stoned!" When teen-agers use that word they mean a youngster high on drugs. But when God uses it, He means a lifeless form left crumpled in the dust. Just think of it! A young person stoned to death for refusing to mend his ways after his parent's efforts to discipline him have failed. That's shocking. Especially when you realize he is stoned for—**stubbornness and rebellion!**

Nothing I will sugest in this book could be as harsh as that. We won't be carrying out God's Old Testament recommendation in this book. However, it is possible that a few stoning by the elders of the city could have a magical effect on many irresponsible youths. In Moses' day this was a necessary precaution to protect the nation from idolatry. He knew the up coming generation would one day rule Israel, so he would rather slay them, than have them emerge as the nation's leaders. He couldn't afford to have the control of Israel fall into the hands of dissident youths.

In our day God is NOT trying to preserve nations. He is not likely to preserve this one much longer. But He is building His church, the body of Christ. Death by stoning would not be the safeguard for the invisible church that it was for His visible nation. However, God does have a drastic device for the protection of the "body of Christ," and it is just as severe. I won't touch on it now. It is reserved for later in the book. It is to be applied ONLY when all else fails.

● Aren't those Scriptures something! What a responsibility they place on parents. God expects fathers and mothers to insist on **implicit** obedience. They are to use discipline to get it. The purpose, of course, is that the children will ultimately submit themselves to the Lord. Any youth who refuses to bend to the authority of his parents, will hardly surrender his whole life to the Lord. It is almost guaranteed that those growing up in self-centeredness WILL NOT submit to God's authority later on. It bears repeating: if children will not obey mothers and fathers whom they can see, how much less will they obey God Whom they cannot see?

But punishment alone is not enough.

GOD ALSO WANTS YOUNG PEOPLE INSTRUCTED

God's Word further insists that parents pass on to their children the wisdom of the Christian life. They must be counseled in the practical steps of godly living. We have already noted certain items. We discussed them as the "Parent's Package" in Chapter Four. Now listen to the way God instructs parents to plant these things in the lives of their children. These passages are also from Proverbs:

"My son, attend to my words, incline your ear and submit to my sayings. Let them not depart from your sight; keep them in the center of your heart" (Prov. 4:20, 21).

. . . Then Solomon goes on to tell why a son should heed his father's words:

"For they are life to those who find them, healing and health to all their flesh. Above all that you guard, watch over your heart, for out of it are the sources of life" (Vss. 22, 23).

. . . Then Solomon mentions some specifics:

"Put away from you false and dishonest speech, and wilful and troublesome talk put far from you. Let your eyes look straight ahead so that you learn how to concentrate and are not easily distracted . . ." (Vss. 24-27).

"My son, Keep your father's (God-given) commandment and forsake not the Law (of God) your mother (taught you). Bind them continually on your heart, and tie them about your neck (for they shall guide your ways). When you go, it (the counsel of your parent's God) shall lead you; when you sleep it shall keep you, and when you awaken, it shall talk with you" (6:20-22).

. . . No youth can ignore counsel which has been diligently planted in his heart. It will stir his spirit day and night to affect his decisions and habits.

"A wise son makes a glad father, but a foolish and self-centered son is a grief to his mother" (10:1).

"Be wise my son and make my heart glad, that I may answer him who reproaches me (for having failed my parental duty) (27:11).

PUNISHED AND TAUGHT

Can you guess why I separated the Scriptures which spoke of punishment and teaching? It was to emphasize the fact that God wants His children BOTH punished and taught. Today people tend to go to extremes. There are those who would use REASON only and leave out punishment. Then there are those who would employ PUNISHMENT only and leave out the teaching. **But God wants them used together.** Actually, one is no good without the other.

Watch your pastor or visiting evangelist. As he nears the end of his message, see if he doesn't give a heart-stirring illustration. Why? He knows people will DO NOTHING about his words **unless they are moved.** So he tells a story which touches the emotions. If he can get people to cry or respond with aroused feelings, he has a good chance of getting them to act. This is not trickery on his part. It is necessary. Why? People do not respond on the basis of FACT alone. Mere knowledge rarely makes people do what they should.

● Your tax bill arrives in the mail. It is due and should be paid. Do you sit right down and make out a check? Hardly. If you are like most of us, you wait until the last minute before filing. If it were not for the late penalties, you probably wouldn't pay it then, but go past the due date. Now those penalties constitute a threat, they are punishment. It is the threat of punishment that makes us pay those taxes on time.

Is it any different when we come to the Word? Most of us know what God expects of us. That is, we have a head knowledge of what He wants us to do and be. In fact, we know more Bible than we care to live. Then what holds us back? We simply do not respond to knowledge alone no matter how wonderful it is. Facts do not stir people to action. It takes an emotional prod such as a threat or emotional story.

That's why the preacher closes with a tear-jerking illustration. He is not happy to have people merely approve or disapprove of what he says. He wants them to DO SOMETHING about it. He knows they won't unless their feelings are fired, unless they are MOVED. Therefore, he uses stories which stir the imagination and arouse feelings. Yet, if he used stories only, his people wouldn't know what to do. Extremes simply don't work.

• Those parents resorting to **reason only** ignore the fact that teens are being wooed by the world at the **emotional** level. Sexy stories and wild music appeal to them more than the Word of God. Those who apply **punishment** only (emotion), overlook the fact that discipline without teaching merely widens the generation gap. Punishment without counsel produces bewilderment and hatred in a child. More than one has run away from home because of it. It takes both reason and emotion—IN COMBINATION—to do the job.

Now you can see why I devoted an entire chapter to the **parent's package** (teaching) and another whole chapter to fear (emotion).

> **NOTE:** Some parents wait until they are driven to it before they will punish a child. Then they are angry. It becomes a matter of vengeance rather than discipline. Such parents are merely striking back at their children. They are retaliating for something done **to them.** By waiting until they are moved to the heat of anger, their actions are likely to be hard and cruel. Children with such parents soon learn to lie to escape brutality. Yet, parents must punish to instill "godly fear," but discipline given in fits of anger creates terror instead. Those who terrorize their children should not be surprised when their children become schemers and cheats through devising ways to escape that kind of punishment.

• Does the New Testament back up the wisdom of Solomon? Does it confirm that both reason and emotion are needed in rearing God's children? Hear the words of the apostle Paul:

> **"And fathers, do not provoke your children to anger; but bring them up in the discipline and instruction of the Lord"** (Eph. 6:4 NAS).

See? The two elements are there. The rod of correction ("discipline") supplies the emotional elements. The parent's package ("instruction") supplies the intellectual elements. When we put the two together we have exactly what God wants. Once we understand both are necessary for the proper development of young people, we are in a position to consider how they work together. Used in combination, reason and emotion are like the two arms of a—**nutcracker!**

A NUTCRACKER . . . ?

Yes. Take a walnut. Now pick up a nutcracker. Insert the nut and squeeze . . . "ccrraaaacckkk!" That's the way to handle a rebellious teen. Put him in the nutcracker and squeeze. Something will give—you can be sure of that. Can't you see the shell of that walnut crumbling under the pressure of those jaws? Well, that's what happens to your boy or girl when you follow the plan set forth in this book.

We're going to consider the NUTCRACKER TECHNIQUE.* Don't be alarmed. It is not going to hurt their personalities. Only the **shell** of their RESISTANCE will be cracked. The kernel (person) won't be damaged at all. You've used a nut-cracker. You know its purpose is to crack the shell only. That's what makes it a perfect device for dealing with resistant teens.

Who hasn't used a nutcracker at one time or another? Surely every reader is familiar with it. It's simple to position a nut between the jaws and bear down just hard enough to crack the outer shell. What you couldn't possibly crack with your fingers, yields easily in the nutcracker. Why? It provides so much leverage that shell has to crumble. Teen problems, which otherwise seem insurmountable, give way easily in the nutcracker.

Now look at our nutcracker for teens.

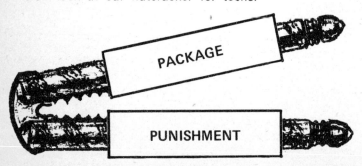

---

*The "nutcracker technique" was first introduced in the author's book, UNEQUALLY YOKED WIVES. There it forms the basis of a plan for winning unsaved husbands to Christ. The same principles can be employed in dealing with young people. The two elements are different, of course. Whereas the wife uses her testimony and submission to squeeze her mate, parents use punishment and godly teaching to salvage a teen.

Our two words PACKAGE and PUNISHMENT are now the jaws of our nutcracker. Ah, but see how they are held together at one end? That is the Holy Spirit's part. He is the One Who holds the jaws together so that they work in combination. He makes the leverage possible. He is faithful to back up mothers and fathers who want to obey God's Word. Because He is steadfast, you can bear down on those handles to get all the squeeze you want. Without Him, there would be no leverage at all.

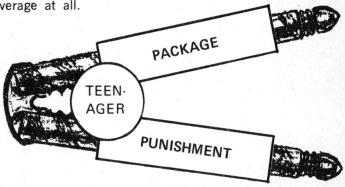

Next consider how the nut in the middle is your resistant teen. Once you catch on to using reason and emotion together, you can start putting the pressure on his rebellious shell. Naturally it is increased gradually until you have just the right amount. If necessary, you can exert tremendous force by bearing down hard on the handles. The Holy Spirit will not fail. He will see that the leverage is there. There is hardly a teen anywhere who can withstand the total pressure parents can apply in the power of the Holy Spirit.

CRACKING THE SHELL

You told your son to rake the front lawn when he got home from school and put the leaves in a barrel. You want the job done before you get home from work. He has plenty of time to fit it into his schedule. He gets home from school hours before you reach home from work.

But as you wheel into the driveway, there are the leaves— **untouched!**

He didn't do as you told him. Now that you have begun the nutcracker technique, you know a time of discipline is ahead. Will he have an excuse? Sure. You know that before you ask. But you also know you are going to punish him— IN LOVE. It is because you do love him, that you cannot allow disobedience to go unpunished. There's no turning back now. **Every offense** must be dealt with sincerely. Why? Each one is an OPPORTUNITY to install more of God's truth in your boy's life, truths which will guard his way later on and prepare him for eternity.

There's your boy now. He's glad to see you.

"Hi pop." He's not perturbed about the unraked lawn. He must have a dandy excuse.

"How come you didn't rake the front lawn, son?"

"Oh, yeah . . . well . . . dad, the coach told some of us there was open time on the basketball court this afternoon, and he'd like us to get in some practice shots. I meant to get home in time to do the leaves, but I got to playing with the other guys and forgot. I sure didn't mean to, Dad."

NOTE: Did you catch the "accident" ring in that excuse. The way teens tell it, it sounds as if it couldn't be avoided. They have a way of putting it, so that it sounds as if they couldn't help it. But teens are easily careless, thoughtless, and forgetful. It's the nature of the critter. However, since excuses don't count with God, they don't count with you either. They may have worked on you before you began the Nutcracker Technique, but they can't now. At the same time, you let your boy know you understand the situation. You realize he didn't mean to disobey you deliberately. See how easy it would be to let him off this time? Sorry, LOVE demands you deal with his carelessness.

90

"Had I thought you meant to disobey me, son, I would be forced to discipline you far more than I am going to now. I believe you when you said you didn't do it deliberately. But because I love you, I can't allow you to be careless with my orders. I want you to go to your room right now. I'll be in shortly."

You know what happens next, don't you? You remember from the last chapter. You want to be alone with Jesus for a few minutes. There you will ask Him for wisdom and the strength to be a real man of God to your boy. You will also get rid of any feelings of anger or hostility, so that your discipline is motivated by love and is not a reaction to his disobedience. When you punish, it must not be a matter of retaliation, but for the sake of your boy's eternal welfare. To punish him for disobedience only, is too short range.

THE MOMENT OF DISCIPLINE

By now you have come to understand that the moment of discipline is the prime time for teaching. You will use the nutcracker. That means the emotion generated by the punishment will be harnessed to a truth from the parent's package. You're going to teach your boy, not just discipline him. You are ready to go to him. You will be using the rod of correction, as Solomon called it. There's no anger in your heart, only love.

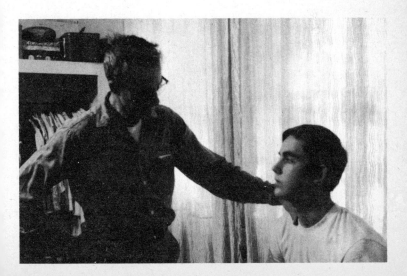

"You know son, even though you have been careless with my orders, I can't be careless with God's orders. I don't dare. I have to be careful when God gives me something to do. I'm going to punish you because God's Word expects me to. However, it is not for disobedience, that is, not for deliberate disobedience. I take your word for it, that you forgot.

"It's a serious thing to be careless with an order given you by someone who has both the power and the right to punish you. I have the power and I am going to use it. Later on you will be working for people who will have the power to penalize you when you are careless with their orders. And one day you will stand before God who has the power to punish you eternally if you are careless with His orders.

"Excuses don't count with God. I can't accept them either. One of the worst things I could do for you, would be to let you feel it didn't matter if you were careless with my orders. If I let you grow up thinking all you need do to avoid punishment is have some good excuse, you could easily adopt that same view toward God's orders. Do you understand what I'm saying son? I don't want you growing up thinking excuses can be substituted for obedience?"

"Yes Dad."

"Do you know why?"

"Well, like you said. You don't want me using excuses to get out of obeying God's orders."

"That's right. So I am going to use this strap on you. It will hurt, but not nearly as much as if you had deliberately disobeyed me. God deals with us the same way. He accepts our good intentions, but He does not overlook our disobedience. We have to suffer the consequences of our carelessness with His orders."

Then you administer a few good swats with your belt. If you have already secured some of those green, bamboo garden sticks, that's even better. He'll feel the pain sharply through his britches. It hurts. It has to. Token punishment is a joke. It is useless. Why? There is no pain. Where there is no pain there is no penetration. And where there is no penetration, there is no communication. There is no way to reach a boy without pain. His carelessness must cost him something. So you hit him hard enough to hurt. Two or three times are enough, as long as it hurts.

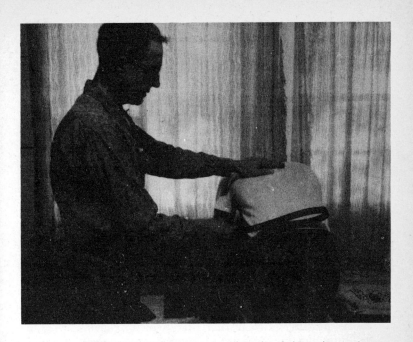

NOTE: Does it startle you to think of a father using a strap or switch on a 15 year old? It is the most effective way. Why? Its work is done in seconds. Yet, it is PACKED with emotion. What is more emotional than a father taking a strap to his son? No other form of punishment can be delivered so fast with forgiveness following instantly. Confining a boy to his room, denying him the TV or making him forfeit some school activity extends the penalty over a period of time. While it sounds more adult or more dignified to use social pain (penalties), it is not nearly as merciful or effective as corporal punishment. A moment of physical pain is the most rewarding type of discipline if you have the ability and courage to use it.

When it comes to the different types of punishment parents may use, I'm ready to leave the choice with the parents. God's way is clearly the "rod of correction." However there are three other forms which may be used in connection with the rod. I will discuss them in the next chapter. Regardless of what psychologists have had to say, nothing is as effective as physical pain. Keep in mind that we need EMOTIONAL CONTENT to make the nutcracker work. Without emotion there can be no squeeze.

NOTE: Tears may come to your boy's eyes. Yours too, perhaps. Particularly if he is a good boy. It is not easy to be a man of God in such a situation. But it is absolutely necessary if one is going to be a godly father. The FEAR OF GOD must motivate a man to make him such a father. He must be one who dares not disobey God. But, oh what marvelous results follow when this punishment is administered in love. A good boy becomes even better. Had you accepted your boy's excuse and failed to discipline him, you would then be letting his excuse become **your excuse** for disobeying God.

Your boy is in the nutcracker. He is feeling the pain of punishment, which supplies the needed emotion. He has also heard his Dad say he couldn't afford to disobey God's orders. That was the teaching. Your boy has now acquired the truth that carelessness with his father's orders or God's orders carries a penalty which **cannot be escaped with excuses.**

Clothed with the emotion generated by punishment, that truth will go into his NEW NATURE. A bit of the fear of God stirs within him too. His father didn't flinch from doing his duty, and He knows God will not flinch from penalizing His either. In the drawing below, note how the "truth about carelessness" and the "pain of punishment" combine to make the nutcracker work. The pressure on the jaws crumbled his outer shell. His resistance was in the form of an excuse. It didn't take much pressure. With little effort, this father penetrated his boy's spirit with a wonderful teaching. The Holy Spirit will have that truth to use in guarding the boy's steps in the future.

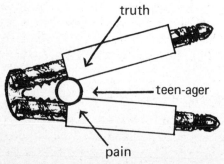

truth

teen-ager

pain

THREE RULES FOR THE NUTCRACKER

94

A nutcracker is a simple tool. It's features are familiar to everyone. That's what makes it a swell teaching device. If I can take what you already know about using a nutcracker and show how it applies to handling youngsters, the principles will be clear and easily remembered.

1. Equal force on the jaws.

When you squeeze an ordinary nutcracker, you apply equal force automatically. You don't even stop to think about it. It won't work unless you do. If you didn't do this, would you be able to crack a walnut? No. The shell gives way because it is caught between equal pressures. The squeeze is the same on both handles. How does this apply to a teen?

This means the amount of teaching given a child should match the emotion generated by his punishment. The father who merely hands out spankings (or other penalties) as needed, wastes the experience if he does not incorporate matching truths from the parent's package at the same time. On the other hand, those who merely REASON with their youngsters at the time of an infraction, might as well save their breath.

> **NOTE:** Truths cannot be implanted apart from emotion. Yes, there might be superficial learning, but it quickly passes away. At the same time, any emotion generated at discipline time is wasted unless it is harnessed to specific truths. To use one without the other is like trying to crack a nut with only one jaw of the nutcracker. It can't be done. Thus, we have a general rule: The more punishment that is called for, the greater the truth you may implant with it. It goes without saying that punishment should NEVER exceed the crime. It would be awful to apply excess punishment for the sake of trying to implant a larger spiritual truth. Discipline must always be geared to the misdeed.

2. Squeeze gently at first.

Not all nuts offer the same resistance. It would not do to come crushing down on an almond. It would mash the kernel as well as the shell. Yet, a Brazil nut requires real pressure before the shell gives way. This provides our second important principle for handling teens.

No two teens are alike. Therefore, no two resist their parents and the things of God in the same way. The variable can range from those who are actually cooperative and enter into some phase of the family's spiritual life, to those who angrily resist everything their parents ask of them. Whereas some are merely reluctant, others are downright defiant. Therefore, it pays to squeeze gently at first to test the resistance of a teen's shell. Some young people need severe pressures, others do not. It would be a shame to come crashing down on your child if he didn't need it.

Besides, a gradual approach gives you a chance to get acquainted with the method. Parents should go easy at first to find out how it works. They should make their mistakes with small matters and gain a little skill before tackling the more critical matters of discipline. It does take some skill to dovetail teaching with discipline. But it will come quickly if you EASE yourself into action. In the next chapter I will show you an easy start.

CAUTION: It is one thing to discover a successful plan for dealing with teen problems, quite another to make it work in your own situation. Desperate parents could be tempted to go overboard and apply the plan in wholesale fashion. Don't let that happen. You have a lot to learn about inserting the parent's package into your children's lives. Besides, they'll think you have "flipped" if you go all out with heavy pressures in sudden moves. Give yourself time. It will take a little experimenting to match punishment with teaching. As you become more familiar with the technique, you can ease on more pressure. Then you can deal with the more serious problems.

3. Take one area at a time.

Watch a person using a nutcracker. Does he attempt to crack two or three nuts at a time? No. He cracks them one at a time. Oh, it can be done. We've all tried it at one time or another. But it makes an awful mess. One of the nuts usually gets crumbled to bits, while the other isn't sufficiently cracked. Why? A nutcracker is designed to break one shell at a time. This introduces another principle for handling teens.

Don't try to revamp your boy or girl with one full swoop. Can you imagine trying to reshape a boy's way of life in one day! You'd end up with a bewildered lad. True, you have the authority to try such a thing—even the power—and now the technique. But what a shattering experience it would be for both of you. The shock would likely drive him out of the house and leave you in the valley of despair.

Instead of a BLANKET approach, become selective. Instead of demanding submission in all areas at once, pick an area where the changes are the EASIEST for him. As soon as you gain victory in one area, you will be encouraged to try another. After success in a few things pertaining to his surroundings (yard-work, for example), you might consider the kind of companions he chooses. Or if you are dealing with a daughter, you can see how restricting her time on the telephone is far less threatening than forbidding her to see a certain boy.

AFRAID TO TRY?

It's possible that the nutcracker scares you. Unless you read about it in one of my other books, the truth is probably new to you. But don't let the newness frighten you. It is nothing more than a device for taking what you already know of God's Word and putting it into a form familiar to you.

What is more obvious than the fact that God wants His children disciplined and taught? When you are able to do both **simultaneously,** you have a powerful tool for dealing with teens. So don't be afraid to try. We will start off gradually. You will be able to test for results as we go. It is going to bring you much joy to be able to infect your child with truths the Holy Spirit can use. You will draw deep satisfaction from using discipline that really changes lives.

Once you plant these truths in your teen's life with emotion, the Holy Spirit will use them to direct his steps. You will see him making decisions and choosing his companions, guided by principles you have planted in him. Then you will hear the Lord's "Well done," in your soul. That's what you want, isn't it? Now let's start learning how to use the nutcracker. That's next.

Chapter Seven

THE FIRST SQUEEZE

"Everything in the modern home is controlled by switches, except the children."—Evening Tribune, Surrey, England.

Professor Ross K. Toole, of the University of Montana wrote an article for the Billings, Montana **Gazette.** It was titled, "I'm tired of the Tryanny of Spoiled Brats." It was so constructive, it was entered into the Congressional Record. The magazine, **U.S. News & World Report** thought it was so much to the point, it reprinted the article. A paragraph belongs here:

> **"I assert we are in trouble with the younger generation . . . because we have failed to keep that generation in its place, and have failed to put them back when they got out of it. We have the power; we do not have the will. We have the right; we have not exercised it. We need to reassess a weapon we came by the hard way as parents and teachers—FIRM AUTHORITY. The best place to start is the home."***

You agree? Good. Then you are ready to see that generation return to its place. You have just learned of the nutcracker technique. The task doesn't seem so formidable once you realize your authority in Christ and have techniques for doing the job. In any event, you are presently absorbing some know-how which will make the job a lot easier. Before we're finished, you'll really know how to deal with testy teens.

BUT HOW TO BEGIN?

We've already agreed you can't move in on a son or daughter to change his whole life in one swoop. You don't deal with anyone that way. Instead you go to work on one area at a time. You wouldn't be reading this book if there weren't some changes you'd like to see. Some family rules are no doubt being violated. With that, I want you to consider

---

*U.S. News & World Report, 13 April, 1970, p. 78.

that **every infraction** of your family rules is an opportunity for the nutcracker. But again, where to begin.

In the last chapter we said it is easier to change something in a person's routine than in the individual himself. Getting a teen to turn off the TV by a certain time is a lot easier than getting him to quit his smart alec talk. Therefore, we will NOT begin by working on personality defects. Instead we will select something from his routine that is easily corrected and TEACH HIM TO OBEY **in that particular thing.**

> **NOTE:** We keep returning to the matter of obedience. That is the key—implicit obedience. It could be brand new to you—and your child. So we start off with easily made adjustments. The beginning point must be something as minor as removing his wet towel from the bed after a shower or slamming the back door when he goes out of the house. It will be a shock for him to obey you ON COMMAND or be punished. It will also be a big change for you to get into the habit of speaking once—and expecting to be obeyed. Yet, that's the point of obedience, isn't it? That's what obedience means.

Years ago Art Linkletter hosted a TV show called, "People, Places, and Things." That title presents the order of human interest. People are indeed the most fascinating item of God's creation. We're next interested in places, and finally we care about things. Ah, but that is also the order of **threat.** It is not so threatening for your boy if you tell him to change certain THINGS in his life. It is more threatening if you restrict the PLACES he can go. He is most threatened when you forbid him to be with certain PEOPLE, particularly a girl he likes very much.

Therefore, we will begin using the nutcracker to change some THINGS in his life. But where, exactly? A boy's routine moves about four centers:

1. His home.
2. School.
3. Social activities.
4. Church.

It is less threatening for him to make changes at home, before he is required to make them some place else. Every lad has a routine at home. We'll begin with your boy, Jerry.

HINT: Millions of youngsters grow up with little or no exposure to the discipline of work and productivity. They simply don't know what it is. Not only is their time wasted in foolishness, they pick up frivolous and wasteful habits. The habit of WORK is one which leads to success. But it is one children must be taught. On a farm there are so many chores to be done, it is hardly necessary to make this suggestion. City-raised children can be taught to care for the yard, vacuum carpets, scrub floors, and help out with housework. Every child should be taught to keep his own room clean, make his own bed, and put things in order before leaving for school. If he doesn't, he will develop the habit of leaving the work for someone else. That does not make for responsibility or self-discipline.

You go into Jerry's room. As usual you have to straighten up after him. He is always in such a dash to get off to school in the morning. He claims he doesn't have time to do it himself. You have asked him about it often enough.

"This seems like the place for me to start using the nutcracker. There's no reason why Jerry can't do this, even if he had to get up a few minutes earlier. Now that I think about it, it would be good for him to get up in time to share in the responsibility of our home. I'm going to talk to him about this when he gets home from school."

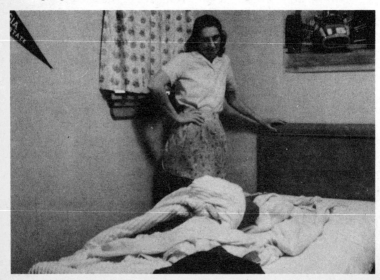

NOTE: It is possible there are other things in Jerry's life that displease you. For the moment, however, we're thinking only of a place to START the technique. He may be smoking, running with the wrong crowd, dating questionable girls, careless with his money, lying to you, as well as hostile to the things of the Lord. But you don't begin with those. They are too serious, too threatening. You need to experiment with the technique before tackling difficult matters. The way to begin is to get him to submit to your authority in little things first. Also, you need to "get the feel" of the Spirit's backing as you bring this kind of discipline to Jerry's life.

In essence you will be teaching Jerry obedience to a **single** command. That's dramatic. Very few children are taught that. Yet, it is not obedience unless the first command is obeyed. Once Jerry learns to obey you in little things, you can move gradually to the harder areas. In time he will become more and more submissive to your authority. If he had learned this as a child, it would be much simpler. However, it is still not too late. If you go about it gradually, you can establish considerable TEACHING and DISCIPLINE in him before he leaves your control.

"Let's see now. How will I relate this to the parent's package? What teaching will I bring as I explain to Jerry the necessity for cleaning his room? What discipline will I be prepared to use if he disobeys me?"

Perhaps we should pause here and think about the kinds of punishment which can be used. I have already said that God prefers the stick. He prescribes corporal punishment in His Word. However, there are other ways too, three of them.

THREE OTHER PUNISHMENTS

1. Allowing young people to bear the consequences of their folly.
2. Isolation from friends or family.
3. Depriving them of some pleasure or privilege.

Some educators advocate **criticism** as a form of punishment. It's true that criticism hurts, especially from parents. Young people yearn for the approval of their folks. This is natural since they identify with them. They want their mothers and dads to be proud of them. But I prefer to AVOID criticism as a form of punishment. I think it is risky to punish a child by withholding approval. True, it is good to criticize a boy's **actions**—even to the point of letting him see your disapproval. But it's a little tricky to distinguish between disapproval of an action and the boy himself. Parents could have the distinction in mind, but youngsters might not.

> **NOTE:** A parent's love is absolutely essential to a teen's security. He must always be assured that you love him no matter how firmly you discipline him. Regardless of what you do or say to him, he must feel that underneath everything, is your love for him. That is the rock of his life, until your love is replaced by that of the Lord Jesus. The love of a father or mother must **never** be negotiable. That is, it must not rise and fall with the tide of his behavior. It must be constant, rock-like.

Disapproval or criticism used as punishment, comes dangerously close to disapproval of the boy or girl. Should the child feel that he himself is the object of disapproval, that would be awful. I feel it is safer not to use it than risk confusing a teen. As always, though, you are free to do as you please about my suggestions. In all of His dealing with us, the love of the Lord Jesus remains constant though we know He disapproves of some of our actions. Anyway, four kinds of punishment are enough.

Now a word about the other three. I've already covered corporal punishment in the preceeding chapter.

1. Bearing the consequences

Jack Kerr, one of our directors, was telling me of an experience he had as a teen. He wanted to eat a green banana, but his dad warned it would make him sick. Jack insisted it wouldn't, so his dad let him eat it. He became very ill. Today, he doesn't eat a banana without remembering the lesson of discipline by consequence.

That was an easy lesson. Carelessness with a musical instrument at school could result in its being stolen. What then? Does dad rush out to buy him another, or does he bear the consequences and go without? Suppose he breaks someone's window? Does he pay for it himself, or does an over-protective parent hasten to replace it for him? What if he is arrested for stealing? Do his anxious parents keep him out of jail, or do they feel it is right for him to pay the price of his own error?

Short-sighted mothers and fathers can't stand the thought of their teens bearing the consequences of their own evil. Yet, they will be on their own at the Judgment. Should they be raised without any painful knowledge of what it means to pay the price of folly? God clearly says . . . "Every man shall bear his own burdens" (Gal. 6:5). There are things we all suffer because of our foolishness. Boys and girls should learn that. One of the best ways to teach them is to let them pay the price in controlled situations and not rush in with over-protective first aid. I'll cite specific cases later on.

2. Isolation

Isolation can be effective when circumstances warrant it. If a teen is abusing other members of the family, for example, isolation in his room is a form of punishment. Again, there might be a squabble over TV. Isolation from the rest of the family would be fitting punishment for the offending member. Or take the uncooperative teen who wants his own way about a family outing. If the family isn't going to be away too long, he could be left home. Missing the outing could be sufficient penalty if the occasion promises to be fun. Parents shouldn't hesitate to apply this kind of discipline.

3. Deprivation

"If you don't eat your dinner, you can't have any dessert."

"If you're not a good girl, we won't go to Grandma's house."

Sound familiar? Such threats represent the most common intimidation of little ones. The sad part is, the threats are seldom carried out. In some cases, the execution of such a threat would produce lasting results. Teen-agers don't like this form of punishment, but it is effective.

 Your daughter has made plans to go shopping with some friends. But then she displays a rebellious attitude when you ask her to do something at home. It would be painful for her to phone her girl friends and explain why she can't meet them as planned. Or take the boy who gets on his high horse when told he must do something. He'll feel it if you deny him use of the family car for a planned outing. This form of punishment puts a stiff price on disobedience and rebellion.

But corporal punishment is the best.

A mother can slap a girl, she can use a switch on a boy. Rarely will a son use violence against a mother who loves him—no matter what she does. He will take a sound thrashing without raising a hand against her. But just suppose he does react. What if he grabs her hands and shoves her aside so that she falls or bumps against the furniture? He may leave the room with his up tight feelings, but minutes later he is sick in his spirit. That is punishment, too. It can be harnessed as well as any other.

The same is true for the father who administers corporal punishment. He's the one who should do it, no argument about that. Even if he is of slighter build than his boy, he should try to deliver the punishment. A boy who resists his dad with violence will feel as bad as if he had resisted his mother. That is, if he knows his dad really loves him. The likelihood of a lad using force to resist a father's discipline is 100 to 1. It is a strange youth who engages his father in an actual fight. If he does, it indicates the relationship between them was broken long ago. The fight will merely be the symptom, not the cause.

I won't forget a whipping my stepdad gave me when I was seventeen, though now I forget what I did. I think I sassed my mother. He took me into a large closet where she couldn't hear me yell. He didn't want her coming to my rescue. Now my stepdad was rugged, a powerfully-built man. But I myself weighed 175 pounds and was on the senior boxing team at school. I knew I could give my dad a rough time. But I didn't. I let him bend me over his knee (actually a half-standing position) and swat me hard as long as he cared to. It brought tears to my eyes. Even so, I couldn't possibly bring myself to square off with him. I knew he loved me. It would have torn up my insides to lay a fist on him. I wasn't saved then, but I once found him praying for me. I knew he loved me.

In the course of using the nutcracker, you will be using all four of these methods. There will be times when one fits the situation beautifully. Most important, is remembering that you need a lot of emotion to make the technique work. It is emotion that makes the nutcracker function as it should. The less emotion there is, the less effective your teaching. Truths do not penetrate apart from emotion. Therefore, the punishment selected for any situation should not only match the crime, it should also stir enough feeling to operate the nutcracker. A teen's resistance will not crack without it.

NOW BACK TO JERRY

I left you standing in the middle of Jerry's messy room. You were thinking about starting the technique when he came home from school. You were asking yourself what part of the **Parent's Package** would apply to the situation. You also need to be ready with discipline should he refuse to carry out your orders.

> "Let's see. If I make him clean up his room this afternoon, and see that he does it each morning after that, it will be a nice start in securing his obedience. I will be teaching him responsibility by making him RESPONSIBLE to do this every day. And I can teach him the principle of accountability as well. He will have to account to me for the orderliness of his room, even as I have to account to God for the way I am raising him."

Jerry comes home. He goes to his room to get rid of his books. He should study them, but you know he won't. You follow him. You are going to confront him with the new requirement.

> "Jerry, just look at this room! See how you left it this morning? I've asked you repeatedly to make your bed and put things away before you leave for school."

> "I know, Mom. But there just isn't time in the morning."

He's probably surprised to find you haven't straightened it up for him. You usually do.

"You know it isn't right for mother to have to pick up after a big boy like you. I'm not helping you a bit when I do it for you. But I didn't realize that until today. During my prayer time, the Lord showed me how I am actually hurting you by not teaching you to obey me in things like this."

"Yeah . . . ?" He's wondering what's coming.

"Yes Jerry. The Lord has been speaking to me about the way I have been raising my son. I want to be a good mother. To do that, I have to obey the Lord and insist that you obey me. So Jerry, I want you to make your bed and straighten this room right now. You are not to leave the room until you do. And I want you to do the same thing each morning before you leave for school."

Then you put some teeth into your expectations:

"Not only does the Lord want me to see that you do this, Jerry, He also expects me to discipline you if you don't. So it's up to you, son. Do as mother asks, or you will put her in the place where she has to punish you. You know I don't want to do that."

Jerry could react

"Wow, Mom! How come all of a sudden you would punish me for not cleaning up my room? You haven't done it before."

Cleaning his room seems so trifling to Jerry. He doesn't realize you have selected an easy beginning for the technique. And you don't tell him, of course. He's not to know you are carrying out a plan for securing his obedience. He's a little startled, but that's fine. It adds seriousness. Jerry's question provides an opportunity to bring the Lord into the conversation once more:

"If I have to punish you, son, it will be for refusing to obey me. Failure to clean your room will simply be the point at which you disobeyed me. Even though you disobey me, I don't dare disobey the Lord now that He has put it on my heart. He expects me to punish disobedience. And I will, if you force me to. But I'd much rather think you want to obey me, even as I want to obey the Lord. Mother prefers to believe you are that kind of a boy."

NOTE: The technique has a positive side. A healthy ring is added in the form of expressed CONFIDENCE. Each time you give an important order or place a responsibility upon a youth, tell him you have confidence in him. Then it becomes a challenge. Often, youngsters will rise to meet such a challenge. It is this feature of stated confidence that has led some psychologists to conclude that parents should use confidence exclusively to direct their children's lives. While it is powerful, it is NOT that powerful. Positive motivation (confidence and rewards) simply cannot compete against Satan and the old nature. While it can be used in connection with punishment, it must NEVER be substituted for it. There is NO substitute for punishment.

NOW YOU'VE STARTED

Once those words come from your lips, the plan is under way. Purpose not to turn back. Determine to be consistent. Anticipate that it means a new way of life for you. Sure it will take effort. There'll be some heartache. But what do you have now? The situation isn't pleasant as it is, or you wouldn't be reading this book. It's not easy to watch a boy or girl go down the wrong path. It is painful to see your children drift from the way of the Lord. So don't let a little distress keep you from applying the necessary discipline. You won't be sorry if you obey God. The reward could be a salvaged son or daughter.

However, you must be consistent.

Let me say that again. The plan will NOT work unless you are steadfast. To punish your boy for an infraction one day and allow him to get away with it another day, frustrates the technique. To build the HABIT of obedience, you must develop the HABIT of punishing EACH infraction. If you do not sell yourself on the need for determined consistency, you'll end up punishing only when . . . "I've had it with that boy." The foundation you seek to build in his life comes only as you proceed with calm, firm, systematic discipline EVERY TIME an infraction occurs. And each time that discipline must be accompanied by teaching. Both jaws of the nutcracker must be operating to get the job done.

So be sure you speak only once.

Parents who say, "Did you hear me?" are those who speak more than once. Those who say, "If you do that again, you are going to be punished," also speak more than once.

> **NOTE:** Many parents are fooled by kids who simply ignore them when they speak. It baffles folks when youngsters pretend or act as if an order had not been given. A boy who does this, wants you to think he didn't hear you. He's hoping you'll give up, not bothering to say it again. And then he's off the hook. But it is amazing how sharp their hearing becomes if you have the habit of speaking only once and reward disobedience with IMMEDIATE punishment. As soon as this plan has been in operation a short time, the moment you say . . . "Go to your room, I'll be in in a few minutes," they'll know exactly what is coming. It could be you will develop the habit of clearing your throat before acting. If you do, they have a warning. This allows them to jump to obey rather than have certain discipline come upon them.

Never give up.

Once the technique is started, never give up. If you find that the first discipline doesn't do the job, apply a second. If the second fails, apply a third. Don't hesitate to do it four or five times if necessary — or even more. Never give up simply because a child rebels, seeking to manifest a stronger will than yours. That rebellious spirit can be broken if you stay with it. It MUST be broken. It is easier to give up than be steadfast in discipline, but it is disastrous for the child if you do.

> **NOTE:** Teens can be taught to respond to a single command. That may seem like a dream at this stage. Not only can it be accomplished, it must. You shouldn't settle for less. God expects no less, we shouldn't either. Of course, it may take some getting used to. And it might shock your friends to see your son or daughter act instantly on your command. But you will get accustomed to it in time. And you'll like it. Soon it will seem there is no other way to raise young people. Take my word for it, there is nothing abnormal about obedience, certainly not in a godly home.

BUT WHAT IF JERRY REFUSES . . . ?

If he submits to his mother then the first bump passes easily and the plan is under way. But that might not be the case at all. He may be used to having his own way. It could be he has done pretty much as he pleased, though making a pretense at being a cooperative son. Kids are not dumb, you know. They know how to operate. They know how to get what they need from their folks. But Jerry is still a teen-ager and not ready to make his way in the world. He needs the "establishment" to survive. And you're part of it. It could be he has learned to work the "angles" to get by until he can leave home. Many kids reason that way.

> "I wish I could stay and clean up my room, Mom, but Eddie and George are waiting for me to come and help them take the engine out of George's car. What do you say we start tomorrow. Okay?"

There. See the stubborn self-will? He's determined to do things his way. There's no submission. Instead there's a promise of tomorrow with which he hopes to get around you. It doesn't matter that you are seeking to obey the Lord. He thinks you should be satisfied with his talk of future cooperation and let him off the hook.

"SLAP!"

That was the sound of your open palm striking him full across the cheek. It was a good blow. His skin reddens where your fingers landed. He's surprised. Shocked, is a better word. You've never reacted to his scheming words this way before.

"Son. Mother just told you she had to obey the Lord. That means I must make you obey me. You are not to leave this room until you have done as I asked."

> **NOTE:** Don't hesitate to administer the slap. The female slap is the equivalent of the father's strap. A stinging slap from a boy's mother has a penetrating effect equal to the blow of his dad's belt. You were prepared to do this, so it is NOT retaliation for his remark. Before you spoke to Jerry, you were ready to do what was necessary to secure his obedience in this matter. You are simply carrying out your plan. You are dealing with defiance, not reacting from wounded pride.

● Now what will Jerry do? The slap will either stun him into submission or bring out his real feelings. If he becomes hostile, it will simply be the surfacing of hostility ALREADY THERE. If he doesn't start at once to straighten the room, he will probably go storming off, slamming the door as he stalks out of the house. Don't worry—he'll be back. He'll get hungry. He has to come home. Even if he has enough money for a snack or two, he's nowhere near ready to make his own way in the world.

As soon as your husband gets home, tell him what happened. Enlist his cooperation. Hopefully, both of you are concerned about the trend in Jerry's life. I am assuming your husband is a Christian and you have agreed together that the nutcracker should be tried. It would be a mess if you began the action and your husband refused to back you. One of the most sickening situations is where one parent nullifies the instructions of the other. Or where one parent sides with a youth, feeling the other partner has dealt with him too harshly.

It is bad enough for a teen to suffer his own conflict with his parents and the Holy Spirit, without witnessing a conflict between his parents as well. That really tears a youngster apart. It also makes it impossible to remedy the situation. In those cases where parents are at cross-purposes with each other, with respect to training the children, it would have been better had no children been born into that family. Such children have practically no chance of growing up to be obedient, respectful, or emotionally sound.

> **HINT:** If your husband is unsaved and he will not give you the needed freedom to begin the nutcracker technique with Jerry, it could be God's will for you to use the technique on your husband first. In that case, however, the plan works a bit differently. The ARMS of the nutcracker consist of the wife's submission on the one hand, and her words which credit Christ for her sweetness on the other. It is very effective. To use it, you would need a copy of the author's book, "Unequally Yoked Wives." The plan can be put into operation the moment you get a copy. What you have read in this book will add that much more to your understanding. Once your husband is saved, he will agree that any problems with the children should be handled from God's point of view.

● When will Jerry be back? Don't worry about it. The Holy Spirit will look after him. That's part of the deal. If you obey God, He will back your action and take care of Jerry. Trust Him for it. It's natural for you to wonder if he is all right or getting into trouble. Satan will seek to annoy you with his suggestions . . . "What if this or that happens . . . ?" The devil will exploit your motherly instincts. But it is better to obey God than your motherly instincts. You see, even animals have those instincts.

But what is Jerry doing? Stewing. You can be sure of that. He's fuming inside at first, but then those feelings turn to restlessness. Finally they become agonizing. The Holy Spirit will pierce his heart with bitter conviction. He'll feel awful. So relax and let the Lord work in Jerry. The more time He has, the better.

If there are four members in your family, only set places for three at the table. Don't plan on Jerry for dinner. Until he submits to cleaning his room he should get NO FOOD at your house. You're not going to feed a rebel. See—this is the **isolation** form of punishment, only now it is working in cooperation with the SLAP.

HINT: As you prepare the family dinner, have something in mind that Jerry can fix for himself later on. It might be a glass of milk and a sandwich. It is possible he may not like being hungry and will come home around mealtime. "After all," he says to himself, "what's the big deal about making my bed. I'll go do that and then I can eat." If he does get home in time to straighten his room and join the family for dinner, fine and dandy. But if he thinks he can come at his own convenience, fix his room, and then expect you to feed him, he should have another think coming. Don't do it. You must not cater to his wishes or timing. He is the one who must obey YOU. You do not obey him. That's been going on long enough. Today is the day you put a stop to it.

● Does it seem terrible that your boy should miss a meal or two? He won't starve. People can live over 30 days on water alone. Actually this is a painless way to handle the problem. The only reason he is going hungry is because he is too rebellious to submit and clean his room. Why should you make it any easier for him? Let him stew. The more emotional he gets, the better the nutcracker will work. Chances are you've been over-protecting him anyway. It has produced his cantankerous ways. You've babied him and made him feel it was all right to grow up a self-willed, spoiled brat. If I'm wrong about that, I apologize at once.

When he comes home

Finally Jerry will have had enough. He'll come home. Don't feel sorry for him even if he acts like a whipped dog. He gets no bonus for feeling as he should. He deserves no special attention. Therefore, subdue all your motherly instincts UNTIL you have squeezed all the profit you can from this situation. Later, you can indulge yourself and fawn over him. But for the moment, don't pity him because he displays a little meekness. It's really good for him. If he arrives at dinner time, and finds no place for him at the table, let him be shocked. Don't jump up and set a place for him. If he finds the family has eaten with nothing left for him, that's good too. He will say to himself, "They didn't even expect me!"

"Where's my dinner, mom?"

"Well, son, when you refused to obey me, I went to the Lord about it. It became clear to me that if my son would not obey me, I had no right to support his rebellion. The way you went out of here, I didn't think you were coming back. However, if you want something to eat, go clean your room. Then you can fix yourself a sandwich. There are some things in the refrigerator."

"You mean I have to make up my room before I can even eat?"

"That's right. And if you want to eat in this house tomorrow, that room will have to be straightened before you go to school."

There—see now this is why you must not get gushy at the first sign of meekness? It remains to be seen what his meekness means in action. It has to be translated into obedience or it is just a sham.

● Jerry goes to his room. He makes his bed and puts things away. He's not exactly happy. It's a grudging service. He's accustomed to using you. Being in submission is a new role for him. Even so, it's a wonderful start. You've gained the upper hand—plan to keep it. You've won the first round. However, there's still more to be extracted from the incident. The opportunity comes when Jerry sits down to eat his sandwich. Spend a few minutes with the Lord first, then join him at the kitchen table:

"Jerry, you know it would have been a lot easier had you obeyed mother and fixed your room when I asked you, don't you?"

"I suppose so."

"Well, honey, mother wants you to be an obedient son. I want to be proud of you, as does any mother. But more important than that, is my obedience to God. I have been disobeying God with my failure to make you mind me. So don't be too upset with me for dealing with you this way. I'm in the same position you are. You have to mind me or suffer the consequences, I have to obey God or suffer the consequences."

"What consequences could you have to suffer, Mom?" Jerry's sure the situation is all one-sided. It's news to him that you have to obey God or be sorry.

"Honey, you're not my son. (That gets his attention.) That is, you are not my son alone. God sent you into this family. Your father and

I are responsible to raise you the way God wants you raised. His Word makes it clear what He expects of me and what I am to expect of you. The Bible says God chastens (disciplines) those whom He loves. He loves, me and I know He will do as He says. I don't want the chastening hand of the Lord to fall on me, so I must see that you obey me. From now on when I tell you to do something, you should know mother really means for you to do it. I don't have any choice, Honey."

"I'll try Mom. I'm sorry I acted the way I did. I shouldn't have run off like that."

HIS SHELL HAS CRACKED

The nutcracker has done its job. The squeeze wasn't really so hard. His resistance at this point has been overcome. It might be another story when we get to the harder areas. However, you have started and your first efforts have been rewarded with Jerry's tenderness. That's not bad for a beginning. Of course, we deliberately started with an item where Jerry's surrender was likely. That's only wise.

So far you have installed a wee bit of the parent's package. He has learned of obedience in connection with the Lord. The idea of consequences for disobedience has been lodged in his understanding. There is something you must do now that Jerry has apologized. God wants that boy—**FORGIVEN.**

No boy or girl should be left with the impression he is **still guilty** once you have his repentance. As soon as your discipline has done its work, Jerry should be restored to the good graces of the family. It should be built into your plan and Jerry's mind that forgiveness awaits as soon as his punishment has brought about his repentance. The very act of forgiveness is a precious teaching time. But it must be forgiveness as the Lord forgives. That is, mothers and fathers should forgive the same way He does—completely and **without recall.**

> **NOTE:** There is a lot you could have said to Jerry while the two of you were at the table. But I will skip the dialogue in order to get to the forgiveness scene. Your boy has experienced physical (slap) and emotional (isolation) pain. He's now sorry for the way he's acted. With the penalty paid, he is ready to be forgiven. His heart is tender. Yours most definitely is. You reach across the table for his hand.

"Son, do you understand that mother has to discipline you because she loves you. I do you know, very much. And I'm ready to forgive you if you want me to."

"Of course I do, Mom. I really do."

Jerry may be one who likes to present a tough appearance. If so he will hold back his emotions. The Holy Spirit is using your obedience. He is backing your words with a witness to Jerry's heart. Jerry knows you love him. God's Spirit says so. Jerry feels it. Your anointed words will now have a terrific effect on him. It is surprising how thoroughly a youth will repent of a misdeed in such a moment, and go all out to assure you he is sorry.

It is not uncommon for a boy who has been punished, as you have dealt with Jerry, to put his arms around his mother and tell her he loves her. When you speak of forgiveness, it is something for which every heart yearns. Jerry is melted by your words. Punishment and forgiveness go together. God's forgiveness is based on the punishment Jesus took in our place.

"Forgiven"

"I'm glad you asked me to forgive you son. Until you did, I couldn't express it as I would like to. But now that you've asked me, I not only forgive you, but as far as I am concerned, today's incident never happened. The reason I forgive you this way, is because that is how God forgives us when we repent of our evil and ask His forgiveness."

Such a scene is full of teaching and emotion. Jerry's spirit is penetrated with a wonderful truth as he embraces his mother. Secular educators have nothing to offer that matches this moment.

SUCCESS?

Sure. At least with your first squeeze of the nutcracker. The plan has worked. You have made a penetration. It remains to be seen what Jerry will do in the days ahead. If he is faithful to straighten his room for a period of two weeks, plan on rewarding him. People love to be rewarded. A useful emotion goes with it.

"Jerry, your father and I are quite pleased with the way you have obeyed us. We want you to know we appreciate it. We are proud of you and we don't want your obedience to go unrewarded. Tonight, at the dinner table, we have a special surprise for you."

HINT: Since it was from the dinner table that Jerry felt his isolation, it is a good place to reward him for his obedience. Does he have a favorite cake? Bake him one. Then secure a little gift that he can either wear or hang up in his room. It should be something he will see all the time so that it can serve as a reminder that "obedience pays." Just before you give him his gift, bring out a crudely fashioned crown made from cardboard and put it on his head. This adds a terrific touch to the teaching you are going to bring him.

"Son, it is biblical for us to reward you for your obedience. The Bible teaches us that the Lord is going to reward each of us for our obedience unto Him. It calls our rewards crowns. Since this is the hour of your reward, here is your crown. And since your cooperation has made it possible for us to obey the Lord as we should, we honor you with this gift."

116

Jerry will feel foolish, perhaps, when that crown goes on his head. But he will eat it up. A tremendous amount of emotion is present to this scene. Don't worry if it seems childish or ridiculous. That only adds to its strength. The emotion he feels will be harnessed to two great truths: (1) disobedience brings discipline, (2) obedience brings reward. See now what you have accomplished by taking something as simple as straightening up his room?

You wisely selected an item from the THINGS in his routine to get Jerry to yield to your authority. It really wasn't too hard for him. Still, it took some pressure and he didn't give up without a struggle. That's what made it a marvelous teaching. Enough emotion was generated for you to penetrate his spirit with truths from the parent's package. Are there other THINGS in Jerry's domestic routine which need changing? No doubt there are. I will leave it up to you to decide how long you want to work at the THINGS level before advancing to the more threatening matter of the PLACES he goes.

> **CAUTION:** Do not think to use this plan to gain COMPLETE control over a teen's life. That is not the purpose at all. We are interested solely in installing truths from the parent's package. To do so, we merely select a FEW rough spots and use them in the nutcracker. God does not seek to control our lives. He wants us to align our desires and ambitions with His **voluntarily.** For that, He uses pressures and circumstances in a FEW areas to plant His truths. God has a nutcracker, too. He uses sickness and tragedy to touch our hearts. And the corresponding emotion drives the truth of His Word deep in our hearts. So it is with our teens. We work on a few areas to get the truths installed, but it is their VOLUNTARY submission to the will of God we really seek. The plan of this book is a means for installing truths. It is NOT a device for dominating youngsters.

Now that you know how the plan works with THINGS, we're ready to consider PLACES. But let's give Jerry a break and deal with his sister. She is not perfect either. So now to try the nutcracker on a girl. That's next.

Chapter Eight

INCREASING THE PRESSURE

"Parents spoil their kids today!"

That's what 88% of all young people think, according to a recent Harris Poll reported in **Life Magazine.** Another 75% said, "Parents have become too permissive." Isn't it interesting how youngsters perceive this? They sense that rules and discipline do belong in the home.

Rules are vital. No home can function without them. A child cannot be taught to obey unless first there are rules for him to obey. Youngsters must have specific guidelines, otherwise, they do not know what they can and cannot do. Behind those rules must be parents ready to enforce them with FIRM discipline.

There is never a time when fathers and mothers can let up in their responsibility to discipline their children, any more than there is a time when the police department shouldn't enforce the law. However, that doesn't mean that parents should stand over their youngsters dictating every move they make. That would be an awful bondage for both parent and child. Instead, the rules should be like a fence inside which a teen can discipline himself, but beyond which there is danger. Teens need freedom. Without it they cannot mature as they should. But the **limits** of their freedom should be as rigid as a fence.

The freedom of the fence.

We once lived on a busy boulevard. A family moved into the house next door. They had a little fellow only two years old. It was summer and he wanted to be outside. He knew how to open the screen door. There was no fence about the yard and every time he got out that door, he made a bee line for the street. He was fascinated by the cars whizzing by.

This terrified his poor mother. More than once she found

him off the curb, edging closer to the fast moving traffic. Consequently, she had to watch him like a hawk. She had to know where he was every minute. She didn't dare let him out of her sight for a moment. It was a nightmare for the nerve-wrought mother, an awful bondage for the boy.

Then the father ordered a chain link fence. It went all about the house providing a safe yard for the little fellow. Now his mother could turn him loose and relax. It was just great for the youngster. It gave him considerable freedom. He was out from under his mother's thumb. True, he was confined inside the fence, yet he could play for hours with total freedom—within those safe limits. He enjoyed far more liberty with the fence than without it. The fence actually set him free, providing safety and liberty at the same time.

TEENS NEED SIMILAR FENCES

If the 2 year old was endangered by the busy street, teens are endangered by late hours and the company they keep. There are things young Christians should not be permitted to do and see. There are places they should not be allowed to go, and habits which they should not be allowed to develop. No matter how old a boy or girl might be, if he lives at home, he still needs rules which will give him liberty and protect him at the same time. Family rules can provide a fence inside which a young man can grow into a healthy, contented adult.

At the same time he is protected from going where his impulses and imperfect judgment might take him into danger.

The family rules of a Christian home should be a good strong fence. As the children mature, the limits of the fence can be pushed out further and further. As long as the boundaries are clearly defined, a youth can relax inside the limits of his freedom and mature as he ought. The teen who knows exactly what he can and cannot do, is healthier and happier and more contented. But without a fence to establish those limits for him, he has no way of knowing what is safe and what isn't. That leads to insecurity.

It becomes obvious then, that parents must establish clear-cut rules for the regulation of the home. The moment a mother and father begin to enforce those rules with consistent discipline, they become a FENCE. A well established fence, one that does not yield to testing, is a marvelous thing for a teen-ager. Not only does it show him the safe limits for his activities, he soon learns those rules are for his protection. Inside the fence he has all the freedom he needs for maturity, but outside that fence lies **danger.**

THE FENCE MUST BE FIRM

Have you seen an electric fence? Usually it consists of nothing more than a strand of highly charged wire running around a piece of property. Such fences are useful for keeping livestock within the limits of a compound. Every time an animal tries to go beyond the limits of the fence, he gets a shock. Since it is a real jolt, he usually won't try it more than once or twice. He soon learns to let that fence alone and doesn't try to get past it.

Now our children are not animals. And we don't treat them as livestock. But the discipline we install in our homes ought to work as automaticaly. The moment a youth tries to go beyond the rules of the home, he should get a shock. Every attempt to wander beyond the fence should be met with discipline. It should be a stiff jolt, one which discourages future attempts. That way, he won't try it more than once or twice. Discipline in the Christian home should be as **automatic** as an electric fence. That is another way of saying it must be **consistent.**

What is it that keeps a boy from acting on impulse when temptation arrives? Is it the little talks you've had with him? No. He forgets all about your words and reasons in the heat of passion. REASON hasn't a chance when he's faced with an EMOTIONAL situation. But he won't forget PAIN. Pain is not theory. It isn't forgotten. It lingers in his nature. The Holy Spirit can bring it to mind. If your boy knows for sure that impulsive actions can bring PAIN as the swift consequence, he'll think twice before plunging into evil. He learns about pain from discipline. Discussions do not build fences, PAIN does.

Little chats with your son or daughter are nice. They are great for fellowship. It's a swell way to inform them of holy ideas. You can easily get them to agree with you while you are talking to them, but when they are being impelled by one of their drives to do evil, that agreement means nothing. Logic is a poor competitor with emotion. Nearly everyone who does wrong, KNOWS IT AT THE TIME.

I recall an evening when my grandmother was telling my brother and me about a boy in our town who was sure to end up in trouble. He was running with the wrong crowd, defying his parent's wishes. She said he would finally end up in jail. Grandma's counsel on bad companions impressed me. I loved her and respected her wisdom. But what poor grandma didn't know, was that I was planning that very night to break into the bus depot. An "evil companion" and I had schemed to get the ticket agent's cash box. Yet, as I listened to grandma's words and knew they made sense, they couldn't compete with the excitement and adventure that lay ahead.

I went that night. I wasn't caught. No one ever knew. I expected to get away with it. I had been getting away with plenty at home. You see, inspite of Grandma's wise counsel, she never spanked me. She never disciplined me. It never occurred to me to consider the consequences were I caught. Consequences, were something I never thought of—**I didn't have to.** It was natural for me to think I could get away with anything I planned carefully enough. I know from experience what the lack of discipline can do for a youth. I was a seasoned criminal by the time I was sixteen. Had there been a fence to teach me the consequences of self-will, it would have been a different story.

GIRLS NEED FENCES TOO

"Sugar and spice and everything nice," is the way that old poem describes them. But boys are made of "dirt and snails and puppy dog tails," they say. Little girls are thought of as nice little angels, while boys are pictured as little demons. Don't you believe it. There's not the slightest difference between the old nature of a boy and that of a girl. Both are selfish and mean and capable of terrible evil. To be sure, they express their evil in different ways, but it all stems from an identical nature. Both require firm discipline. A girl may not go storming from the house, slamming the door behind her, but she knows how to pout and make life miserable for everyone around her.

That brings us to Jerry's sister. Judy is 14. Jerry was in the nutcracker because he left his room in a mess. But Judy has telephonitis. She forgets all about time when she's on the phone. You think an hour is too long for girls to giggle into the mouthpiece. Besides, there are better uses for her time. So you are going to break the habit by placing a 10 minute limit on her calls.

You can almost hear the squawk that will come when you tell her. But you have talked it over with the Lord and your husband, and you're convinced it would be a fine place to begin the nutcracker technique in Judy's life. It's not a life or death matter. Rather it is one to which Judy should be able to adjust without too much trouble. Though you don't really expect a lot of fireworks, you are prepared to back the new rule with discipline. Sure there will be some emotion. You are counting on that for the sake of the teaching you want to bring.

"Brrrrnnnnnnggg!"

There goes the phone. And there goes Judy. The moment to install the technique may have arrived. Could this be one of her girl friends? It is. That means another hour of her life will be squandered on the phone. While she talks to her friend, you go to the Lord. You have plenty of time.

You want to make sure all hostility is gone from you. There mustn't be a speck of resentment stirring when you talk with Judy. What you do and say must be out of love ONLY. You ask the Lord for the wisdom. You trust Him for the counsel you'll need when you talk to her about her waste of time on the phone.

At last she's finished.

"Judy, do you realize you spent over an hour on the phone?"

"Oh Mom, what's wrong with that? Don't be a square!"

Her flip reply could have thrown you off guard, had you not prepared yourself. It can't be allowed to trigger a reaction from you. You've reached the moment when you have decided to be a godly mother rather than a permissive parent. The easiest way to handle the whole situation would be to shrug it off with . . . **"I'll be glad when she gets past this stage."** But you know permissiveness of that sort makes for juvenile delinquents. After talking things over with the Lord, Judy's snip reply doesn't sound so "cute" today.

"Sit down a minute dear, I want to tell you something."

"What is it, Mom?" She senses something's up. You didn't brush off so easily. Her tone becomes different. She's not so flip now.

"I've discussed this with your father and we've decided you are spending too much time on the telephone. We've agreed to set a time limit on your conversations. So beginning right now, you are to limit yourself to 10 minutes."

"I don't see what's wrong with talking on the phone. That's what it's for. Besides, you aren't using it. I don't see why I should have to limit my calls. It's not hurting anybody."

"Now that's a firm rule, dear. It doesn't mean 11 minutes, it means 10. If you break it, mother will have to discipline you. However, you are entitled to know why we're making this rule."

NOTE: Youngsters need an explanation for rules imposed on them. They cooperate better when they share in your reasons. They may not agree, but they feel more secure when they know WHY they cannot do certain things. What they really want, is to feel the love behind the rule. They want to make sure that love is still there, even though the rule seems like an arbitrary decision. If they are informed that it is in their best interest, as well as important to others in the family, then they have a REASON to discipline themselves. The goal of all imposed discipline is self-discipline. Explanations aid in the self-discipline process.

"You know it isn't because we don't want you to enjoy your friends. We realize friendships are important, but you do see them at school. There's no need for hour-long conversations on the phone after you get home. You tie up the line and prevent any incoming calls. Besides, it's poor discipline of your time."

"I've got plenty of time. And I get my work done, don't I?"

Judy is more emotional now. She feels the restriction is unreasonable, even though you have stated your reasons.

"You don't have a lot of time, Judy. What you mean is, you're not using it for anything important. Whether you realize it or not, time is the most important possession you have on earth. However, your father and I feel that staying on the telephone for an hour is an abuse of the privilege, and we're going to insist that you discipline yourself and limit your conversations to ten minutes."

NOTE: If Judy should ask why time is her most important possession, it would open the door for a teaching on the fact that we have but one life to live for Christ. Why? When it is gone, we will never again be able to lay up treasures for OURSELVES (Matt. 6:20). Judy may think that household chores and homework fulfill the demands on her time, but she is ignoring the Lord's claim on her life. If a conversation about the use of time develops, you could say a word about the investment of her life in Jesus as being necessary to get ahead in heaven. Truths from the author's book, WHY DIE AS YOU ARE! would fit perfectly into such a conversation. They show how every minute of one's life should be used for Christ. We are called to total Christianity.

● Judy won't like it, but she'll do it. She has to. Your reasons are good enough and she knows it. It's natural for kids to complain when denied something they've gotten used to. It is an easy adjustment, actually. She'll grumble some, but down deep she knows you are right. When the phone rings again, glance at the clock. I don't mean for you to play detective with her, but keep tabs on her for the first half-a-dozen calls.

HINT: When her first calls come, after the regulation is in force, it would be helpful to hold up 10 fingers as a signal to her when she runs to answer the phone. That will have the effect of saying, "Don't forget, dear—10 minutes." After two or three such reminders, the rule will be fixed in her mind. After that, if she has a lapse of carelessness, you won't be puzzled about using discipline. If she disobeys you deliberately, then you must deal with disobedience. If she merely forgets, then she should be disciplined for carelessness. It will help you to decide which is the case if you see that the rule is firmly fixed in her mind before an infraction occurs. Those hand signals are for your benefit as well as Judy's.

● Judy slips. She's been talking on the phone for 20 minutes. You go to the Lord to make sure your heart is ready to deal with her in love. Then Judy looks up and sees you standing in the doorway. **"Oh oh, sorry Jan, I've got to hang up."** The phone goes back to its place. What happens next depends on Judy's attitude. If she is defiant, protesting the rule is unfair, use the slap. Follow it with a conversation about obedience. Let her know that you have no choice in the matter of discipline. God requires it of you and you dare not disobey Him. As a penalty she should be denied the use of the phone for a period of three weeks.

Is Judy tender hearted? Is she sorry she forgot? Then your action is different. Your attitude is the same—loving yet ready to do what you must in the situation. She should be denied the use of the phone for one week. In both cases you are gentle, even tender—but firm. Do not reduce either penalty before the stated time has passed.

NOTE: Children want their parents to be steadfast, even though they set up an awful howl of protest. Teens identify with their parents, but they want that identification to be with strong people who show good control of themselves and the situation. Through all of the shifting attitudes of bewildered teens, they look at their parents and get a glimpse of the kind of people they will be when they are adults. You can be sure your child will grow up to be more settled and secure if you remain firm in your promises and prohibitions. In moments of discipline, you are like God to them. They don't ever expect Him to weaken. Deep within themselves, they don't want you to weaken either.

LET'S CONSIDER SOMETHING MORE THREATENING

Remember we said the order of threat ran from THINGS to PLACES to PEOPLE? Within each of those categories is another scale of threat. That is, some THINGS are less threatening than others. Making Jerry fix his room was not very threatening to him, though he made a big fuss about it. It wasn't a lot to ask of him. Had you told him to get rid of his mini-bike that would have been more threatening. To make him quit smoking, would be a still higher form of threat. That gets closer to his personality. Smoking is usually related to a personality disorder.

Let's now select an item for Jerry which has quite a bit of threat. It's still in the THINGS category, but we can expect some fireworks when you exert your authority over his **long hair.**

Jerry has been influenced by the hippies. He has let his hair grow out where it is hard to tell from a distance whether he is a boy or a girl. It is a source of embarrassment for the rest of you. It doesn't enhance his looks a bit. In fact, he seems down right messy. You've gone along with him for a time, hoping it was a passing fad. But now it appears he isn't likely to cut his hair at all. You want him to return to a more conventional style. So we'll make Jerry's long hair our next item for the nutcracker.

NOTE: The long hair and far out dress styles of modern youth are SYMBOLS. Of what? Rebellion. No one enjoys hair in his face or itching his neck. So why do kids endure it? It is contrary to the established way. It's an act of defiance, a protest against the status quo. What is the kid's gripe against the established order? They didn't establish it. Our permissive society has brought up a generation which rebels against everything it doesn't initiate. They want to do "their own thing," and are ready to defy all authority to do it. Consequently, they seek to overthrow or change things which are none of their business. In spite of the fact that they have no experience nor have made any contribution, they'd like to run the country. Symbols of defiance are now seen in the speech, dress, and mannerisms of American youth. Long hair is one of these symbols.

With his Christian background, your boy doesn't exactly approve of the sordid things occurring in his peer group, but he has a longing to be "in." If long hair helps him to be "in" with the crowd, he'll let his grow. So far you've gained control over his room maintenance, and we'll assume you've been successful with some other items such as yard work. Now you're ready to try a bigger squeeze with the nutcracker. This time we'll let Dad handle the situation:

"Son, your mother and I have been talking about your long hair. We think you have been wearing it that way long enough. We'd like you to get a more conventional hair cut."

"You mean, just like that?"

"Right. We want you to go to the barber and get a regular hair cut. We'll give you one week to get rid of long hair. We don't feel a Christian has any business wearing his hair so long, you can't tell whether he is a boy or girl."

"Hey! Wait a minute! Don't I have anything to say about it?"

"No. In fact, I expect to see you wearing a conventional hair cut one week from today. And you don't have any choice about it."

"What if I don't want to do it. Suppose I just don't have it cut. Would you hold me down and cut it off yourself?"

"If you refuse, Jerry, it will be an outright defiance of your mother and me. I don't want to threaten you with punishment. I'd much rather you'd trust us to know what is best for you. However, if I have to punish you I will. And I will deal with you in precisely the same way God deals with me when I disobey Him—ROUGH!

"Once we agree that something is right in the Lord's sight, we don't defy God by refusing to carry it out. Your mother and I are not about to defy God in this. We think it is right in His sight for us to have you cut your hair. You think about that, Jerry. I'm sure you will find yourself a lot happier by going along with us, than by refusing to get your hair cut."

> **NOTE:** You were not only prepared to talk to Jerry like this, you are also prepared to punish him should he disobey you. You made it something of a commitment to God even before you spoke to Jerry. There's little point in talking about the nutcracker unless you are ready to use both jaws. Threats are meaningless. Anyway, by this time, Jerry has become familiar with the pattern. It is more than a suspicion that punishment comes automatically when he disobeys.

Jerry's real decision now is: **"Shall I test the fence?"** He's wondering if you will stand firm or will he be able to find a way around the rule without having to pay the price. In the past he used to get away with things. He might just try it again to see if the fence is as strong as it appears. It's up to him. The charged wire is there—**"Get rid of that long hair!"** What he is asking himself is: **"Will I get a real jolt if I defy my folks in this?"** If you have been steadfast in applying discipline to this point, he should know that discipline follows disobedience. If he doesn't, he soon will.

A week goes by.

Oh no, it appears Jerry is going to test the fence. He did get his hair cut some. It's not quite as long as it was. Likely he thinks to squeeze a compromise out of you. Kids are sly, especially 16 year olds.

> **HINT.** Check some of the weekly magazines. They'll give you an idea of the latest fashion. There would be nothing wrong with letting Jerry follow the current trend in men's hair styles. What you want, is a shift from the outlandish modes which mark the rebellion. If he wants his hair to cover the back of his neck, that should be okay if it is neatly trimmed and coincides with the

conservative element of his peer group. You are not trying to make an "odd ball" out of him. He does have to live with those kids at school. You want him comfortable with them. Along with that, you want to be comfortable around him too. That's why you are landing on his rebellious ways with both feet.

But Jerry's hair remains too long. He's still more hippie than human. That means he is determined to keep his identification with the teen-age rebellion. That rebellion is now against you. Jerry is going to test the fence. That's obvious. He hoped to get around you with the slight trim he did get, but you clear the air on that score:

"Well son, I see you did trim off a bit of the surplus, but you didn't get your hair cut as mother and I asked. Why not. Don't you intend to obey us?"

"I don't think it's fair for you to make me have it cut way back just because you don't like the way kids wear it today. I did have it trimmed some. Doesn't that show I'm trying to cooperate?"

He thinks that should get him off the hook. But of course it can't.

"I told you I would have to punish you if you didn't do as I asked. Now you have deliberately disobeyed me. You don't leave me any choice. I want you to go to your room, son. I'll be along in a few minutes."

Yes, you've already talked to the Lord about this. You were all prayed up before you spoke to Jerry. But you want him to sit alone in his room for a few minutes before you come in. This way he can be alone with his thoughts. It gives him a little time to determine how far he wants to carry this rebellion. Also his emotional buildup will be greater. Your words, "I'll be along in a few minutes," have a familiar ring. He knows what's coming.

Though you spent time with the Lord before you talked to Jerry, you now talk to Jesus again. This way you make sure you have divested yourself of all resentment and bitterness. You definitely do not want your discipline to be retaliation in any form. What you do must be in love. This is a point I must stress repeatedly. Nothing fills a father's heart with love for his boy like talking to the Lord about him.

NOTE: We may have reached the point in dealing with Jerry's rebellion where he will refuse to go to his room. There's a lot of threat in this item. He may take his stand and defy you right on down the line. He might even dare you to make him, thinking you wouldn't go so far as to use force over something as trivial as a haircut. If that's his thinking, he's made a mistake. He doesn't know how much courage and determination the Holy Spirit can give a mother and father to do what is pleasing to God. You know you have the authority, you also know that shell must be cracked. If you hope to make a penetration with the truths of God, you've got to reach a tender spot with discipline. You've found one and with God's help, you're going to see it through.

HINT: If Jerry refuses to go to his room, he will have to be disciplined openly. Make sure, though, all hostile feelings are dumped in Jesus' waste basket. Inasmuch as having a rebellious son in the house is a family matter, there is no need to escort Jerry to a private place. Punish him right there in front of his mother. If his sister is home, let her be present also. God's hatred for rebellion is so great, He required the city to witness the death of a rebel. After that, the victim's body was hung on a tree for one day as a public testimony to God's vengeance. God despises rebellion. Christian parents must act godly in such cases. Plan to use your belt as I will describe below.

"You really hurt your father when you disobey. And I know I don't want to hurt my heavenly Father by disobeying Him. He's too good to me for me to hurt Him with my disobedience. He has made it very clear to me that I must discipline you when you disobey me; therefore, I am going to obey God and punish you."

"But dad, I don't see that cutting my hair is all that important? Everybody wears his hair like this. I don't think you have a right to punish me for something that is normal for our times. If I had stolen something or burned down a building I could understand it. But you see people wearing hair like this everywhere!"

"We discussed that when I first told you to have it cut. We're passed that kind of a discussion now. Once I gave you the order, you were responsible to obey it or suffer the consequences. We've come to the consequences, son. It is for refusing to obey me that I must punish you. If you've got the courage to defy me, then I'm sure you've also got the courage to take your punishment like a man."

"All right dad, you can try. But I'll tell you this. You can punish me all you want, and I'm still not going to cut my hair."

> **CAUTION:** Oops. His last remark could trigger a reaction in you. Lift your spirit silently to the Lord Jesus asking for the grace to let any further defiance roll past you. The boy is now very upset. Don't indulge in any more words. The time has passed for talking. Proceed systematically with what you have to do, not letting his words determine the quality of the punishment you are going to inflict. You want to put the right price tag on his rebellion without retaliating against his words. It is going to cost him to defy his folks, but the price must be fair. Punishment for the sake of punishment is out now that you have learned to couple it with the truth of God.

● Off comes your belt. You fold it in half, making sure the buckle is in your hand. Whap! Whap! Whap! Whap! Whap! Those were good blows. They hurt. He felt them, but good. He manages to hold back his tears. He figures he can take whatever you dish out. Perhaps he can.

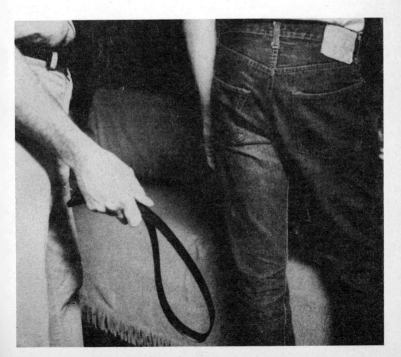

"You can hit me all you want to, dad, but I'm not going to cut my hair."

"No more hitting right now, son. I have no delight in punishing you. If the belt won't do the job, I will use another means. Because I love you, Jerry, I must find a way to break your rebellious spirit. The Lord will show me what to do. You see you are not only resisting your mother and me, you are also defying God.

"God says you are to honor your father and mother. And do you know why? '. . . That it may be well with you!' I can assure you this rebellion guarantees it won't be well with you. God will show me how to deal with it and you won't like His methods. He means it when He says, 'Obey your parents in the Lord, for this is right'."

> **NOTE:** What a fine teaching situation this is. Jerry has defied you. You applied physical pain, a healthy dose of it. And squarely in the midst of Jerry's defiance and pain (combined emotions) you bring the Word of God as it relates to the situation. Those verses, now clothed with emotion, sink home. They won't break his spirit, but they do go deep into his new nature. In one way, it looks like the present scene is a failure. However, it is actually a whopping success whenever you can apply the Word of God at a critical time.

Only the beginning of Jerry's suffering.

The first squeeze on the nutcracker did not break his shell. However, he did feel pain. You know he didn't like it, even if he can take it. You could elect to use the strap some more, and keep on until you break his spirit. In some cases that is the thing to do. In this case, however, we will go to another method of punishment. It will allow us to put a different type of pressure on Jerry. And a different type of pressure will allow us to bring more teaching. That's what we're really after. Breaking his spirit is important, but getting the parent's package into his life has the priority.

> **CAUTION:** If you elect to whip your boy until his spirit is broken, do so as UNTO THE LORD. Let your mind go to the Lord Jesus so that you are actually punishing him in the Lord's presence. You should feel the Lord's eyes on you as you do this. That way, each stroke is something of a prayer request for the Holy Spirit to deal with Jerry's heart. This task should never be done

in the flesh. That is, you should do it only in the closest cooperation with God's Spirit. Be as conscious of the Holy Spirit as you
would be in dealing with a lost soul. Trust Him to bear witness
to your words to Jerry. Do that, and your counsel will penetrate
Jerry's spirit. If you find you cannot whip him as in the Lord's
presence, then do not attempt to break his spirit with extended
lashings. It could be a cruelty rather than a spiritual ministry.

So Jerry's rebellion continues. He feels he's won the first
round. Even so, he's not happy about it. Rebels are not happy.
Why? Rebellion is itself a sickness when the cause is not just.
You, on the other hand, are at peace. You are ready to do the
Lord's will. You know He is backing you. He will give you what
you need to salvage your boy. Your one regret is that Jerry
is bringing so much needless suffering upon himself. As his
rebellion continues, the price tag gets bigger.

● Once more you go to the Lord. You ask for wisdom. You
plan your next move. You are determined it too will be carried out in love. Your wife may think the step is a bit harsh,
but what could be worse than having a rebellious son? Particularly when you realize you are facing a situation for which
God's Word prescribes death by stoning (Deut. 21:21). Now
you're ready to speak to Jerry again.

> **"Jerry, don't plan on eating dinner with us tonight."**
>
> "Why not dad? You still mad about my hair?"
>
> **"Son, this has gone beyond the matter of your hair now. Your
> mother and I are concerned about your rebellion against our will. That's
> the one thing God hates most in a child. We've decided we dare not
> feed a rebel in our home. We cannot use the daily bread which God
> provides to feed someone who defies His will. As long as you persist
> in this rebellion, you will not eat in this home. Your mother is not
> to fix another meal for you until you get your hair cut as we have
> asked, and apologize for your rebellion."**

"Okay, if that's the way you want it." He talks big. His
stomach isn't empty yet. He prefers to carry his arrogance a
step further. He won't feel quite so tough around dinner time.
But, if he'd rather be defiant than eat, that's up to him. He
won't go too many days like that.

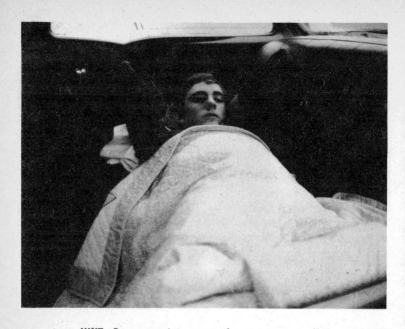

HINT: Be prepared to go as far as necessary. If Jerry tries to steal food from the refrigerator and you catch him at it, bar him from the house. Give him a blanket or two and let him sleep in the car. That way you can keep tabs on him. He can get water out of the garden hose. Naturally, he will have to come in to use the bathroom or go to a nearby gas station. But don't feel sorry for him. **This is his choice.** He is suffering by his own free will. Missing a few meals will do more good than harm. The human body can go for 30 days on water alone and the benefits are remarkable. Fasting sharpens one's senses and quickens his thoughts. This could help Jerry harken to the voice of the Spirit.

NOTE. Does this seem like cruel and unusual punishment? It isn't. Anytime Jerry wants relief, he can apologize and cut his hair. Only his stubborn will extends his suffering this way. He is the one making it tough on himself, and over a slight matter. Hair style is not the greatest issue facing a young lad. It is something he could easily give up if he wanted to. So the issue is not his hair, but his EGO. His ego has clashed with yours and the real issue is REBELLION. Now he has to work it all out within his own spirit. Don't feel sorry for him. And don't be upset if his friends (especially the grandparents) take his part against you. You are doing what is right in God's sight, and that's what counts.

Jerry finally breaks

It had to come. He has felt pain and discomfort due to disobedience. He has suffered the loss of his family's presence. He has gone hungry. It's no fun sleeping cramped in a car. We'll assume his stubbornness took him that far. He's had time to consider the price tag on his rebellion. It gets more expensive with each passing day. It should. Between the physical pressures and the Holy Spirit's jabbing at his soul, Jerry doesn't have a chance. Finally it comes to him . . . **"If you can't lick 'em, you might as well join 'em."** That's what you want.

> NOTE: If you are forced to go this far with Jerry, he will have gained an enormous lesson. He now knows the extent to which his folks will go to see that he is the kind of a boy he should be. What he has suffered is also a measurement of how much you care for him. Never once has he detected any bitterness or meanness in your words. Everything you have said has reflected your love and concern for his best interest. This is what makes it easy for him to yield. He is not surrendering to harsh enemies, but a mother and father who love him enough to deal with him as they should.

> "Dad, mom. I've been thinking it over and I have decided to apologize and get my hair cut. I don't know why I was so stubborn. It seems like something gets into you and you hate to give in even when you know you should. Can I come back in the house, please?"

● We're looking at a different Jerry now. He's been through the wringer. It shows. But that stubborn will has been broken. Praise the Lord for that. You've made real progress. Not that you hope to revamp him into a model Christian. We've already noted that complete control of him is not the purpose of this plan. Jerry has tasted the FIRMNESS of his folks. Deep inside he is proud of you. Secretly he says, **"That's the kind of a dad I'm going to be when I have children—strong and uncompromising."** He's pleased to identify with Christian parents with such conviction and courage.

Likely he will go to his mother's arms first. There he could cry. Pent up emotions must come out sometime. Forgiveness often brings tears where a beating can't. It sometimes makes me cry to think of all that Jesus has forgiven me. When the tender love of a father and mother reflect that same forgiveness, it can melt the heart of the toughest teen.

> **NOTE:** This tender scene does not mean you will be compromising in the future. Quite the opposite. Now that you have gained the upper hand, keep it. Plan to be just as firm should a similar matter arise in the future. It is possible you may never have to do this again—unless you relax the fence. In which case it would be your fault, not Jerry's. Jerry has learned BY EXPERIENCE how far his parents will go in obeying the Lord. He does not want any more miserable nights in the car, much less hunger and a whipping. Things should fall into place more easily after this. They will if you maintain a strong fence, punishing every breach of the family rules. You must not relax discipline, even once.

● There's more to be extracted from Jerry's repentance. After feelings have settled down and things are somewhat back to normal, make a trip to his room. He looks up and smiles as his dad enters the room. This time he sees a book in your hand instead of a whip.

"Hi pop, whatcha got?"

"Something you said, Jerry, made me think you might be interested in this book."

"Yeah, what was that?"

"You said, 'It seems like something gets into you and you hate to give in.' I thought you might be interested in learning where rebellious ideas come from."

"You mean there's a book on that?"

"Not every idea that pops into our heads originates with us, you know. We have a powerful enemy who is able to put ideas into our minds. We don't suspect them as coming from someone else, for they seem like our own ideas at the time. But they're not. If we buy this other fellow's ideas, we end up doing what he wants us to do.

"We've all found ourselves doing things we shouldn't, and most of the time we thought it was our own idea. The truth is, Jerry, it isn't always. But until we learn how to distinguish between those ideas which are our own and which are his, the devil has the power to make us do his will by suggestion. To be able to do that, we have to learn how he

136

works and to recognize his ideas the moment they pop into our thinking. Once we learn that, we can even catch him in the act."

"Really dad? How can you catch the devil in the act? And what would you do with him if you did?"

"The Lord has given us authority over Satan, Jerry. We have the power to send him away from our lives. And when he goes, it is quite an experience. Things we thought were important, aren't at all once he leaves. A lot of kids would not be involved in what you see today if they knew how to deal with the devil. That's why I thought you might be interested in reading this book. It's called, DEALING WITH THE DEVIL."

"You mean it really tells a person what to do about the devil?"

"Yes. It's got a four step plan that really works. I think you'll get quite a kick out of being able to rid yourself of some of the hang-ups that bug kids today. It's a real experience to tell Satan to 'bug off.' It's an adventure when he goes!"

> NOTE: Jerry will be curious. If you had said these things to him at another time, he would have dismissed it as so much religious talk. Now he's fascinated by the idea that someone could have engineered all his trouble. He wonders if he could have been the victim of satanic suggestion. He would like to think it wasn't entirely his idea to fight against his parents. Of course, Jerry is the one to blame. Even though Satan did put the suggestion in his mind, Jerry still had to APPROVE it. The devil DOES NOT have the power to by-pass the human will. Even God does not allow Himself that privilege. It would cancel the human program if He did.

"Dad, do you really think Satan can put ideas in kid's minds like that?"

"Of course he can. Just think. Why would any boy want to defy parents that are good to him and go all out to see that he has the best? On top of that, there's no way for the kid to win. He simply gets hurt in the process. Why, even on the surface it is something a person wouldn't do unless he were led into it in some mysterious way. Isn't that right?"

"I never thought of it that way. Maybe you've got something there. I'll have to take a look at that book."

NOTE: It is a fantastic thing to get the anti-satan skill into a young life. Not only is the teen equipped to recognize the devil's workings in every day occurrences, he learns to conquer some powerful drives. Satan knows how to use that vast reservoir of evil in the old nature. But a teen who knows how to deal with him can have victory over the flesh. This in turn affects his behavior at school as well as the things he likes to do and the places he likes to go. Those parents who equip their teens with the anti-satan skill, give them one of the finest advantages for walking in the Spirit. I consider the truth of dealing with Satan to be one of the top requirements of the New Testament.

How about Jerry's sister?

I mentioned her telephonitis. But perhaps we should select some THING from her life which would mean as much to her as Jerry's long hair meant to him. What might that be? Let's see—miniskirts, perhaps?

 We'll asume Judy has a good figure for a 14 year old. She likes the miniskirt fashion. And it's not be-cause she is sex-minded, she likes to be appreciated.

To her mind, there's nothing evil in displaying the respectable limbs God has given her. But you don't feel right about that elevated hemline. So far you haven't done anything about it. You are a little perplexed. You know how much a girl suffers when she is out of step with the others at school. To be judged or ridiculed by her peer group is almost unbearable for a girl. More than one has said, **"I'd rather die first."**

> **NOTE:** The miniskirt fashion, at least in the extremes, is as surely a rebellion against the moral code as long hair is a defiance of authority. If hair in the face and rubbing the neck is uncomfortable, miniskirts are chilly and make sitting awkward. A woman who reveals too much of herself when seated in a chair is not really a pleasant sight. Few are happy about that. Mothers who refuse to let their girls go dancing (and rightly so) often permit them to wear uncommonly short skirts. Again, fashion is the stated excuse, but the matter goes deeper than that. The ultra short skirt is a defiance of our puritan tradition, thus a symbol of rebellion.

At 14 Judy may not be conscious of the sexual implication. (Though we shouldn't be blind to that possibility.) Being in step with other kids is likely to motivate her more at this age. Whether she realizes it or not, she is invoking the principle of provocation. Short skirts do arouse feelings in the opposite sex. What a howl she'll make when you insist her hemline conform to the lower limits of fashion. This makes it an item for the nutcracker as surely as Jerry's long hair. It can be handled in the same way.

> **NOTE:** I won't state where the hemline should be, fashions change continually. But there will always be upper and lower limits in every trend. The nutcracker will operate well when you require your girl to conform to the lower limits of FASHION, without resorting to an extreme of modesty. While we are in this world, little is gained by making a spectacle of the Christian and the Gospel by insisting on opposite extremes. However, if a person is inclined to extremes, the safe one is that which covers the body.

CREATING THE CRISIS

Surely you have noticed how the United States never gets to pick its battlefield? Our enemies have that privilege. They know we will not wage an aggressive war, but wait until we are provoked. Therefore, they are free to select the trouble zones for the planned wars of attrition against the U.S. We didn't choose Viet Nam or Korea. We will not choose the next site. Our enemies pick the time and place and we oblige with a military reaction.

It doesn't have to be that way with your teens. You can take the initiative. You can select the "hot spots," the items for the nutcracker. Being able to pick the time and place guarantees your success with the nutcracker. It is a controlled situation. Jerry's room, for example, had been a mess for some time. But you didn't make an issue of it until you were ready. The same was true of Judy's telephonitis. No real problem had developed. You waited until YOU were ready. Then you **created the crisis.**

Was that not the case with Jerry's long hair? You could have waited him out. In time the fad may have passed. He might have grown weary of it. You could have dismissed the whole thing as part of the strange times in which we live, but you didn't. Instead you made an issue of it. When you were **spiritually ready,** you used it as an item for the nutcracker. And you were assured of victory.

There are some impressive advantages in taking the initiative:

1. You are spiritually ready before you create the crisis.

2. You can select a situation in which you are sure to win.

3. You can pick non-threatening items before going to those which are more threatening.

4. Victories gained in minor areas of your teen's life pave the way to victories in major areas.

5. When you create a crisis over a minor issue, your teen can afford to submit. He doesn't want to pay too high a price in a small matter. Yet, he is not aware that a series of little surrenders is leading him to larger ones.

6. If you started off with something which seemed a "life or death" matter to your teen, the issue might be more important to him than living at home. He might then be tempted to run away rather than submit to your authority. Lots of teens leave home because parents have not approached key issues gradually.

> **CAUTION:** By now you can see how this plan could be applied to EVERY area of a teen's life. DO NOT attempt such a thing. Do not try to produce a perfect child by using the nutcracker on every aspect of his life. It would turn you into a legalistic watchdog. It would rob you of your delight in your children. Instead, BE SELECTIVE. Take only a few items from each of the three areas—**things, places and people.** This book is not a plan for raising perfect sons and daughters. It's purpose is to install the truths of the **parent's package.** That's all. God does not press on all areas of our lives, neither are we submissive to him in every aspect of living. We should not expect MORE from our children than we give to God. We turn into harsh taskmasters when we try.

There are many other THINGS we could have chosen for the nutcracker. But I have selected these, thinking they might be representative. They do let you see how the nutcracker works. We have yet to see what happens to a youth who is so stubborn he'd rather leave home than surrender. That is not likely to happen with the items we have selected so far. However, when you start dealing with PLACES your teens can and cannot go, the squeeze is greater. Let's see what happens then. That's next.

Chapter Nine

PLACES AND PRESSURE!

The once popular **Collier's** magazine carried a cartoon which satirized modern youth's demand for unlimited self-expression. It showed three people—Adam, Eve, and their son, Cain. On the ground was the body of the other son, Abel. He had just been killed by his brother.

In the scene, Adam is showing considerable excitement over the murder of his son. Eve is trying to calm him down. Cain is standing off to one side, a cigarette hanging from his lips. He is looking down at the dead body of his brother, completely indifferent to the whole thing. The caption gives Eve's words to Adam:

> **"Now Adam, don't carry on so. You simply don't understand Cain. He belongs to a new generation. He is trying to solve his problems in his own way. He's facing the facts of life fearlessly, dealing with things as they really are."**

Sounds ridiculous doesn't it. By how much does it exaggerate what is happening in homes today? Kids are getting away with "murder." Permissiveness is spawning the present rebellion. What is occurring on the streets and campuses has its roots in the permissiveness of parents. But that also tells us where the solution lies—in the restoration of FIRM authority in the home.

We should be warned by what we're seeing. Young people are denouncing the guide lines of older generations as "road blocks" to social progress. To hear them tell it, we should place the destiny of our land in the hands of youngsters who have PAID NOTHING for the privileges they've inherited, and who have yet to contribute ANYTHING to our nation's welfare. If we're wise, we'll move quickly to curb this trend by dealing with it where it starts—in our homes.

YOU HAVE STARTED.

You've installed the nutcracker. Jerry and Judy are beginning to feel the squeeze. If all goes as it should, not only will the spirit of rebellion disappear, but the truths of God will be at work in their lives. To this point we have covered one-third of the plan. We have dealt with THINGS in your youngster's routine. Now we are ready to move up the scale of threat to apply the technique to PLACES.

We'll consider Judy first. She's sixteen now.

"Mamma, Mary Jo Rogers is giving a pajama party at her dad's beach house in Newport. It's a real swanky place and I've been invited."

"Who is Mary Jo Rogers? I don't recall your mentioning her. Is she a recent acquaintance, dear?"

"I met her at the beginning of the semester. She's in my English class. Her father has this groovy place down on the water and she's invited six of us girls from school to spend the weekend with her. Can I go?"

"Is there a Mrs. Rogers? How about Mary Jo's mother?"

"Her folks are divorced and she lives with her dad. He's an attorney here in town and makes lots of money. He also has a boat and is going to take us sailing Saturday afternoon."

"Will Mr. Rogers be there all the time?"

"He has a case he's working on and can't come down until Saturday. But we'll be all right. After all there will be seven of us girls. There's safety in numbers, you know."

"Is anyone else expected?" (By that you mean, will any boys be coming around?)

"Mary Jo's boyfriend might stop by."

"I'll talk it over with your father and let you know."

Judy gets her answer.

"Because we don't know Mr. Rogers, Judy, we don't feel we can let you go. We just can't turn our responsibility over to a man we've never met. Besides we don't really know what we're letting you in for, so our answer has to be no."

"Oh mom! You folks are so old fashioned. I'm 16 now. I can take care of myself. Don't you trust me?" There now, we're getting some emotion. A nice situation is developing for the nutcracker.

"Let's talk it out, dear. You're old enough to explain what you really feel. I'd like to hear your side of it. I'm quite interested in knowing why you think protecting our daughter is old fashioned. I want to hear all of your reasons. Then you can hear more of our reasons for not letting you go."

> **NOTE:** You could have reacted to her accusation of being old fashioned by silencing her with an order not to speak to her mother that way. But that would merely close the lines of communication. You want her to bring out her feelings. That gives you a chance to share yours with her. Since you have all the power and authority on your side, there is no need to clamp her mouth shut. She is NOT going to go, but she still needs to FEEL the basic reason is because you LOVE her. An arbitrary "No, and that's the end of it," closes the door between parents and children. Judy knows she can't go. Now she wants evidence that your "no" is not an arbitrary one. The way to do this is to hear her reasons first, and then show her how yours are in her best interest.

It would be so easy to say, **"You're not going and that's all there is to it."** But that is an autocratic use of your power over her. Sometimes it is necessary, but in this case it would accomplish nothing. On the other hand, talking it out protects the mother-daughter relationship and gives you a chance to plant some truths into her life. That won't take away her disappointment, of course, but you want those feelings. You're going to use them in the nutcracker. After Judy gives her reasons, you give yours:

"First of all, Judy, you asked if we trust you. We do, but trust is a two-way street. You also have to trust us to know what is best for you. It's not fair unless you do. It would be one-sided if we merely trusted you and you didn't trust us. Also, it is not wise for us to trust you too far. If we do, we put too much responsibility on you. While you live at home, the Lord wants you to have the benefit of our guidance.

"The Lord holds us responsible for you. He will not let us shift our responsibility to you or someone like Mr. Rogers. It would go hard with us if we did. We don't want to feel the chastening hand of God, so we play the game according to His rules.

"It's possible you could go to this beach party without any harm done to you. But to take that chance on people we don't know is a terrible way for us to discharge our responsibility. The Lord wouldn't be pleased with us if we did that."

Will Judy understand all that?

Perhaps not. Her emotions may blind her to your reasons. But she will get the impression you trust her—up to a point. That point has been pushed out further and further as she got older and demonstrated her ability to regulate her life according to the standards of her home. If she will not discipline herself by those standards, then she cannot be trusted with much responsibility.

"Don't you trust me?" That's a phrase youngsters use as a lever to get their own way. But when they understand that you DO trust them to the limits of their ability to handle responsibility, it is a different matter. Sixteen year olds want very much to be adults. Christian mothers and fathers should NOT allow that desire to carry their youngsters into situations where they have neither the strength nor wisdom to restrain their own drives.

"But mom, what do you think is going to happen? I suppose you think we've arranged for some boys to come down and meet us there?"

"No dear. I told you I trust you. I believe your plans are innocent. Why should I think anything else? What concerns me are the standards of Mr. Rogers. I don't know what he thinks constitutes a good time. He may be a very respectable man, but his idea of what is right in God's sight might be quite different from ours. He may not even care what God thinks.

"Now that may sound old fashioned to you, Darling, but the devil is looking for ways to get his hands on you. A 16 year old girl is a choice target for him. Already he has put the suggestion in your mind that I don't. Because you're disappointed about not going to the beach, he'd like you to think that you know what is best for your own life and I don't. Because your disappointed about not going to the beach, he's sure you will buy his ideas."

"I doubt if the devil pays any attention to me."

145

"He knows teen-age girls will one day be mothers themselves. He works doubly hard to influence the thoughts of girls like you. If he can lead you into something that will affect your life, he knows it can influence your children. He sets clever traps for girls that sometimes imprison them for the rest of their lives.

"If Satan could accomplish what he has planned for you, he knows his work with your children will be a lot easier. You may doubt that he has such power, but he has. You are at one of the most vulnerable points of your life right now. So if the notion enters your head that mother is keeping you from this beach party because she doesn't want you to have a good time, the devil put it there. Think about this Judy. If the devil can do things like that while we're here talking together, what could he put in your mind if you were away from us and in an exciting situation?"

"Gee mom, can the devil really do that?"

"Next to God, he is the most powerful person in the universe. He has the power to thrust tempting ideas into our minds as easily as God can inspire us. For instance dear, if it ever occurs to you to wear your neck line a little lower or your hemline a little higher, so that you will be noticed or admired, you can be sure the devil put it there. If you find yourself thinking it would be good to go out with certain boys to discover how the other half lives, that will be another of Satan's tricks.

"The most vicious thing about it, Judy, is that he can make you think it is YOUR idea. He can affect your conduct at home and school, and particularly when you are out on dates. Dating gives the devil one of his best opportunities for securing control over a teen. But honey, a beach party can be just as deadly. Not because you are deliberately involved with boys, but when you are away from the influence of your home, he makes it easy to try things just for the fun of it, or because others in the group say it is something great.

"I want you to listen to mother. I know this enemy. He can lead you into trouble without your once suspecting him. You don't realize he is manipulating you until you know how he does it. Therefore, I want you to learn about him, and when you do, you'll understand my concern."

> **NOTE:** It's healthy for young people to learn that Satan is the author of many of their rebellious feelings and resentments against their parents. Also, it helps them to appreciate their parent's caution against letting them go into situations where

drives and passions can be awakened beyond the point of control. Once a son or daughter catches Satan in the act of trying to turn him against his parents, he has an entirely new appreciation for them. He realizes they have to contend with Satan's dirty work too. It can be shocking for a child to learn that the devil stirs him to revolt against his mother and father. The sooner he learns it the better. This would be a good time to place a copy of DEALING WITH THE DEVIL in Judy's hands. Once she is wise to Satan, she won't let him stir up resentment against her mother for not letting her go to the beach party.

● If Judy is submissive and cooperative after hearing your reasons, that in itself will be a precious reward for your soul. It would be nice if you could REWARD her. Maybe you could let her invite one of her girl friends to stay overnight. But remember: this is a REWARD for her **attitude.** It is NOT to be used as a device for offsetting her disappointment. If she is NOT cooperative and tenderly submissive, DO NOT give her this benefit. Do not try to compensate for her "lost weekend." You do not have to ease the pain caused by doing what is right.

If Judy's attitude is such that your own soul has been rewarded, then it is wholly proper to reward her. Let her know it is a reward. Tell her she is a blessing to you, that you are pleased with her attitude and want to reward her. It will add emotional content to the truth that obedience brings blessing.

> **NOTE:** See again how the technique isn't negative only. Teens should be rewarded when their ATTITUDE toward your authority is what it should be. It can be an emotional experience to receive a reward. A teaching can be harnessed to it. What teaching? The truth that the Lord rewards us for our joyful submission to Him. Even as you reward your girl, you can speak of the Judgment Seat of Christ, that day when God rewards faithful Christians for their works. It is simple to say, "Just as I reward you for obeying me, so will the Lord reward you when you submit to Him in the same sweet way."

> **HINT:** When your children feel they must always be going "some-place" in order to have a good time, something is missing from the joy in your home. Families should play together. Mothers and dads should LISTEN when youngsters talk, especially at the dinner

table. The TV should be turned off when they have questions. Dads should teach their boys to enjoy masculine things. Down inside, they want to emulate their dads in things and working like a man. A boy learns quickest from his dad how to sweat and get things done and not be a coward. If you center a good deal of your children's activity in your home, they won't be shaken when told they can't go some place. Also, it develops a family close- ness which can mean much over the years. It helps them to pic- ture the kind of a home they want for themselves later on.

But suppose Judy isn't all that nice?

In the scene just described, it sounds as if Judy is ten- derly submissive to her mother's wishes. But Judy may not be like that at all. In fact, for the sake of teaching, let's suppose she is a self-willed person who insists on having her own way. She thinks she is quite grown up and has a right to do as she pleases. Some sixteen year olds feel they are ready for total independence. So our Judy, instead of meekly yielding to her mother, is impudent, often coarse at times. She likes to assert her own will. To illustrate this different Judy, we'll change the scene.

Lately she's been going to the local park with some of her girl friends. It's a gathering place for malcon- tents and dissident youths. In addition, off beat young people collect there to display their weird clothing styles and listen to soul-shattering music. Seemingly, they all have an utter disdain for neatness and cleanliness. It is probably the drug scene as well. The park has become the headquarters of rebellion.

You are at a loss to know what the attraction is for Judy. Perhaps she identifies with the spirit of rebellion pervading the place. In the past you have let her go, because she was accompanied by girls whose families you knew. But more and more you feel it is no place for a girl from a Christian home. The influence is anything but godly. You have refused to let her attend most of the modern movies. So you feel the Lord would have you put a stop to her going. As soon as you try, we'll have an item for the nutcracker.

● This time you don't mind facing a "knock down, drag out" affair, knowing you can use it to penetrate Judy's life. You have learned that a "fuss" can be useful for the Lord. In the past, you've been tempted to let her get away with murder rather than be firm. But now you know firmness can be used for Christ to plant important truths in her life. So you fortify yourself in the presence of the Lord. Then you talk the matter over with your husband.

He agrees. He too, feels the park is influencing her in the wrong direction. The two of you agree that forbidding her to go to the park is the next item for the nutcracker. So you prepare to take a stand against Judy. You are ready to apply the needed discipline, should Judy give you a bad time. Remember, we're dealing with a tougher Judy who is not above coniving to get her own way.

> **NOTE:** If your husband is unsaved or you are raising your children alone, your job is a lot harder. Not impossible, just harder. It's a handicap when one parent is missing or uncooperative. But the Holy Spirit will strengthen you and give you great authority with your children—if you do things HIS way. I understand that a woman alone has her hands full just providing for her family, but that cannot be used as an excuse for tolerating disobedience

or lowering the standards of her home. God will make up for the lack of a mate if she is faithful to do what she can in the matter of discipline. But if she throws up her hands in despair, saying, "What can I do?" God will do nothing for her. He will let her stew in the mess. She still has to obey and do things God's way.

● Judy comes home from school. She goes to her room to change her clothes. You know she is dressing to go to the park. But this time it is going to be different. You have been with the Lord in prayer and you are ready to tell her she cannot go—and why. The scene could be emotional, but you are prepared in Christ. You have set yourself to deal with the spirit of rebellion already prominent in her life. You go to her room. Your own spirit is under control.

The Scene with Judy.

"**Getting dressed to go to the park, Judy?**"

"Yeh mom, Betty and Carol are going to meet me there."

"**Sit down a moment dear, I want to talk to you about going to the park.**"

"I can't mom, there isn't time."

"**Judy—sit down!**" (There's authority, but no anger in your voice.)

Your girl stops. She looks at you, trying to size up the situation. She has a hunch what is coming before you get out the words.

"Okay, what is it?"

"**Your father and I have decided the park is not a good place for our daughter. We're not happy with the influence there. So, beginning right now, you are not to go there any more.**"

"Oh mom, wake up! Don't be so old fashioned. Times have changed since you were a girl. You don't like it because the people there aren't square like you!"

"**Pow!**" Your hand slaps hard across the side of her face. You were ready to do that, so it is not retaliation for her words. She needed it. You wish you had done it long before. But Judy is tough. She's startled, but she doesn't cry. She looks at you like a calf staring at a new gate. She doesn't know what to make of it. That's the point. It was a surprise move.

There was no anger behind your blow. It was a tactic, not a reaction. You know your daughter well enough to guess what kind of words would come from her upon such an order. With this element of surprise you have the advantage. Your emotions are in complete control as you make your next move.

> "I didn't slap you, honey, because I'm angry with you, but because I love you. You may think that's a strange way to show it, but it is the best way, because it is God's way. I have prayed a lot about what I am going to say to you."

Judy is silent. She listens. You have her attention but good.

> "Because I have allowed you to speak to me that way in the past, doesn't make it right. However, I can't punish you for my mistakes. That wouldn't be fair. I slapped you just now, because God expects me to deal quickly and sharply with impudence. He has been showing me some of my mistakes as a mother, and one of them has been allowing you to go to the park when I knew there was a bad influence there. From now on, I want you to stay away from the park altogether."

"But why, mom? I don't really understand."

> NOTE: Judy is on the verge of unloading her feelings. You can tell she's ready to defend her views about the park. Good. Listen to her side of the argument. Be sympathetic as she explains. Let her feel you are really LISTENING. That's so important. It keeps the lines of communication open and protects your relationship with her. A girl responds more to her RELATIONSHIP with her mother, than to any particular act of discipline. The relationship is enhanced when Judy senses your love and careful attention to her point of view. Even though she doesn't get her own way, Judy wants to feel what her mother does and says is prompted by love for her. The tone of the voice and the patient listening serve to communicate that love and strengthen the relationship.

● Judy is upset. Her feelings are all over her face. She's wondering what the other kids will think. She hates to tell them she can't go any more because her mother won't let her. She has been trying to be so adult all along. On the other hand, her mother has made it very clear this prohibition is in accordance with God's will.

Judy refuses to give up easily:

"I suppose if I took a bunch of tracts to the park and witnessed to everybody, you'd think that was great. You'd want me to go then, wouldn't you?" (See—she is clever.)

"Yes, I'd let you go with other Christians. I'd know then you were an influence on the park, rather than being influenced by the evil element there. I would not only let you go, I'd supply the tracts and pray for you as you went. But that's not your reason for going. You're attracted to the influence there. That's what makes it dangerous for you. You are exposed to just the opposite of what you should be.

"Now that you've mentioned it, Judy, let me ask this. How would you feel about passing out tracts and witnessing to the people there about Christ?"

"I'd feel like some kind of a nut. They'd laugh at me and think I'd flipped out."

"That's my point exactly. You've explained the situation yourself. The world hates people who are openly identified with Christ. When you go to places like the park where you are ashamed of your relationship with the Lord, you are actually mingling with the enemy. God does not want me to bring up His child to feel at home in the midst of those who hate Him."

NOTE: Now is the time to mention that you are raising her as "unto the Lord." You are meeting that responsibility by making the park "off limits" to her. If you cared to, you could go on to show how Christians are a persecuted minority. It all depends on whether Judy will listen to you as well as you listened to her. It is better not to teach too much, but it would be great if a few strong points could be quickened by her stirred feelings and go into her new nature. Since Judy is a Christian, and the issue is the park, your main point should be that Christians must be careful about the PLACES they go. It is dangerous for a child of God to enjoy a place where people are acting like children of the devil. The believer's stand for Christ is wiped out if he appears comfortable with such a crowd.

"Do you understand what mother is saying, Judy?"

"Sure mom. Say—if I can't go to the park, do you mind if I go over to Nancy's for awhile? Her mother won't let her go to the park either."

"Yes, I think that would be all right."

This time Judy goes out of the house without her "rock rags." There's no point in wearing them to Nancy's. You breathe a sigh of relief as she goes out the door. You might have made some progress. At least she has been squeezed between your counsel and her kindled emotions. Let's hope something from the parent's package has been lodged in her spirit. We'll see.

Brrrrrnnnnnnng . . . !

That's the phone. **"Hello?"**

"This is Nancy's mother. Could I speak to my daughter for a minute?"

"She's not here. Isn't she there with you? Judy went over to your house some time ago."

"Yes, Judy was here, but then the girls left to go back to your house. At least that's where they said they were going. The music shop just called to say her violin was fixed. I wanted her to pick it up on the way home from your house."

Oh no. You hate to think the worst, but you can't escape the conclusion that Judy went to Nancy's house with the idea of going to the park from there. You'll have to check it out.

"I don't have a car, Mrs. ...., but if you'd care to come by for me, I think I know where the girls might be."

You and Nancy's mother drive to the park. Sure enough, there are the girls. It doesn't do your heart any good to see your daughter there. You know she has deceived you. That hurts. It's hard to keep down your reaction, but you must.

CAUTION: It would be easy to wade into this situation with your feelings boiling. Satan would whisper, "You ought to give that girl a good piece of your mind. She has it coming." He'll try to get you to say things inconsistent with a godly mother. So

153

deal with those bitter thoughts the instant he plants them in your mind. He may even suggest you are wasting your time trying to correct Judy's rebellion, that your efforts are doomed to failure. But of course they're not. Instead of failure, you have just come upon a more powerful opportunity for the nutcracker. Before you get out of the car, let your thoughts go to the Lord Jesus. As you walk toward the girls, make sure your feelings are tempered by the Lord's presence.

Avoid saying too much to Judy there in the park. She's been caught with her hand in the cookie jar. It gives you a splendid advantage. Now it is not a matter of her arguments versus your arguments. She has performed a deceitful act and gotten caught. The advantage is all yours. You must use it wisely.

"Come on Judy, we have to go home now."

Say very little in front of the others. Face-saving is so desperate with teens. It would be an unloving act to embarrass her before her friend. You must avoid doing anything that would damage your RELATIONSHIP with Judy. So you reserve your words for a private moment. You say nothing to her about her deception while driving home in the car. There should be no hint of discipline until after Mrs. . . . . has dropped you off at your house.

Judy's discipline.

You go with Judy into her room. She's not so brash now. Normally she is able to talk her way out of a situation, but this time it is different. She seems to sense it. That makes her meeker than usual.

"I'm sorry, mom." She could mean it. Again she might mean she's sorry she got caught. Her voice quivers a bit this time.

"I'm glad you are, dear. That is encouraging to mother. I'd feel awful if you just didn't care. Even so I have to discipline you. I cannot deal with you any differently than God deals with me. When Christians do evil, God is ready to forgive and does, but He never takes away the consequences of their folly."

NOTE: What a truth that is. Judy will sense it as soon as the words come from your mouth. A Christian girl, for example, may date a man of the world to become the victim of his scheming advances. We'll assume she sins and becomes pregnant. While God readily answers her plea for forgiveness, He nonetheless does not remove the pregnancy. Her guilt is gone, but the consequences remain. She must bear the child or abort the pregnancy. Either choice could have a serious affect on her life. Similarly, while you are ready to forgive Judy's deception, she must still bear the consequences. It would not be fair or right to let her get away with both rebellion and deception with no price attached. Such an action would deny the truth of God. It must cost Judy something if God's truth is to be upheld in your home.

"I am going to punish you, Judy. But I want you to tell me what the punishment is for. I want to make sure you understand why you are being punished."

"Well, I guess I sort of lied to you. But I didn't mean to."

She's quick to add that.

"Oh? How do you mean?"

"All I wanted to do was go to the park to tell Betty and Carol why I couldn't join them. I was planning to go right back to Nancy's."

Listen to that, would you. See——she's used to talking her way out of tight situations.

"Let's see if I understand you, Judy. You are telling me you disobeyed me in order to keep from disappointing your friends? Is that a fair explanation of your reason?"

"Yeeesss . . . but I wouldn't put it quite like that."

"I see. Regardless of how you put it, dear, it must have meant more for you to advise your friends why you couldn't join them, than it was for you to obey me. And you felt it was such an urgent thing, that you even deceived your mother to do it. Isn't that about the size of it?"

"I guess so."

155

Judy knows she isn't going to get away with it no matter what explanation she gives. But she has had a chance to give her reason and her mother listened. You make it a point to be sure you understood her reason. That's important! You didn't act like a tyrannt. You didn't tear into her with tongue lashings and blows, simply because you had the right and the odds were all in your favor. No matter what punishment comes now, Judy's relationship with you is protected and preserved. She knows a loving mother is dealing with her.

> **NOTE:** Perhaps I will not be able to convince many mothers they should spank their sixteen year old daughters. I wish I could. I spanked mine and the results were miraculous. If you are willing to give it a try, use a green bamboo stick such as nurseries sell for propping up new plants. They are about 3 feet long and about 1/8 inch thick. But oh do they sting! Because of their frail size, they do no physical harm. Test one across the palm of your hand first. It hurts plenty, but will not break the skin. That's what you want—PAIN. It is ideal when you can make PAIN the PRICE of disobedience and rebellion. It allows forgiveness to follow fast.

If you elect to whip Judy, let the stick strike across her bottom. She'll really jump with the first swat. Likely she is not used to pain. If you spank through her clothing, the hurt will be dulled considerably. If she jumps about, let some of your swats fall on her legs. That hurts too. About four real good swats should be enough, provided the pain is there.

> **HINT:** If Judy's father is cooperative, it would be in order to defer the whipping until he gets home. As the head of the wife, it is his duty to administer punishment. We have drifted a long way from that principle, but it is a dandy one. When BOTH parents are involved in discipline, it is much more effective. Nothing is worse than having one parent deliver the discipline, and find the child going to the other for sympathy. That is disastrous. Agree with your husband ahead of time, so that there is no danger of his saying, "Since this is the first time, why don't we let her off with a warning? If she does it again, then we'll punish her." If there is any chance of that, say nothing to your husband and discipline Judy yourself.

STILL—JUDY MUST PAY THE PRICE

If you cannot bring yourself to whip her at least once, then your choice for discipline lies between deprivation and isolation. You should ground her for a week and confine her to her room. Or you can deprive her of a privilege she enjoys. If you take away her TV privilege, it should be for at least one week. The price would be higher still were she also denied the use of the phone for that week.

The point is—you MUST do it. Judy's deception cannot be without price. Rebellion has to be costly at your house. She must learn that disobedience brings discipline. If you let her get away with it, you will be defying God and allowing her to grow up thinking it is safe to shun your will—and God's. It would be a crime against Judy were she raised to believe rebellion has no price tag. Should she reach adulthood without learning the consequences of disobedience, God will hold YOU responsible.

WARNING: If you refuse to raise your child in the "discipline of the Lord," prepare for grief. It will come. Not only will you witness the devil's takeover of your child's life, you can expect God to afflict your household. It's bad enough to watch a son or daughter become more and more worldly, but to be in God's woodshed because of it—OUCH! This very moment, God's heavy hand is being felt in many Christian homes where the parents have withheld the rod. As I said earlier, God can play rough. On top of that, we meet the matter again at the Judgment Seat of Christ. There we receive the consequences of our disobedience. There it will affect our reward where we will have to wear the price tag of our own rebellion against God's will—FOREVER!

A PLACE JERRY OUGHT TO GO

So far I have mentioned two places Judy could not go. Since she WANTED to go, telling her NO produced the necessary emotion for the nutcracker. Now let's see the technique work in the other direction. There are places where teens SHOULD GO. When we COMPEL them, we also get a useful emotion.

> **NOTE:** I hope you are not disappointed that I didn't select items such as forbidding Judy to attend school dances or go to shows. Christians are so divided on such things, that were I to select one, the focus would shift from the nutcracker to a debate over the right or wrong position. The technique would get lost in the shuffle. I'm close enough to the battlefield when I speak of girls' short skirts and boys' long hair. To have parents take issue with me on the ILLUSTRATIONS I select, would frustrate the purpose of the book. Mothers and fathers might ignore the principles in their hurry to challenge me. I seek only to show the principles. You can apply them to any situation you like.

There are places where parents should insist their children accompany them. If, for example, a father and mother must leave home for several days, it is not good to leave teens alone. They have neither the moral strength nor judgment to handle large opportunities for evil. Idle minds and hands are the devil's workshop, and added to an empty house, mischief can easily follow. You should insist that Jerry and Judy go with you, rather than leave them home alone.

158

Another place where most readers will agree with me that young people should go is church and Sunday school. I don't expect to get into trouble with that suggestion. Although, I am not sure how many will agree with me when I say they MUST go whether they like it or not. We have reached an issue where I am ready to take a strong position.

 I appreciate the directness with which F.B.I. Director Hoover deals with this point:

"Shall I force my child to go to Sunday school and church? Yes! And with no further discussion about the matter! Startled? Why? How do you answer Junior when he comes to the breakfast table Monday morning and announces rebelliously, 'I'm not going to school today.' You know, Junior goes! How do you answer when Junior comes in very much besmudged, and says, 'I'm not going to take a bath'? You know, Junior bathes!

"Why all this timidity, in the realm of his spiritual guidance and growth? Going to let him wait and decide what church he'll go to when he's old enough? Quit kidding! You didn't wait until he was old enough to decide whether or not he wanted to go to public school and get an education—or until he could make up his mind as to whether or not he wished to take the medicine that would make him well.

"What shall we say when Junior announces he doesn't like Sunday school or church? That's an easy one. Just be consistent! 'Junior, in our house we all attend Sunday school and church, and that includes you.' Your firmness and example here will furnish a bridge over which youthful rebellion may travel into rich and satisfying experience in personal religious living.

"The parents of America can strike a most effective blow against the forces which contribute to juvenile delinquency, if our mothers and fathers will take their children to Sunday school and church regularly."

YOU'VE HEARD THIS BEFORE

"My parents brought me up so strictly it turned me against religion. They crammed it down my throat and made me sick of it."

Can you imagine what Mr. Hoover would say to that?

"Did your folks teach you to be honest."

"Yes."

"Were they strict about it?"

"Yes."

"Has that turned you against being honest?"

"Did they make you take a bath when you needed it?"

"Yes."

"Were they strict about it?"

"Yes."

"Has it made you hate to be clean today?"

What child ever learned the multiplication table for the sheer delight of it? None. Yet, who hates the 12 x 12 table because his teachers and parents made him learn it? The same reasoning applies to almost every noble and good thing we have ever learned.

I agree with Mr. Hoover 100%. As long as a teen lives under your roof, he ought to attend church with you. There should be no argument about it. He goes and that's it. Talking of hating the Lord because one has been forced to face what he should, is nonsense.

Going for the sake of going?

No, that's not what I mean. Forcing youngsters to church for the sake of being churched is bondage. They get the impression that Christianity is more medicinal than joyful. No one should go to church just to participate in a drab set of rules. Teens who are made to "sit there and listen, because it's good for you," can end up with an awful impression of the Christ-life.

Therefore, the church you select for your teens must be one that GLOWS with the Spirit. It is not enough to find a fellowship that acknowledges Christ as God and treasures the Bible as His Word. It should be a church that enjoys the testimonies of young people experiencing the thrill of Christ. The church must be ALIVE, faces should radiate the joy of Jesus.

Until young people sample the EXCITEMENT of Christ, Christianity is hardly more than a religion to them. They need the convulsive experience of meeting Christ ALIVE. After that, to THRILL to the adventure of moving in His POWER. They should be introduced to the FUN of serving Him, for that is the dessert of the Christian life. Once they taste it, living for Jesus can provide the biggest KICK in life! You know how kids love kicks!

> **NOTE:** Don't insist on finding a church that conforms to your doctrinal system. Doctrinal exactitude should NOT have the priority over spiritual warmth and vitality. If you find a church where the people love Jesus and radiate the joy of the Spirit, you have located a good spot. Thrills in the Spirit will do more to involve young people with Christ than the sterility of precise doctrine. It can be demonstrated that joy in the Lord involves teens with the Christ-life quicker than a head full of doctrines. Discount your doctrines if need be, to get into a glowing church. Let your children become infected with the FUN of living for Christ.

● When you find a glowing church, make your children go with you. They may fuss a while, but it won't be long before the infection takes hold. If you differ with the church on some points of doctrine, turn it to your advantage. Use the differences for stimulating discussions about the dinner table. Make sure the church has an active youth group with plenty of witnessing outings. It won't be long before your youngsters join in the testimonies and report the thrill of Christ in their own lives.

> **NOTE:** If you have to go to such a church for a year, do so. It is worth the sacrifice to involve your kids with the adventure of Christ. After that, if you wish to go to another church which coincides with your doctrinal position, fine. You might feel more comfortable in a formal church, but spending a year in an "on fire" church is a small price to pay for what it can do for your teens. Once they experience the fun of MOVING in the power of the Holy Spirit, they might bring it back to your old church. That would be a nice dividend, wouldn't it?

● Earlier we had a scene with Jerry. He wanted to go to the beach instead of church with the family. His father insisted that he accompany the family or forfeit his class in driver's education. Jerry went. The price for staying home was too stiff. That's as it should be. Having now moved up the scale of threat, you can make the price higher still. He must go with you and no argument about it.

Regardless of HOW you get Jerry to church, he should understand you are compelling him to go because you are responsible to God for his spiritual development. You dare not fail when it comes to Jerry's participation in Christian fellowship. Your fear of God's displeasure should move you to take whatever measures are necessary to see that he goes with you. As always, let him know you are in the same boat he is, i.e., he has to obey you, because you have to obey God. You can refer back to chapter five to see how the father made that fact clear to his son. I won't repeat the dialogue here.

> **NOTE:** Don't let Jerry talk you into allowing him to go to one church while the rest of the family goes to another. Your responsibility is not discharged simply by seeing that he goes to SOME church. He must go with you so that you not only know what he is receiving, but can watch his participation and provide whatever encouragement is needed. That's part of your responsibility too. Going to church is a family experience. This is vital in our time when the family altar is all but extinct. Gathering for dinner is about the only time most families meet as a unit. On Sunday afternoon, for example, the father can ask, "What did you think of the message today?" The spiritual conversation that follows could be something of a family altar.

We're ready to consider the PEOPLE with whom you do not want your children to associate. That's next.

Chapter Ten

PEOPLE AND PRESSURE

I couldn't believe my eyes. On the TV screen, a newsreel camera showed a group of young people tearing down a U.S. flag and ripping it to shreds. The scene was taking place on the campus of one of our great universities. In the interview which followed, the students openly advocated the overthrow of our government. The reporter didn't flinch when a spokesman for the group boldly asserted that democracy had failed and it was time to get rid of it, by force if necessary.

Where do young people get such ideas? Are we seeing a satanic plan for the destruction of our nation being carried out by young people? How can the devil get away with it? He couldn't without the cooperation of fathers and mothers who unwittingly help him by refusing to discipline their children. When a young person is allowed to grow up thinking right consists of what he can get away with, Satan is supplied another agent. Permissive parents are giving Satan an unbeatable force for bringing about the collapse of our country.

Why unbeatable? It is futile for authorities to get tough with rebellious youths as long as American homes cultivate them. Soon these self-willed youngsters will be holding public offices, serving as campus administrators and presiding over our courts. The whole society will become permissive. Then it will collapse. The lack of authority in the home will finally produce a breakdown of law and order in all areas of American life.

It does little good to go about checking outbreaks on the streets and campuses as long as the main source of rebels continues to produce them. It's like trying to put out the lights in a town by turning off each one instead of shutting off the power. America is in real danger unless we move on the source of her problem—the lack of discipline in the home.

THE HIGHEST LEVEL OF DISCIPLINE.

At last we come to PEOPLE. When we tell our boys and

girls they cannot be with certain people, nothing upsets them more. Why? The greatest satisfactions come from being with others and receiving their approval. The ego drive is the strongest of all. When young people can be with those who accept them as equals, nothing is more satisfying. To restrict a young person's contacts, is to invade the most strategic area of his life.

> **NOTE:** Augustine said, "Man was made for Thee, O God, and his soul is restless until it rests in Thee." But God is a PEOPLE. (I could have said—PERSON.) It was God's intention that we should live to satisfy Him and He us. It is a perversion when we find satisfaction in people who are UNLIKE God. We frustrate the divine intention when we enjoy the company of the ungodly. We violate the very purpose for which we were made when we find pleasure in those who are not in Christ. This is a basic rule of Christian existence.

When we regulate the kinds of people with whom our children may keep company, we touch upon one of the most sensitive areas of life. Nothing is more upsetting to a teen-age girl than to be told she cannot continue seeing a certain

boy. Explosive feelings surge through the lad told to stay away from certain youths he has begun to enjoy. We can expect emotional scenes when we start dealing with our teen-agers at the PEOPLE level. However, the more emotion we generate, the better the penetration we can make with the nutcracker.

> **NOTE:** We have now reached an area which does have enough threat and emotion to make kids leave home. A young girl might run off with a boy friend, rather than submit to your rules. A young man can become very defiant when he is told he can no longer see a particular girl or travel with certain fellows. If he is not able to run away and make it on his own, he can resort to devilish scheming to carry out his desires behind your back. The fusses created over bikinis and driving the car are nothing compared to the howls kids can make when you start regulating their social contacts.

 Brrrnnnnng . . . !
This time it was my phone. A distraught mother was calling.

"How do you control a 17 year old boy." Her voice was exasperated and shaky.

"Tell me what happened." Obviously her boy was in some kind of trouble.

"I just received a call from the sheriff's office. My son Jeff was arrested with some other boys. They were out driving and accidentally ran down a woman. The police found liquor in the car, now all of them are in jail."

"Who was driving?" I asked.

"Fortunately Jeff wasn't driving. But he wasn't even supposed to be with that bunch. I've told him repeatedly to stay away from those boys. I thought he was at the library. That's where he told me he was going. What can I do?"

> **NOTE:** You and I know this situation didn't develop overnight. It takes years of permissiveness and lax discipline to produce that kind of disregard and deception in a boy. You can be sure Jeff's arrest was only the climax of a history of disobedience and self-assertion. He had reached the place where he felt his own desires

had the priority over his parent's orders. He had no fear of punishment. He wouldn't have been with those boys if he had. In time, disrespect for rules in the home always brings boys and girls to trouble.

I hurried to Mrs. .... house. She was very upset. The thought of her boy being in jail was shocking. He hadn't been in trouble with the law before. However, it was only a matter of time. That time had come.

I knew the situation. This mother had been easygoing with Jeff. She waited on him hand and foot. She made excuses for his failures and disobedience. He had no trouble getting anything out of her. In spite of his spoiled antics, he was clearly her favorite. Though he was only 17, he lived like a king. His mother was his servant.

"Do you know a good lawyer?" she asked. "We just can't let Jeff stay in that awful jail." She was still ready to coddle him. "He's not really a bad boy, you know."

"Since you called me, I'll make a suggestion. You may not like it, but I wish you'd ask the Lord about it anyway. Let Jeff stay in jail. Since he is not really guilty of a crime, he'll be out soon enough. But he is guilty of something worse. He has lied to you and deceived you. That should be punished. I think a day or so in jail would be a fair price for that."

"You can't be serious!" The mother was astonished. "You mean I should let my boy stay in that terrible jail? I wouldn't think of such a thing. There's no telling whom he might meet there. Think how it would look on his record!"

NOTE: It's obvious which record she meant. Not God's, of course. She was worried about his social standing. To her thinking, it wouldn't do to have a black mark against Jeff's record among men. It might interfere with his future. Not his eternal future, his temporary future on earth. However, when one views such things from God's point of view, a day in jail can be a marvelous thing for an undisciplined boy. For Jeff's mother to rush in and secure his early release, might easily frustrate a divine teaching situation. This would be an ideal time for the CONSEQUENCES method of discipline to be harnessed to truths from the parent's package.

166

"You can go down and have Jeff released to you, if you want to. But I wish you'd pray about my suggestion first. He's already in the place of discipline. I agree it is better for a boy to learn discipline at home, but Jeff's already in a place of punishment. Why not use it for Christ? It will teach him something about the world's method of punishment. It could make him more inclined to submit to your ways at home."

"Shouldn't I even go down to see him?"

"Sure, but pray before you go. Ask the Lord to USE your visit. When you see Jeff, let him know you love him and are sorry to see him suffer. But also let him know he is going to stay there until the authorities release him. When he asks why, give one answer—'Your experience is the result of disobeying God.' The Lord says, 'Honor thy father and mother that it may be well with thee.' He has dishonored and deceived his mother. Now jail is the consequence. He is tasting a sample of God's discipline in the world."

> NOTE: If the mother and father allow the boy to stay in jail until released by the judge, it can be a valuable lesson. If Jeff gets the idea he is suffering the consequences of disobedience and tasting God's discipline, the Holy Spirit will use the stress of jail to BURN the truth into his new nature. Once lodged there with feeling, the Spirit can use it again and again later on. A boy can come home from such an experience shaken but effectively disciplined.

Some would warn you to get your boy out of jail fast. There's a bad element there, they say. It's true, all kinds of tough kids end up in juvenile hall. But here again you must trust the Holy Spirit to guard your boy. The Lord is ready to shield him if you commit your action unto HIM. However, if you have no thought of cooperating with the Holy Spirit to exploit this situation, there is no guarantee of protection. It is your motive that makes the difference with God. It is your submission that invokes the Spirit's protection in such cases. He is faithful to KEEP that which is committed to Him, but it must be committed.

When the boy comes home.

"Won't he feel I've let him down?"

Satan will try to bother you with that thought. But the opposite is true. Jeff knew he was in jail because he disobeyed his mother. He's the one who is worried. He wonders what you are thinking. All along you thought he was hoping you'd come running to bail him out. That just isn't so. Deep down inside, Jeff was hoping YOU WOULDN'T. He was praying you wouldn't yield and rescue him as always. For once he'd like to find you strong—**like a rock.**

It is marvelous when a young person finds his parents standing firm in a crisis. He knows you can't put your approval on rebellion and disobedience. He knows you shouldn't. The Spirit tells him that. Jeff wants you to do what is right. He expects it. If you stand firm, he'll draw strength from you. It will give him a picture of what he can be like when it is his turn to raise a family. Every time you bail Jeff out of a bad situation, he secretly hopes you wouldn't.

> **NOTE:** As noted, Jeff had the habit of doing as he pleased. He never met consistent discipline at home. He could always pressure his mother into giving in. Finally his rebellious ways took him into trouble outside the home. Had his mother and father built a fence for him, firming it up with discipline, he would have already known that PAIN follows disobedience. As it was, he did not receive these lessons at home. Therefore, he had to learn them in the world. How much better for young people to learn to submit to authority within the loving environment of their homes, than the cruel world outside. There is no love behind a policeman's badge.

JUDY STARTS TO DATE

In the last chapter, Judy was disciplined per the park incident. She deceived her mother and ran off to that PLACE to end up in the nutcracker. Now we come to Roger, the PERSON in her life. She met him at church. He's 17, a senior in the same high school. They have frequent chats on campus. Roger has a part-time job at a local gas station. He also has his own car. On several occasions he has been allowed to take Judy to the young people's meeting at church.

Now he wants Judy to accompany him to a night function at school. This is the first time she has been anywhere with the same boy to a different event. It's time to establish a new rule for Judy. Dates need deadlines for getting in at night.

"Judy, I'm going to let you go with Roger, but you must be in the house no later than 12 o'clock. That doesn't mean you can get home by twelve and park in front. I want you in the house."

"Okay mom."

● There shouldn't be any problem on the first date. Judy and Roger will make a point of being in on time. If they start dating regularly, they will be careful with your rule for a while. But it won't be long before they will try testing your fence. The first clue will be when Judy protests the time limit. Hold your ground. Midnight is late enough for a girl still in high school. An exception might be when they secure permission to stay out for a particular event that would keep them past the deadline.

Judy's boyfriend professes to be a Christian. He says he has received Christ. On that basis you have allowed Judy to see him. After all, she does need to learn about boy-girl behavior from experience. But time tells you more about Roger. Since he has a car, he has been bringing Judy home from school each day. Until he has to report to work at the gas station, they sit on the front porch or come in the house. You're glad for that. It makes for a closer look at Roger.

> **HINT:** Some girls get into trouble because they have no place to take their boyfriends. A youngster who was about to give birth to an illegitimate child told me recently, "I never had anyplace to bring my boyfriends. My folks said we made too much noise, so they wouldn't let me bring them to my house. Since I couldn't return the favor, I was ashamed to keep going to other girl's houses all the time. So I just went out with my dates alone and finally I got into trouble." Many a girl's life has been marred by being alone too often with the same boy. So letting Roger come to your house is a good idea. It allows you to keep tabs on any seriousness that might develop. Besides Judy is only 16.

So far so good. Roger and Judy have attended a few school affairs. Each time they've gotten home by midnight. But Judy has begun to protest the rule. Now you are alert to the possibility she might test the fence. Then it happens. They went to a basketball game at school and it is well past midnight. You look out the front window. No, they're not parked in front of the house.

It's 12:45 when you hear Roger's car in the driveway. In comes Judy on tiptoe. She walks softly, no doubt hoping all are asleep and nothing will be said. But you are awake. You have been all along. You've been talking to Jesus about the counsel and discipline the situation calls for.

"Judy?"

"Oh mom, are you still awake?"

"What time is it dear?"

"It's a little after 12:30. I know we're late, but the game was so exciting and everybody stayed until the last minute. We had trouble getting out of the parking lot, it was so crowded."

"You know the rule, Judy. You were to be in by midnight."

"I know mom, but it just couldn't be helped."

CAUTION: It's natural for a mother to worry when her child is late getting home. But the more one worries, the more her emotions build up. The later the hour, the worse it gets. As soon as you hear the car come in the driveway, discard your aroused feelings in heaven's wastebasket. Do it by thanking Jesus for her safe arrival. Then ask Him for the wisdom to make the most of the situation. Your feelings will subside when you think more about Christ and serving Him than about yourself and how worried you've been. Ahead of you is a time of discipline. You must have your emotions under control. If you find you CANNOT divest yourself of the upset feelings, defer your discipline until the next morning. Do not try to counsel your child while you are upset. You will only say the wrong thing, your punishment could be unduly harsh.

● Judy has an excuse. You expected that. You have also planned the kind of discipline you are going to bring. You and the Lord have agreed on that. The strength of the FENCE is readiness with the discipline required to make it firm. If you determine in advance the kind of punishment you are going to apply, you avoid the danger of assigning punishment when you are emotional.

"I know how you feel dear. I can remember when I was a young girl and had to face the same thing. I know how hard it is to tear yourself away from a game just to get home on time, especially when it is coming to an exciting conclusion. But it is an important choice young people have to face. Most kids have to decide between obeying their parents or staying to see the end of the game. I know it is a hard decision when everything is so exciting."

NOTE: See how that response identifies with Judy's feelings? That's important. Modern young people think their parents do not understand the pressures on them. But they do. What is vital is SAYING SO. And expressing it so that the kids know they do. This is what preserves the relationship. You do understand what Judy is saying—you've been in that situation yourself—you can identify with what she is feeling. When young people KNOW that you understand their FEELINGS, they accept punishment more readily. The agony of today is expressed as . . . 'BUT YOU DON'T UNDERSTAND.' You erase that notion by maintaining rapport with them at the **feeling** level.

Understanding doesn't eliminate discipline

We had a beautiful black cat named "Smokey." She littered and we gave away all her babies except one, which we named "Smudgy." When Smudgy was six months old and nearly as big as his mother, he ran into the street and was almost run down by a car. His mother watched the near tragedy from the front porch. Her tail switched in anger. As soon as Smudgy was within reach, Smokey whacked him a good one across the face and gave out a scathing meow.

With some animals it is a matter of instinct to guide their cubs until they are able to take care of themselves. How much more should God's image, gifted with reason and divine instruction, discipline their youngsters? God has not made it a matter of instinct with us. He has clearly told us what to do, and we must be at it. If a cat will swat her kitten which is nearly as big as she is, parents shouldn't hesitate to discipline their children even though they are nearing maturity. But you were answering Judy:

"Mother is also faced with tough decisions at times. I have to make one right now. Do you know what it is?"

"You're deciding what to do about my coming in late?"

"Yes. You see, I could let you off this time and give you another chance, or I can do as God instructs me and punish you for disobeying me. I appreciate your excuse. I can remember when I made the same one to my mother. And don't think I'm not tempted to overlook your lateness this time. I really am. But what excuse would I give God? How would I explain my disobedience to Him?

"Since mother is a little older and wiser than you, honey, she knows it is better to obey than to try offering an excuse. So I must discipline you for breaking the midnight deadline for the sake of a good time?"

"What are you going to do, mom?"

"You are not to go out with Roger for the next two weeks. I know you will see him at school and church, but you are not to get into his car or go anyplace with him. That means you will have to ride home on the bus for the next two weeks. He can come over as he always does. I am not trying to isolate you from him. But you will lose the privilege of going places together for two weeks. I have talked this over with the Lord and feel the punishment is fair."

172

This time you chose the deprivation method of discipline. Likely Judy would prefer the whip. Then the whole business would be settled in seconds. Now that we are at the PERSON level, more squeeze is made with the nutcracker by using social pain. It is more intense when boy-girl emotions are involved. The lesson, once again, is obedience. Your girl must obey you, even as you must obey God. If a child fears to disobey you, because you fear to disobey God, you have secured a most important truth of the parent's package.

● Will Judy hate you for this? Never! She will love you. She senses you established the fence for her sake and enforce it because you love her. It is because you do love her that your act of discipline does no injury to the bond between you. You have gone out of your way to understand her feelings. She is convinced you know her side of the story, even though you disagree. There is only love and warmth between you. That bridges the generation gap. She won't agree with your reason, perhaps, but it doesn't matter as long as she is secure in your love for her.

> **NOTE:** Parents of teens must face the truth that a day is coming when they will finally emancipate them, removing all controls. As that day approaches, the control span gets wider and wider. Even so it remains bridged by the bond of affection. It is NOT bridged by reason for there is never agreement on all things. As young people mature, they are entitled to a difference of opinion. This is why it is so important for parents to TALK to their children. The lines of communication must be kept open and room left for a difference of opinion. It is by such conversations that young people know their parents care for them. That care is demonstrated when mothers and dads show increasing respect for their youngster's advancing maturity. Respect does a great deal to maintain the bond of affection long after the controls have disappeared.

What if Judy comes in late again? If she does, and her excuse reflects she has again placed her desires above your authority, the discipline will have to be more strict. The fence must be charged even higher. If Judy is going with a boy whom Satan is using to get her to defy the rules of her home, she should be cut off from him completely. That will raise a yowl of protest, but it must be done. Satan has a lot of traps for teens. It is the duty of parents to spot them and deliver their children from evil.

● Modern teens do not feel "IN" with the crowd unless they are going steady. In many places it is the "in" thing to do. As a result, there are more unwed mothers than ever before. The National Office of Vital Statistics recently announced the shocking fact that one in 18 births in this country is illegitimate. Social scientists offer the following reasons:

1. Modern psychology, which says, "any repression of the sex drive injures the personality."
2. The H-bomb philosophy, which says, "Live for today, tomorrow may never come."
3. Broken homes, robbing teen-agers of moral guidance and discipline.
4. The custom of going steady.
5. Startling displays of sex in plays, movies and magazines.
6. Society's permissive attitude toward sexual misconduct.

> **NOTE:** More than sexual involvement is to be feared from going steady. We tend to become like our associates. The happier we are with certain people, and the more intimate, the greater their influence on us. There is no way to prevent the TRANSFER of ideas and mannerism from those with whom we share good times and excitement. Knowing this, parents should steer their boys and girls away from those who are beneath them in social grace, ambition and moral standards. Even more important is the date's relationship to Christ. A girl should set her sights high, looking on each date as the possible father of her children. That notion may be the farthest thing from her mind in the beginning, but the situation could easily end up that way because of the power of personal influence. More than one has ended up with an unsaved partner in life, because of this very thing.

If it turns out that you finally disapprove of Judy's boyfriend, and feel he might be leading her down the garden path, you have a responsibility to break off the contact. It will be an emotional time. Judy will get upset, but that only makes it ideal for the nutcracker. It's true that dates come and go, so parents are right in hesitating to cry "fire," before there is one.

If Judy displays serious interest in a boy of whom you disapprove, your love for her should compel you to act in her defense. You must not allow her to continue in a situation where she has to battle the biological urge without supervision or spiritual help. To turn a 16 year old girl loose with a scheming lad, is like sponsoring a fight between a baby kitten and a bobcat. She wouldn't have a chance.

Will Judy rant and storm? And how. But the more she carries on, the more effective the nutcracker. She feels pain. There's no doubt of that. Her spirit is caught between the jaws of discipline and teaching. Of course, you hate to see her suffer, but neither do you intend to let her agony be wasted. A lot of good counsel can be squeezed into her new nature for the Spirit to use.

● You're ready for Judy's agonizing cry, "Why, mom, why? I just don't understand it." Don't reply with, "It's for your own good, Judy." Kids hate that phrase. Instead let your words reveal your love for her:

> "Because we love you, honey, we're willing to let you endure this pain. We know it hurts to break off with Roger. We feel it too. It's hard for us to watch our girl suffer. But we love you enough to let you do it. It was the same with God when He had to watch His Son suffer on the cross. He didn't like it a bit, in fact He suffered along with His Son, but it had to be done."

If you quoted John 3:16 at this time, it wouldn't be preaching. It would be sympathizing. She would feel some of the agony herself, and the penetration would be marvelous. Equally important is the fact that you are suffering with her. Why? You love her. You don't have to tell Judy this separation is for her own good. She knows that. But it sure helps to know you are suffering too. If she believes that, the bond between you and her will be even greater—akin, perhaps, to that of the Suffering Son and the heart-torn Father in heaven.

> **NOTE:** If Judy cannot accept your love as sufficient reason for breaking off with Roger, but defies your authority, be prepared to go as far in dealing with her as you were with Jerry when he refused to cut his hair. Of course, you should try the gentler disciplines first. If none of them works, don't be afraid to go the

route with her just as you did with Jerry. The minor disciplines could include cutting off allowances, denying the use of the phone, confinement to her room, depriving of social contacts, isolation from the rest of the family with no T.V. privileges—finally no food and sleeping in the car. At no time, though, should Judy sense anything but compassion and love for her in your heart. Be tender as you speak to her. Let her know it hurts you to see her suffer. It does. She'll break in time. At some point the price tag on rebellion over Roger will be too high.

NOTE: Some kids in this situation run away from home. Fortunately they are a tiny minority. Most girls do not. Judy will NOT run if she has been made to feel the love behind your action. If you have been careful to protect your relationship with her during the THINGS and PLACES squeezes, there's no danger of her abandoning her godly home for the sake of a boy her parents consider unworthy of her. However, if she should bolt and run off with the lad, do not punish yourself with guilt feelings. She has a free will. It will be a matter of her choosing to be with that boy rather than remain in the loving care of parents who adore her. Any girl who makes that choice, does so entirely on her own, forsaking all the great lessons built into her so far. Passion is a powerful force. If such a thing should occur in your home, do not punish yourself with thoughts that your strong stand for Jesus drove her away. It just won't be true.

BUT HOW ABOUT JERRY'S FRIENDS?

Jerry is now seventeen. He has just graduated from high school. He has a job at a local supermarket. He is enjoying the first feel of important money in his pocket. You didn't interfere when he decided to buy a motorcycle. Now that he is out of school, you are putting him more on his own. The limits of the fence are shoved out a bit further. One of these days he will be leaving home, and you want the transition to be natural for him. So the reins are relaxed a bit, allowing him more control over his own life. He now has more say about where he goes, and with whom he spends his time.

You weren't pleased with Jerry's decision to buy a motorcycle. Of course, they are fun to ride, and they provide economical transportation. But there are risks too. Jerry has succumed to one of them. He's fallen in with the leather-

jacket crowd. They are a pack of wild riders. Jerry has met a girl. She's one of the wild riders too. She loves the thrill of roaring around town on the back of Jerry's bike. She's pushing him to get more involved with the group.

You are greatly concerned. You note how the crowd's influence on Jerry is anything but good. It doesn't take long to drag a nice boy down. The process is speeded when a girl is tugging too. She wants him to kick off the traditions of his folks and "do his own thing." Every day, it seems, there's further evidence of the wild riders' influence on him.

Oh oh, Jerry has started smoking. You have found grains of tobacco in the bottom of his shirt pocket. You weren't prying. You instinctively check pockets inside before putting them in the washer. There they were. He hasn't said a word about it. Your heart sinks to think of this fine boy, who was showing such promise of becoming a godly adult, now displaying the symptoms of Satan. His language is becoming more coarse. He enjoys suggestive shows on TV. But most disheartening is his coolness toward the things of God. He has not yet rebelled against church, but it doesn't take a mind-reader to see it coming.

"Jerry, have you started smoking? I found tobacco in your shirt pocket this morning."

"Checking up on me mom?"

"No dear, I usually check the pockets before I put clothes in the washer."

"Yeh, I smoke, so what?"

"You know cigarettes aren't good for you, son. Besides, why the secrecy? Were you afraid your folks would disapprove?"

"Well, I buy 'em myself. It's my own business if I want to smoke, isn't it? The reason I haven't said anything about it was, I knew you wouldn't let me smoke at home."

> **NOTE:** That's correct. Jerry should not be allowed to smoke at home. Some parents adopt the attitude, "If he's going to smoke, I'd just as soon he'd do it here as behind my back." To allow something you disapprove is a contradiction. If Jerry wanted to drink, would you apply the same principle? If so, would you also allow him to take drugs at home? If your home is built on Christ, the standards cannot include that which destroys. When you permit such a thing, you become a party to their smoking, drinking, drug abuse, or whatever. It makes you an accomplice, an undermining influence. Parents must always take a stand for what is right. Both God and their children expect it.

"You're right Jerry, there will be no smoking in this house."

● The rebellion is under way. Jerry's smoking is a defiance of the standard of the home. Even if he doesn't smoke inside the house, he's aware of your stand against it. However, you have extended his freedom fence. It's up to Jerry what he will do about those cigarettes. He knows how you feel. He will be facing bigger decisions before long, he might as well get the feel of them now. So you drop the matter of his smoking. It's up to him. At least for the time being, anyway.

> **NOTE:** Keep the purpose of this book in view. We are not trying to revamp the youngsters' lives, though hopefully there will be nice changes from time to time. We seek to install the parent's package, that's all. We don't want them to leave our shelter without these truths at work in them. Their real education will come during the next 50 years. The Lord will send testings and

trials into their lives. That is when the truths will do their life-changing work. If you do a good job of planting, the Holy Spirit will produce the harvest in their lives. He has a giant nutcracker, one far bigger than the one you are using. He uses sickness, accidents and tragedy. So don't worry about Jerry's smoking. If you get the truths operative in him, the Holy Spirit will take care of his smoking later on. However, it might not be pleasant. Cancer of the lung is a hard way to give up the habit.

You and your husband discuss Jerry a lot these days. It can be trying to handle a high school graduate who lives at home and has money in his pocket. Yet, as long as he is under your roof, he cannot be allowed to flaunt the standards of the home. There's bound to be a showdown before this goes much further. The direction of his life since he joined the "wild Riders," is sure to create a crisis before long.

> **NOTE:** As long as Jerry remains under your roof, he must submit to the authority of the home. True, his fence has been pushed out further, but there are some rules which still apply to him. Even if he were 21 or older, this would be true. Age does not give any child the right to prostitute the headship of his father or be indifferent to the wishes of his mother. When a boy reaches 21 and is still living at home, he becomes a GUEST. He is NOT the lord of the manor. If he feels adulthood entitles him equal rank with his parents, it's time for him to get out and make his own way. It is utterly destructive for a boy to be supported by his parents after he is 21. Unless there are mitigating circumstances, such as physical handicaps, etc., he should be on his own.

Saturday night explosion

It's dad's turn to mention Jerry's cigarettes. You are curious to know how they will affect his ability to participate in the family's church life.

> **"Jerry, your mother tells me you've taken up smoking."**
>
> "That's right, pop."
>
> **"Are you going to be smelling of cigarettes when we go to church tomorrow?"**
>
> "I'm not planning on going."

"You know the rule. Everyone in our home goes to church."

"Beverly wants me to take her to the 'wild riders' picnic tomorrow, I told her I would. It's not going to hurt anything if I miss a Sunday."

Look what's happening to Jerry. His girl friend and the "wild riders" are exerting a destructive influence on him, that's for sure. He smokes and probably drinks. Earlier he was impudent when his mother asked about his smoking. However, she let it pass. But here he is beginning to display contempt for the way of the Lord. That you won't let pass. The situation calls for the nutcracker. Your next words merely restate the family's position on going to church:

"You'd better call Beverly and tell her you are not taking her to the picnic tomorrow; that your family is always in church together on Sunday. Better yet, why don't you invite her to come too. You can still do something together afterwards."

"But we've already made plans, dad. We can worship the Lord just as well in some beautiful spot He's made. You don't have to sit in a stuffy church all the time to be a Christian."

Then Jerry's mother chimes in, backing your suggestion:

"Now son, why don't you go ahead and call Beverly. There's no use arguing with your father. You know he's right. God wants His people in fellowship with each other on the Lord's day."

"Damn it, mom! Can't you people get it through your heads—I'm just not going!"

You can't sit there and let Jerry talk to his mother like that. You move quickly. POW! Your fist strikes him flush on the jaw. The force of your blow drives him backwards against the wall. He slides to the floor in amazement. In seconds the atmosphere has become ugly. Satan is at work.

> NOTE: Parents aren't perfect. They have old natures, too. It would be a shame for me to write a book for perfect parents only. I'd have no readers. There will be times when reason gives way to anger. But is that so terrible? Not in this case. Underneath this very human action is your love for Jerry. He knows you love him. No single act of anger or discipline will change that. Later, when he has thought it over, he will be secretly proud

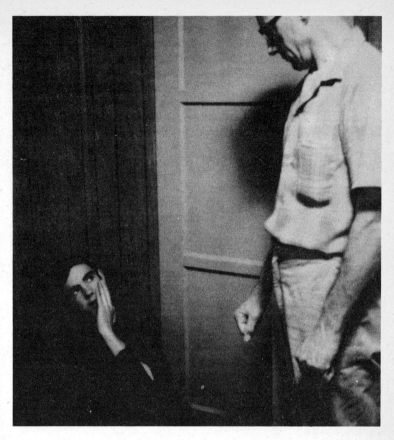

"Parents aren't perfect either."

of the way his father defended his mother. I would rather have parents react to this situation in anger, than to do nothing at all. I approve of that punch.

● Wouldn't it be better to keep your cool and use the lad's profanity against his mother as leverage for the nutcracker? Sure. You goofed. It will happen again. Be assured your action was human and natural. Collect yourself as quickly as possible. Don't let your anger surge a second longer, if you can help it. Reach out your hand to your fallen son. You're sorry by now you struck him. You know that violence is not the solution.

But Jerry remains belligerent:

"You can hit me all you like, dad, but I'm still not going."

"I'm not going to hit you, son. I'm sorry I did that. I don't approve of violence, but I couldn't allow you to talk to your mother that way. C'mon, let me help you up. Then go call Beverly and tell her you are going to church with us. You don't want to let a bunch of ungodly people turn you against the way you were raised, do you?"

"Look! You've already hit me. You've had your say. Now let me alone. I've had it with your making me go to church. You might as well get used to the idea of going without me. If I don't want to go, I'm not going. I'm old enough to decide for myself."

"You mean you'd walk out of your home to be with those 'wild riders,' rather than go to church tomorrow with your family?"

"I suppose that means you're not going to feed me and I can't stay at home anymore?"

> **NOTE:** See—Jerry's caught on. By now he knows the price of rebellion. You can be sure the consequences are turning over in his mind. By experience he has learned that you do not put food which the Lord supplies into the mouth of a rebel. He has already spent nights in the car, because you wouldn't provide the luxury of a comfortable bed to a defiant teen. Your stand for Christ is clear in his mind. He's emotional now. And he's not doing a good job of weighing the results of his defiance. But one thing he does know, that fence he's bucking is highly charged. He's in for a rough time. He knows his godly parents will not finance his revolution against the way of the Lord.

"Well, where would you stay, son?"

"I'll go over to Beverly's house. Her folks will let me stay there."

● Wow, he's serious about it. Did you suspect that gang was having this much influence on your son? Now you know. If he were fully dependent on you for his livelihood, you could forbid him to see the girl or consort with the "wild riders." As long as he has no place to go but home, you have the power to enforce your wishes. But since he is old enough to earn a wage, he is also old enough for this kind of freedom.

Parents are sometimes reluctant to let the leadership slip from their grasp, but it has to come. There is no way to bind

17 or 18 year olds who have jobs and are making enough money to live away from home. So you give them more freedom. But now it is obvious that Jerry has used his freedom to bind himself to the wrong crowd. Did he know better? Of course. You've had episodes over bad companions in the past. He has been penetrated with the truth.

So what do you do when kids reach this stage? You know you can't coddle them or support the worldliness appearing in their lives. You've reached the limit of parental discipline. So what's left to you? Ah, the **warning technique.** I would like to continue the scene, but we have gone far enough for one chapter. Since the warning does require a detailed explanation, let's give it more room. We'll treat the technique as a separate chapter. This time there'll be no introduction as our scene continues in chapter Eleven.

Chapter Eleven

THE WARNING TECHNIQUE

Jerry has just said:

"I'll stay at Beverly's house."

Are you prepared to let him? Indeed you are. He is NOT going to stay in your home and defy the authority God has placed in his mother and father. But there is more to it than insisting he move out—much more.

When you come to the place where you can no longer COMPEL your children to obey you, because they no longer need you for room and board, you reach the limit of parental discipline. Then you have to change your technique. Violence is out. A fist fight with Jerry wouldn't accomplish anything. If you had the power to lock him in his room, a "jail term" wouldn't help either. The only thing you can do is TURN HIM LOOSE. That sounds like failure at the end of the line, but it isn't. You're not through yet—not by a long shot.

You turn Jerry loose, but as you do, you invoke a special program with the Holy Spirit known as the warning technique. When I explain it, you'll see that it is nothing more than a variation of the nutcracker technique. As you reach the limit of parental discipline, it is time for closer cooperation with the Holy Spirit. It is then time for divine discipline.

Instead of your disciplining your teen, the Spirit of God DOES IT FOR YOU. You continue to apply the TRUTH jaw of the nutcracker, but God's Spirit operates the DISCIPLINE jaw. However, He does not do it entirely by Himself. He works only as you work with Him. When you are no longer able to put the pressure on a youth because he is self-sufficient, the Holy Spirit will step in and do it for you—when you ask Him. He is faithful to work closely with mothers and fathers in situations like the one before us. The sad part is He plays rough.

When God uses the stick, it hurts. It would be so much easier for Jerry to submit to your authority while living under

184

your roof, but if that is not to be, he will have to learn the hard way. He must then go into the nutcracker with God supplying the punishment. Now that time has come. Jerry is financially able to walk away from home and make out on his own. He will sacrifice such benefits as home-cooked meals, free laundry, a chance to save his money, family fellowship, perhaps a college education—but that's up to him. All this is in mind as you speak to him next. It's time to see how far he means to carry his rebellion.

"Let's see if I understand you, Jerry. It means more to you to take Beverly to that 'wild riders' picnic tomorrow than being in church with your family. Is that right?"

"Yep."

"And you insist on defying our wishes, knowing God requires us to meet rebellion with firm discipline?"

"I'm too old to have you telling me what to do all the time. I have a right to decide where I want to go and with whom I want to be. Besides, I can make out on my own if I have to."

"Okay, if your mind is made up, that's up to you. Before you leave for Beverly's house, I want to tell you something."

"What?"

"I'd hate to be in your shoes!"

"Why's that?"

"The Word makes it clear we are to bring you up as unto the Lord. I think you know that's what we've tried to do. But now you are turning against that way. We have used all the discipline we can, but now that you are in a position to go your own way, our discipline is no longer effective. When that happens, God has another way of handling rebels . . . and it's a rough one. I must say it again son, I'd hate to be in your shoes."

"Why? What's going to happen?"

"Having your parents discipline you, is God's gentlest way of dealing with people. When you refuse the gentle ways of the Lord, He has rougher ways. He takes over the discipline Himself and you end up in His woodshed. I've been there, Jerry, and it really hurts. There's a lot of things God can do to make us wish we had gone His way instead of our own."

"Yeah—for instance?"

"Well, for one thing, you might not make it to Beverly's tonight. You could have an accident and never get there. I'm not saying you will. I don't know what God will do with you. But it could be one of a dozen things, all the way from getting sick to landing in jail. You can take my word for it, God does spank. I guarantee you won't like it. If you think the discipline I've given you is tough, wait until you feel God's stick. He can hurt!"

> **NOTE:** The warning technique is a precious but neglected privilege. The subject is more fully treated in the author's book, WIN OR WARN, where it is employed as an advanced skill for dealing with those refusing Christ as Savior. The same technique also applies to rebellious teens. I have applied only skimpy details here. Once a teen is warned of God's discipline, the Holy Spirit is in a position to afflict his life. He uses Satan to deliver the actual punishment. The blows (Satan's swats) are limited to specific items, coming against one's pocket book, his business, his body, his family, even his mind. They are, as you will note, the same kind of blows God sends against parents who refuse to discipline their children according to His Word.

GOD'S STICK—OUCH!

"It's a fearful thing to fall into the hands of the living God!" (Heb. 10:31).

As soon as Jerry goes out the front door, go immediately to prayer. Ask Judy (if she has been a witness to the scene) to join you and your wife as you bow before the Lord. Together, the three of you should commit Jerry to the Holy Spirit for discipline. Do not suggest any specifics to God. It is beyond our comprehension to know what kind of punishment God should use. He alone knows Jerry's heart and what is needed.

It is a marvelous thing for Judy to be present when you commit Jerry for punishment. When the event comes to pass, she will remember kneeling to invoke God's chastening hand. Such an experience will stay with her the rest of her life. Not only will it enhance her fear of the Lord, it will prepare her for the day when she may have to do the same thing with one of her children.

NOTE: Earlier in the book we observed how God commanded O.T. parents to stone a rebellious youth to death at the city gates. I said the New Testament provided something better. We have come to it. The apostle Paul speaks of it this way . . . **"Deliver such an one unto Satan for the destruction of the flesh, that the spirit may be saved in the day of the Lord Jesus"** (1 Cor. 5:5). You've read that, haven't you? Likely you wondered about it, too. Now we have an application. The technique of delivering Jerry unto Satan for flesh-destroying work is for the purpose of producing spirit-saving results in your boy. That's the only reason behind your action. Of course this is drastic. It is only to be used after home discipline fails. In Paul's example, the technique was prescribed for a fornicator, but rebellion in a son is worse than fornication, in God's eyes.

Will something serious happen to Jerry. Most likely. Will you worry about him? Probably. But you shouldn't. Once you make the committal, TRUST God. He will do what is best for Jerry. Yes, he may get hurt. God's stick is painful. But you can't use your stick any more.

How fast will God move? His ways are not like ours. It could be right away, or it could be a slow process. The Lord knows the best punishment for the situation. He alone knows when and how the chastisement should be given. Hardest for you, will be believing that what befalls your boy is God's answer to your prayer. It will take real faith to regard the "accident" as taking place according to God's will.

> **NOTE:** Immature Christians feel God wants Christians to have rosy lives. That He desires His people to be in the best of health, have plenty of money and lots of time to enjoy it. To them, the blessed life is one entirely free of stress. The truth is just the opposite. God uses sickness and suffering to accomplish His will in lives. Health and prosperity is the world's idea of blessing. But those things never bring people to maturity. As long as we are in the flesh, it takes pressure and stress to make us CHANGE. Change is the key word in God's program for making men like Christ. So don't be exercised when trial befalls Jerry. Instead, give thanks and look for the precious fruit it produces in his life.

What makes the technique work?

As Jerry leaves for Beverly's house, your words ring in his ears:

"I'd hate to be in your shoes."

That gives the Holy Spirit something to use. Jerry would like to laugh off those words, but he can't. God's Spirit keeps bringing them to mind. **"Awh, that's a bunch of stuff,"** he says to himself. Yet, the gnawing doesn't leave. It's not like his mother and father to give out with spiritual foolishness. Soon his wonderings change . . .

"I wonder if God really would do something to me?"

From that moment on, Jerry will interpret everything that happens to him, whether a flat tire on his motorcycle to missing an appointment with his friends, as the work of God's pursuing Spirit. Even a headache will leave him wondering if God isn't after him.

Dr. F. W. Boreham tells a fascinating story which pictures this precious ministry of the Holy Spirit. He recalls a warm afternoon when he was cradled in the bough of a tree. He was relaxing and meditating when suddenly his reverie was pierced by a terrifying shriek. He turned in his cozy perch for a look. Running at top speed across the field came a frightened rabbit. As the creature raced past him it again emitted a scream of terror. That's when Dr. Boreham learned that rabbits scream.

● What made that rabbit scream? Then he saw it. Traveling much slower, came a weasel. It was pursuing the rabbit. Why should a rabbit fear a slower moving weasel? The weasel has an amazing faculty. It can pick up the scent of a rabbit and never lose it. No matter how many other trails it may cross, the weasel never loses track of his quarry. He stays after that rabbit until he finally catches him. And the rabbit knows it.

The terrified creature panics. He runs until he drops. He knows he's done for once a weasel picks him as the victim. Sooner or later that persistent follower will catch up with him. That's enough to put terror in the heart of any rabbit, **even a man!** It's like that with the Holy Spirit, says Dr. Boreham. In his book, "The Hound of Heaven," he shows how the Spirit of the Lord pursues men in the same way. It can be terrifying to discover the heavenly Visitor zeroing in on your life. Once he becomes aware of God's personal attention, any man or youth might cry with the Psalmist:

> **"Whither shall I go from thy Spirit, whither shall I flee from Thy presence?"** (Psa. 139:7).

Then it happens

God was ready to do something about Jerry. He moved swiftly. He was waiting for you to commit him for divine discipline. The Holy Spirit had Satan poised as God's stick. The answer to your prayer comes a lot quicker than expected.

> "Daddy, it's Jerry . . . !" Judy's all excited. "The hospital just called. Jerry has been in an accident!"

Watch it! Your emotions will surge. If your thoughts race in the wrong direction you'll find yourself saying . . .

"Dear God, what's happened to my boy!"

That's what Satan would like to have go through your mind. But if you are on your toes, your first thought will be...

"Thank you Lord for dealing with him so fast!"

● A nurse gives you the details over the phone. Jerry was involved in a freakish "accident" with his motorcycle. He skidded and spilled, breaking his arm. His arm has been set in a cast. He doesn't have to stay in the hospital. He asked the nurse to call you. He wants you to come and get him. That sends you to the Lord for wisdom.

You go. You find a humbled Jerry sitting in a chair in the waiting room. He's been through God's tenderizer. It shows. He appears relieved to see you. Your time with the Lord has prepared you to make the most of the situation.

"I didn't get very far, did I?"

"No son, but thank the Lord He didn't find it necessary to let something worse happen to you."

"I think I know what you mean now. I didn't take it seriously when you said you'd hate to be in my shoes: But you're right, the Lord can play rough. I had it coming, though. I've been stupid lately. I don't know what's gotten into me. Anyway, I want you to know I'm sorry for the way I acted."

> **NOTE:** There's a lot of emotion attending this scene, and it will dissipate quickly. You want to use it as soon as you can. If you have any privacy at the hospital, don't delay in applying the teaching side of the nutcracker. If there is not sufficient privacy, then reserve your counsel until you are driving home in the car. Jerry will no doubt repeat his words . . . **"I don't know what got into me."** That's your cue for a discussion of the believer's two natures and how Satan uses the ego drive and the sex drive (the gang and the girl) to send flaming ideas surging through his mind. Jerry will be able to understand your explanation for the WHY of his behavior. Once he sees how Satan made a fool of him, it will be a penetrating experience. He won't want it to happen again. At least, he'll know what to look for. If you have already taught him how to deal with the devil, he will defend himself against a similar onslaught.

"This sure has been an expensive lesson, dad. My bike was totaled out and I'm still paying for it."

"It could have been worse, Jerry. Think what might have happened had Beverly been riding on the back. You can thank the Lord this was all it took to turn you from the way you were going. But you can be sure of this—if it did take something worse, God wouldn't hesitate to send it. He can really hit where it hurts."

"Is that why there is so much sickness and tragedy in the world?"

"NO, this is a special situation, Jerry. Your accident would NOT have occurred had I not warned you IN ADVANCE. It wasn't until I said, 'I'd hate to be in your shoes,' and warned that God would discipline you, that this could ever happen. Once you got the warning, you were in a position for God to deal with you. However, if I had not given you that warning, there would have been no accident. God does not send accidents like this unless there is a way for you to behold it as divine discipline."

191

NOTE: What father would smash his boy's bike with a sledge hammer? A rare one, surely. If you had taken the hammer to Jerry's bike, it would have stirred more wrath and rebellion. But when God does it, it is a different matter. He can smash a boy's bike, his body and even his spirit, if necessary. It's proper for HIM to do so. He is the Giver of all things. But had you tried it, it would have produced vengeance and retaliation. There's a point, you see, where it is best to turn the discipline over to God and keep yourself ready to receive your chastened son into your arms. In this instance, note how Jerry wrecked his own bike. That is, the discipline was accomplished in such a way that Jerry appeared to be the one who smashed his own bike. God can arrange such a thing, we cannot. It's a wise parent who makes full use of divine discipline once his own is no longer effecive.

God takes no delight in discipline

Once a rebellious lad receives the warning from his parents, the Holy Spirit is ready to take over where the parents leave off. Without such a warning, His hands are tied. God will not send blows into a teen's life, unless the youth understands what is happening. To do so would be punishment for the sake of punishment. God won't do that. He has no delight in seeing people suffer. He even feels sorry for men when their suffering is the consequence of their own evil. For Him to use Satan to deliver a deliberate blow, with no awareness on the part of the teen-ager, is not like God at all. He just won't do it.

But once that warning is given, God will go to limits you and I would never dream of. He will take any action needed. We already know how He hates defiance and rebellion. Parents shouldn't be shocked at the severity of God's discipline. He knows what it takes to make a heart tender. God doesn't look on a lost leg or arm as we do. To him a body plagued with cancer is beautiful if it produces eternal changes in the soul. A sound body has to die in time, anyway. But a refined soul will be lovely forever. We wouldn't poke out a son's eye, but God would. He even slew His own Son on the cross.

NOTE: God never FORCES anyone to do anything. That is, He is not interested in making people do things against THEIR WILL. He will send affliction only to the extent that it will soften a

192

person's heart. He will send suffering to counteract the fleshly work of the devil, but not enough to violate one's will (1 Cor. 10:13). All of God's discipline is designed to BRING OUT what is already **buried** in one's heart. That's all. He has no desire to overrule our freedom. It would cancel the faith program if He did. God could easily send enough pressure to make every person see things His way, but He is not interested in forcing His will on anyone. He wants people to WANT to do His will. Therefore, all of His disciplines are geared to canceling the power of the flesh, yet leaving the power of choice intact.

Remember Pharaoh? In kindness, God sent evidence upon evidence of His presence and power. The more God revealed of Himself (miracles), the harder Pharaoh's heart became. But God did not put the hardness in Pharaoh's heart. He merely brought out what was ALREADY there. As rain does not put weeds or flowers in the soil, but merely brings up what is already there, so does the working of God. Had Pharaoh changed his mind (repented), Moses would have said, "God softened Pharaoh's heart." In no way did God interfere with Pharaoh's freedom of choice. At any point, the monarch was free to do as he wished. The same process softens or hardens hearts, depending on what is already there.

The same thing could have happened to Jerry. The "accident" with his motorcycle could have made him bitter instead of better. In that case, God's discipline would have merely crystallized something already there. What can you as a parent do then? Pray—and that's all. The Lord will keep an eye on the lad and stay on his trail until the day he dies. The Spirit will be standing by to help should he ever be inclined to repent. But if he remains stubbornly defiant, he is on a collision course with disaster. He will end up in the hands of Satan, and you know how the devil feels about God's people. Had Jerry not repented on this occasion, he could have been headed for a life of misery.

NOTE: Are there not cases where great suffering has brought people to Christ without any warning? Yes, indeed. How do they differ from Jerry's? Jerry's "accident" was discipline. And God's discipline is reserved for His own. He does NOT discipline the devil's children. The blow Jerry received was designed and sent by God in cooperation with his parent's prayers. Had Jerry not turned on the first blow, God would have sent increasingly severe blows until the violation point of Jerry's will was reached. In cases of unsaved people NO DISCIPLINE is involved. There is NO PROGRESSION of blows for the unsaved. Usually they are staggering at the start, such as a terrible disease or the death of a child. It takes a frightful blow to bring an UNWARNED man to his senses, and Satan has them. On the other hand, a WARNED Christian is half-looking for trouble. When it comes, he views it as from the hand of God. Therefore, overwhelming tragedy is not needed to reach a warned Christian. That should be comforting to parents in this position.

The Christian teen-ager who is committed to God for discipline, can come to an untimely end if he refuses to surrender to the revealed will of God. His case is worse than that of the pagan youth. He knows better. Knowledge brings responsibility. His flesh could be completely destroyed (physical death) even though the lad himself goes into the Lord's presence (his spirit saved) an immature creature. Remember how the apostle Paul stated it:

". . . deliver such an one unto Satan for the destruction of the flesh, that the spirit may be saved in the day of the Lord Jesus!" (1 Cor. 5:5).

Now you know how that works. A boy or girl can be committed to Jesus for discipline, but if his heart remains stubborn and rebellious, you can expect the worst. Aren't you relieved that a broken arm and a smashed bike was all it took to salvage Jerry? How awful had he turned the other way. Had he hardened his heart still further, he would have traveled down a rough road. God never lets up on His own.

Delivered by discipline

Jerry was one of the tender ones! What a relief! It would have pained you to see him suffer in the days ahead. But praise the Lord, all it took was one swat from God. What a joy to see his rebellion end. Once more he is the sweet boy you raised. Now you are glad you shifted from parental discipline to divine discipline. It's not easy to make that commitment, but it is worth it.

What will Jerry do about that motorcycle gang now? I wouldn't worry if I were you. The truth of the parent's package has been installed. He knows what to do. Besides, he has already felt God's hand on the seat of his britches. There's not likely to be any further dissent about going to church either.

Look back over the road we've traveled so far. See how the nutcracker has worked in the lives of Jerry and Judy? Isn't the Lord wonderful? It is certain now that your children will leave your home as tender and submissive Christians who honor their parents and their Savior. You are so proud of them. Without doubt you have passed the worst crises of Christian parenthood. But don't relax just yet. I must tell you of something else that should be installed in their lives. What's that, you ask? The FUN of serving Jesus. Your job is not really done, you see, until they have been introduced to the THRILL of Christ! That's next.

Chapter Twelve

TEENS NEED EXCITEMENT

"All work and no play makes Jack a dull boy."

You agree, I'm sure. So far the book has been one-sided, all work and no play. Any plan for correcting a situation has to be that way—at the start. We had to begin by installing the fence and letting Judy and Jerry learn the consequences of disobedience. There is no short cut. There must be a set of rules in the home backed by discipline. Thus, everything to this point has been a matter of:

> **"You can't do this or that."**
> **"You must do this or that."**
> **"If you don't obey, you'll be disciplined."**
> **"I'd hate to be in your shoes."**

When corrective measures are called for, the program is always more negative than positive. But we agree it cannot be all that way. Jerry and Judy would become awfully dull if they knew only a system of don'ts. There is a limit to what external discipline can do.

The Israelites were reared under the Law. They grew up under a system of DON'TS, or "Thou shalt nots." Consequently the Old Testament presents a rather joyless history. Yet, the Law did its job. Paul says it was a "schoolmaster to bring us to Christ." Ah, but after that, the motivation changes. With the coming of the Holy Spirit, people are no longer COMPELLED to do what they should by external threats. They are IMPELLED by the joyous prompting of the Spirit within them. But does that mean the Law was a mistake? Indeed not. It fulfilled its purpose beautifully.

So it is with your external discipline. It has its place. It is indispensible when dealing with a situation that needs correction. You are facing one now or you wouldn't be reading this book. Therefore, we began with the negative approach, installing rules and enforcing them. But AFTER you have gained some control by external discipline, it's time to develop your teen's INTERNAL motivation. When your youngster is internally motivated to live for the Lord, you achieve the highest success as a Christian parent.

Consider the ships of the sea. Remember the days when vessels moved only by the impulse of the wind upon their sails? When the winds were fair, they moved steadily onward. When there was no wind, they couldn't move at all. At other times, gales would drive them off course.

So it is with a lad and the external discipline of his parents. If their discipline is fair and consistent, he moves steadily onward. He can also languish when there is no discipline, or be thrown "off course" when there is too much, especially if it is unreasoning and abusive.

Ah, but then another type of ship came along, the magnificent liners propelled by the inner impulse of their powerful engines. There is an interior force which enables them to move ceaselessly regardless of weather. The lad who becomes infected with the thrill of Christ is like that. He is moved by the FUN of being involved with Jesus. He is motivated by the joy of serving Christ in the power of the Holy Spirit. His compelling force is INSIDE him. That is the greatest discipline of all.

TEENS NEED FUN

The Lord designed us as FUN-LOVING creatures. We perform best when we're doing that which makes us happy. When a Christian finds it delightful to serve the Lord, he is ready to invest his whole life in Jesus. At once there are two kinds of fun, fleshly and spiritual. Spiritual excitement is of a higher order than fleshly fun. Spiritual fun is a work of God. You'll see why in a bit.

God knows that being saved does not quench a person's appetite for good times. Go where people are enjoying themselves. Are there no Christians there? Christian young people are as interested in sports as anyone else. They shout at the baseball games and enjoy themselves in the amusement centers. Are there no Christian youths on the ski slopes, surfing in the ocean, on the fishing boats, racing fast cars or watch-

ing TV? They yearn for thrills as surely as anyone else. Being in Christ doesn't eliminate our hunger for adventure.

> **NOTE:** It is the hunger for thrills that leads youngsters to form gangs and go about stirring up trouble. Usually these kids have no one to show them how to extract joy from life. They have to do it their own way. But do it they will. The passion for excitement is there. When I was a teen, I traveled with such a gang. We stole, shot lights out of houses, and destroyed property for the pure kick of it. I have sampled the excitement of stealing a car, setting fires, as well as putting a gun to a man's head. I have been on both sides of FUN—man's first, then God's. I know from experience that godly fun is the greatest of all. It can be an obsession to exalt Jesus in the power of the Spirit.

Becoming a Christian expands our capacity for FUN! At the same time, life in Christ offers the most fun in this world. Receiving the Holy Spirit is only the first step. Getting acquainted with Him, to find that He is also FUN-LOVING, is a second treat. Then to move in His strength as though it were YOUR OWN is an explosion of FUN you never forget! Moving in the power of God's Spirit has to be the greatest treat on earth. The world can't match it. To me, it is soul-rapturing bliss—pure, holy FUN!

Teens need it

The reason teens are fun-loving is not due to sin. God made them that way. The best way to satisfy the yearning is to get caught up IN something big. God would not create us with this need then fail to provide for it. That would be cruel. That's why He gave us the Great Commission. We have the task of reaching the whole world, introducing people to the One Who made them. If young people want a cause or crusade, here is the granddaddy of them all.

> **NOTE:** The Lord could have arranged for people to be saved by another means, that is, to hear about Him in other ways. He could have used the sunset colors and written His message there. He could roll back the heavens to give men a glimpse of eternity. It would be simple for Him to tell the story a dozen different ways. But He didn't. He gave us the job. He wants us to have the FUN of reaching others in the power of His Spirit.

Is it easy to convince someone that a Man Who died on a cross 2000 years ago is the Creator of all things? That this One Who made them still lives, though once crucified. That He is waiting to come into their lives and save them from a hell? When you come right down to it, the gospel is about the most ridiculous statement a person can make. Why should anyone believe it? Ah—apart from the Holy Spirit, they won't.

Therefore, we need more than a commission to share Christ. We need more than information. We also need the power of the Holy Spirit if men are to believe what we say. That's what makes it FUN. So again I say, it was to meet our need for adventure that God gave us the Great Commission. It was to satisfy our longing for thrills that He gave us the power to carry it out. There is no bigger challenge, no bigger adventure, no bigger kick—anywhere!

> **NOTE:** The day of Pentecost brought individual Christians the privilege of moving in the power of God. The first Christians were drunk with power as they discovered themselves operating in the Spirit's strength. Instantly Christianity became intoxicating— exhilarating and infectious. Everywhere those early Christians went, the truth of Jesus swept like a prairie fire—and it was fun! They quivered with excitement. They were vibrant because of it. My book, "The 100% Christian," presents a full exposition of the FUN

and THRILLS of moving in the power of the Holy Spirit. It shows how to recover the adventure given to the church on the day of Pentecost. It is the same adventure in which your children must become involved if you want them to become 100% Christians.

● When it comes to the passions of the flesh, I agree these should be kept low. But spiritual excitement is of another order. There is honest to goodness fun in Christ. It is as holy as anything can be. Would any Christian say that the joy of exalting Christ in the Spirit should be cooled? I can't believe that. Those churches and leaders who are dedicated to reviving and intensifying our spiritual fever, go to the heart of the matter. I am convinced that those fathers and mothers who infect their children with the FUN of serving Jesus, give them the best of our Christian heritage—"joy unspeakable and full of glory!" (1 Peter 1:8).

HARNESSING TRUTHS TO THRILLS

When we apply the stick to a teen's britches, the message comes across loud and clear—disobedience brings pain. That truth is harnessed to a negative emotion. He understands what you are saying about the consequences of disobeying God. His body feels pain at the moment. By using the negative emotions produced by discipline, we install some great truths of the parent's package.

But look again at the parent's package. See, not all of those items are negative. So a question is in order: can the positive items be installed with negative emotions? That is, can you teach the truth of the Christian's reward, for example, with a stick? No—positive truths require positive emotions. Not everything in the package can be instilled in a young spirit with punishment and discipline. Some of those truths need positive emotions to penetrate the soul of a youth.

What emotion is more positive than the thrill of Christ? What is more stirring to the Christian than being used of God? If disobedience brings judgment and pain, then obedience brings the reverse—blessing and reward. If we install negative truths with negative emotions, then we need positive emotion to install such truths as:

- The moment by moment presence of the Lord.
- The importance of laying up treasure in heaven (rewards).
- That Christians must compete for the best jobs of eternity.
- That one must work to get ahead in Christ, even as men work to get ahead in the world.
- The necessity of making the most of each day on earth in preparation for serving Christ in heaven.

How do we bring such joy to young people?

How do we acquaint teens with the positive emotion of Christianity? How can they experience the FUN of being filled with the Spirit? We must find a way to introduce them to the THRILL of Christ if we would install the positive truths of our package. Without positive emotions, we will not penetrate their spirits. Unless we do, the Holy Spirit will not have those positive truths to use after they leave home.

> **NOTE:** Why do kids try dope? They hope it will give them the KICK they seek. Too late, they discover its promises of pleasure are merely bait for the deadly trap of drug addiction. How precious then to learn of the wonderful excitement God provides in the Great Commission. Those who want to get "high," can "blow their minds" in the power of God. And there are no bad after effects, unless you consider the scorn of non-active Christians a harmful side-effect. Idle Christians always criticize those who get involved with the Spirit to carry out the master's orders. But what is that, when Jesus' "well done" sends your soul on an ecstatic trip.

I stopped by the office of a local businessman. He's a friend of mine, an evangelical Christian and a godly father. He is also the Sunday school superintendent in his church. Whenever we meet, we talk of witnessing and the joy of serving Christ. On this occasion he thought I would be interested in something that happened to his daughter. Janice was fifteen. I knew she attended church regularly with her folks.

Lately, he said, Janice had been complaining of boredom with the Sunday school. He was finding it hard to keep her interest in spiritual things. High school activities held more attraction for her. It had become increasingly evident the routine of church meant less and less in her life. The youth groups had become a "drag," as she put it.

Then one of her school chums invited her to a teen rally. It attracted kids from different denominations. They all had one thing in common—the **thrill of Christ!** These kids didn't care about dress. Some wore off beat styles, a few played guitars, some even wore beads and badges. The significant thing was, not a one was ashamed of Jesus. They sang about Him, spoke boldly of His power in their lives, but most of all —they had FUN witnessing for Him in public places. Every person in the group "did his own thing," but it was for Christ.

Each time they gathered, new ones were invited. Thus, the group was growing steadily. Janice was one of those contacted at school. She went to one of the meetings held in a local park. My friend continued the story:

> "The very first time Janice attended one of their meetings, the group was planning a tract invasion of Palm Springs (a resort community about 100 miles east of Los Angeles). Jan was completely captured by the fun these kids got out of witnessing. She had never seen kids so excited over spiritual things before. She was all wound up when she came home that night. She made her mother and me listen while she told us all about the kicks these kids got out of witnessing for Christ.
>
> "I was dumbfounded," said my friend, "Jan actually begged us for permission to go with that group to Palm Springs to pass out tracts. I have been trying to get her to do this for a long time. She's always been cold to the idea. But the excitement of those kids got her. Whatever it is, I wish we had it at our church."

● Let me tell you about this father. While he liked to talk about witnessing, he never did it. Consequently he didn't really know the thrill himself. No wonder his words fell flat when he spoke to his daughter. She knew he didn't witness. Why should she? His efforts at church were equally unsuccessful. This explains why he didn't know what those kids at the park were experiencing. Sure, he'd like to have it in his church, but he wasn't about to get involved with the Spirit. Here was his daughter "turned on" for Christ and he didn't know what it was all about. Remember, this brother is a Sunday school superintendent in an evangelical church. I doubt, though, if he's alone in his ignorance.

Have you seen the American Cancer Society's TV ads against smoking? One of them is really funny. It fits my friend to a tee. It shows a father complaining of his kid's smoking. He's getting nowhere trying to make them quit.

"I've explained all the evils of this filthy habit to them. I've told them what it does to their lungs and how it can shorten their lives, but they don't pay any attention to me. No matter what I say to them, they just keep on smoking."

Then he took another puff on his own cigarette and continued. . .

"No sir, I just don't understand it. You'd think that all those warnings I've given them would be enough to make them quit. But they go right on as though I had never said a word."

That's funny, isn't it? Imagine a dad telling his kids to quit smoking while he, himself, puffs away. Equally funny was Janice's dad telling her she should witness for the Lord, when he didn't do it himself. It's like the old saw, **"Your actions speak so loud, I can't hear a word you're saying."** Idle parents cannot infect idle kids with the thrill of Christ. It is a psychological impossibility. You cannot ignite others, when you are not on fire yourself.

HAPPY AND HOT

Come with me to the Kaiser Steel plant in Fontana. We'll stand where we can see the huge bucket coming from the blast furnace. Sparks are flying from it. It is filled with bubbling iron. We hold our breath as that enormous bucket is tipped and liquid steel pours into the molds.

In its scintilating form, iron can be turned into almost any shape. So with the Christian. When he is red hot, God can do anything with him. But when his temperature is low, he is as unchangeable as a cold block of iron. If we would fashion our teens for Christ, we must find a way to get them red hot in the Spirit.

How would you like to have Jerry red hot for Jesus? What if Judy wanted to travel with young people hooked on the thrill

203

of speaking out for Christ? Would you be embarrassed to have Jerry outspoken? Would you forbid Judy to go with such a crowd? Or would you pray for them as they obeyed the Lord? I imagine you acquiesce when I put it like that. That's what it boils down to. Youngsters need to be fired with godly emotion—and the hotter the better. One reason we see so little done for Christ today, is because God's people are cold.

 There's gloom over the church of Christ today. His people are not happy. You know that. You go to church. You can see it for yourself. Study the faces in your own fellowship. Do they radiate the joy of Jesus? Do they exude the thrill of Christ? Are they caught up in the wonder of His anointing? You know they aren't. As you speak with the brethren, do their hearts pound as they tell of another exciting week in Christ? Do they breathlessly report the fun of moving in might? Could you honestly say your church GLOWS with the effervescence of the Spirit? Few Christians enjoy such exultation today.

Here's my point: how can we expect young people to be caught up in the HEAT of Spirit-filled Christianity, when the routine of Church proceeds in the opposite direction? Christianity, as revealed in the Word, is a convulsive, revolutionary way of life—which really turns people on. But what do we see? Week after week, Christians drag themselves to church to plop in a pew. They sigh out their weariness, their chins sagging to the seats. As the man up front does his thing, they study the walls and check their watches. How in the world can that routine ignite young people for Christ?

Who wants to be cold and miserable, when Christ invites us to be happy and hot? No wonder kids leave the church in droves. They want to be where the action is. Sadly, there's more of that in the world.

THE ROUTE TO POWER

Witnessing for Jesus is the direct route to the POWER of God. I am not saying that empowering witnesses is the SOLE work of the Spirit, but it is a primary work. The Spirit also seals the sonship of the believer, convicts of sin, certifies the truth, and enables us to live godly lives. But witnessing is the ONLY feature of the Christian life that provides the INSTANT thrills young people need. It is the most direct route to FUN in the Lord. Why? Witnessing can only be done in the power of the Holy Spirit to be effective. It is the one action offering EXCITEMENT day after day after day.

Let young people develop spiritual muscle as they move among the unsaved and they will become red hot. No other experience in Christ can ignite them so quickly. Whereas you and I might thrill to a precious truth from God's Word, young-sters want FUN—fun in the Spirit. Young people are like that. Nothing "blasts" them for Jesus like the HEAT of witnessing. Believe me, that FIRE melts their spirits to the place where they can be penetrated with truth from the package. Their pliable spirits can be shaped easier than iron when fired in the furnaces of witnessing.

I have at hand a letter from a concerned lady in North Carolina. She has relatives here in California. One is a 15 year old boy who says he's saved, but his mother can't get him to go to church. The friend in the East was inquiring to see if I knew of a sound church near the boy's home.

"It could be," she said, "the family has been going to a dead church that offers no spiritual food for the boy and he has simply lost interest."

In the light of what we have been saying, how would you advise this woman? I know of a number of fundamental, evangelical churches in the boy's vicinity. But 15 year olds need more than that. Of course he should be in fellowship with God's people if he is born-again. But the average evangelical church will not meet the emotional requirement of a teen. There is no way to know the thrill of Christ apart from personal obedience to the Great Commission. That is God's ONLY provision for **kicks in Christ!**

So, if we were to recommend a church for a 15 year old boy, it could not be a run of the mill evangelical church. It would have to be one where the ACTION is, in the Spirit's power. But where do you find such churches? They are rare. Even the most sound churches are limited to singing and sermons, lectures and lessons. That's too bad isn't it? Especially when Jesus has made it so plain . . .

"Ye shall be My witnesses!"

WHAT'S GOD'S ANSWER, THEN?

God never leaves sincere people in futility. He always has an answer. For those parents desiring to acquaint their teens with the thrill of Christ, I will list three ways to get the job done.

> **CAUTION:** Do NOT try to bring the thrill of Christ to your teenagers life UNTIL you first establish discipline in your home. You must begin with the negative truths and secure obedience before attempting to install the positive truths. As mankind needed the Old Testament before it received the N.T., our youngsters need discipline before the dessert. The thrill of Christ is the **reward** of an obedient life. Your teens must learn to obey you FIRST, before they can submit to the Holy Spirit. They must yield to your control before they will yield to the Spirit as witnesses. This is the divine order. So I repeat: Do not attempt to bring the positive truths of the package until you have first installed the negative. You do not give dessert to youngsters who refuse to eat their dinner.

I. INVOLVE YOUR TEENS WITH A GROUP OF
YOUNG PEOPLE ALREADY ON FIRE FOR CHRIST!

Not far from me is the "Agape Inn." It is a small building attached to a local church. But the church doesn't use it. It has been turned over to young people who run it to suit themselves. The one in charge is a young man just out of his teens. He saw a need for a special place for kids who "turn on" for Christ. Teens flock to the "INN" from all over. They wear old clothes, sit on the floor at low tables, and have dim light. As the Spirit leads, different ones entertain or testify to what Jesus has done with them that week.

It looks like a coffee house. It's off-beat. The kids wear huge badges which say things like: "Win with Jesus!" or, "Jesus—the bridge over troubled waters," or "Smile—Jesus loves you!" The soft drinks and doughnuts are free. The teens enjoy each other and CHRIST! Souls are saved in a steady stream. It has become the "in" thing to join a group "hung up" on Christ. I know that might shock you, but God is keeping pace with the needs of our young people. Apparently He is not asking them to conform to the ideas of older Christians.

NOTE: All across the nation Christian teens are forming such groups. In some places, the established churches help them. That's so wise. Without question the Holy Spirit is producing this phenomenon. Businessmen and concerned parents seem eager to sponsor them. Even the police have been known to help in some communities. The crime rate recedes drastically in areas where the thrill of Christ spreads like a prairie fire. Originally, it seems, the idea started as an effort to reach the hippies, but now it has proved to be God's answer for teens everywhere.

The backbone of this "off beat" Christianity is witnessing for Christ. Without it these clubs would not survive. It alone provides the kicks young people seek. Where the witnessing is constant, the FIRE travels as it did in the First Century. Some of these clubs grow to the place where they have their own newspapers. They resemble the hippies papers in style, but they have only one purpose—to present Christ.

Such a club exists in Whittier, California. The teens call themselves the "God Squad." It is a take off, no doubt, on the TV series, "Mod Squad." These kids are so unashamed of Jesus they wear their big badges to school. One young man I know was proudly wearing his badge on the high school campus, when a non-Christian called to him.

"Hey Jim! You're not hooked on that Jesus stuff, are you!"

Without hesitation the lad boldly shouted back across the quad,

"Yeah man, I'm hooked on Christ. What are you hooked on?"

Jim, I learned, was one who came to Jesus through the club. With all the members about him witnessing so boldly, it seemed the natural thing to do. It came easily. Witnessing is a lot easier when everyone does it. You can see how this would affect teens. If witnessing is the "in thing" to do, they all want to be "IN." That's the genius of the movement. It exploits the "rather be dead than different" tendency in kids —for Christ.

ACTION

Make some inquiries. See if you can locate such a group of young people in your community. Don't let denominational difference bother you. The effect of such a club on your children outweighs any disadvantage due to doctrine. Usually such clubs do very little teaching, staying on the fringes of doctrine. Their emphasis is on action, figuring the church contributes enough doctrine.

If you hear of such a group, investigate it. Make sure it is Christ-centered and regards the Bible as the Word of God. If it is, you probably won't have to worry about anything else. Next, make some kind of a contact. Call the person in charge. See if you can arrange for some teen to invite your boy or girl. If you have to drive him there, do it. You won't be sorry. If he wants to buy a badge or wear some kind of a JESUS shirt, let him. If he becomes infected, there'll be a changed teen-ager in your house.

Your young son came to the table all scrubbed and shiney. You haven't said a word to him about this. Yet, here he is with his hair combed, nails cleaned, and neatly dressed. Something has come over him, but what? Ah . . . he's got a girl. You know what that does for a boy. The thrill of a new affection grips him.

Well, that's what we're speaking of here—the transforming effect of a new obsession. I submit that having FUN in the Spirit can become an obsession with a child of God. God not only designed us capable of such an obsession, he wants us obsessed with Christ. When Paul said, "This one thing I do," he was speaking of his obsession. Jesus wants us hooked on His power. That's why He gave us the Great Commission in the first place.

There is a limit to what such a group can do for your teen. Therefore, I want you to consider something else. That brings us to the second way of getting the job done.

II.   TAKE THE WITNESSING COURSE YOURSELF.

It wouldn't do, you see, for your teens to come alive in Christ, and then find yourself wondering what the POWER OF GOD was all about. Such a thing would create a GAP between you. To have your teens ignited while you remained a casual Christian, wouldn't do at all. You wouldn't understand them. You know what that does to people—it separates them. You don't want that. Have you ever had a red hot Christian show up at your church? How did the people treat him? They kept their distance didn't they? You don't want that to happen in your home.

If your teen becomes involved with the thrill of Christ, the safest thing is for you to get involved too. Likely, you cannot do this at church. Most churches have no witnessing program that teaches people how to move in the power of the Spirit OUTSIDE the church. There are plenty of churches with warmth INSIDE the building, but we're not speaking of that. When it comes to being ON FIRE for Christ, that is something that has to do with campuses, markets, and gas stations. You can get "turned on" at church, but that does you little good in the world. You need to be ON FIRE for Jesus outside your church. The only way to do that is by witnessing to your own private world.

YOUR PRIVATE WORLD

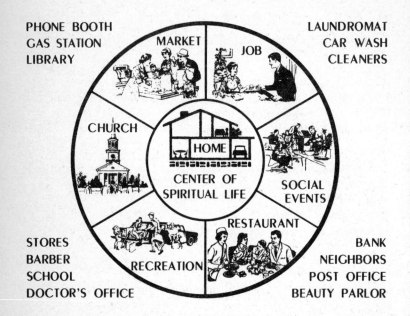

PHONE BOOTH
GAS STATION
LIBRARY

MARKET

JOB

LAUNDROMAT
CAR WASH
CLEANERS

CHURCH

HOME

CENTER OF
SPIRITUAL LIFE

SOCIAL
EVENTS

RESTAURANT

STORES
BARBER
SCHOOL
DOCTOR'S OFFICE

RECREATION

BANK
NEIGHBORS
POST OFFICE
BEAUTY PARLOR

NOTE: On the surface it may sound as if I am knocking the established church. But that's not so. I have dedicated my life to helping her. Before we're through, you'll see how much I mean that. It would be a shame to institute methods that obsoleted the established church. To allow all those dedicated teachers, believing crowds and buildings to drift in the endless routine of church programs would be an awful waste. God is not happy with it. Nothing would please Him more than seeing the established church come alive and on the job before He comes. But it can't happen apart from witnessing. This is the ONE task she was given to do. Some have called the organized church a sleeping giant. I believe that. Once she discovers that Christianity is a layman's movement and gets busy stirring individuals to action, we'll see this land shaken for Jesus!

● The Lord has led me to develop a witnessing course that employs ten action steps. It works like a ladder. You ascend one rung at a time. You climb from silence to the place where it is easy to speak out for Jesus. You start away from people. Why? People scare people. Were it not for ego threat, all Christians would witness openly for the Lord. Once you learn to work with the Holy Spirit IN THE WORLD, the job gets easier and easier. Before long, you are swept up in the thrill of Christ.

You begin with the simplest action possible—leaving a tract in a public place, making sure no one sees you do it. To do that, you go to a public restroom where you can lock the door and be all alone with the Holy Spirit. That's where you make your first move to get acquainted with Him in a FEARFUL situation. An amazing thing happens when you sample God's might with what I call . . . **"The shake test."**

I suppose you smile at that, but you need LOCKED PRIVACY for an important experiment I will assign you. It is one which allows you to prove the Holy Spirit's ability to overcome your fear. You say, what's so fearful about being in a public restroom and leaving a tract there? Try it and as you do, put your hand over your heart. Observe the beat. It will be fluttering 90 miles an hour. Why? You are in the **place of fear.**

See now why this cannot be done in church? Church is NOT a place of fear. Therefore, it cannot be learned in church. We must be in the place of fear if we would watch the Spirit overcome our fear of others. We must be in an actual situation where He can prove Himself to our satisfaction. Anything done in church has to be theory only. That is the nature of things learned in church.

In my book, WITNESSING MADE EASY, I give this definition:

> **"Christian courage is NOT the absence of fear, but the conquest of it in the power of God."**

Listen to this testimony of Mr. Paul F. Sinclair, Jr. of Trenton, New Jersey. He is a graduate of the witnessing course. This statement was attached to his number 10 action report:

> "I will be forever grateful to the Lord for using Personal Christianity and the 'Ladder-Method of Witnessing' for moving me to the place where I could satisfy a very deep, years-long need to obey the Great Commission. There is no way for me to express my gratitude for the joy that is now mine in the Holy Spirit. I praise the Lord He provided this course for me through you!"

Listen also to this word from a mother and pastor's wife:

> "This course has changed my life from a 'want to, but not sure how to,' to an active, joy-filled witness for Christ. I am now encouraging other Christians to obey Jesus' command. Truly it has caused my life to be one of the overflowing abundance. Thank you for giving me the know-how and enabling me to get better acquainted with the Holy Spirit!"
> Marilyn Hall, Wellston, Ohio

● Does that sound like I am trying to sell you a course? I wouldn't blame you if you thought so. I do want you to consider it, but there's no profit motive behind my suggestion. The course costs us more than you pay in tuition. I do not seek your money, but your wealth in Christ. The details for enrolling are in the back of this book.

NOTE: There's another approach to the course. If you wish to confirm the Spirit's leading, send for the $1.00 introductory unit. It consists of the first action step. But don't think it is simple. You'll find it a lot harder than it sounds here. Once you complete this first action step (#1 rung of the witnessing ladder) and are satisfied the Holy Spirit wants you to go to the top, we will give you the $1.00 credit toward the rest of the course. There—doesn't that take the risk out of it for you? A dollar is not much these days for something that really helps you move in God's power.

III. GET A WITNESSING CLASS STARTED IN YOUR OWN CHURCH.

That should scuttle any notion that I am working against the established church. I yearn to see the church roar into action. It could happen in your church after you complete the fifth lesson. By that time you will have had a healthy sample of the Holy Spirit's power. You will have something glorious to share with the brethren. More importantly, you will have the FUN of Christ in common with your children. You and your teens will be in a position to help your church. And you can do it together. Just think what could happen should the thrill of Christ to sweep through your congregation! It can happen.

NOTE: Once you are infected with the thrill of Christ, you'll long to share it with your friends at church. I can help with that too. We not only have a teacher's manual and action kit, but we can supply you with a chart and plan for approaching the pastor to arouse his interest in a witnessing class. If you can get permission to do so, plan on teaching the class yourself. We can supply everything you need. If the Lord has someone else qualified (perhaps the pastor), then you could be used to show him all the helps and tools available. We'll work with you. Yet, it would be nice if you could be the teacher. Your FIRE is what your church needs.

Wouldn't it be great if you and your family could bring revival to every member of your church? After you sample the Spirit's power, you can spread the JOY of it. All it takes is a willingness to be used of the Lord. It could be a family project. Can you think of anything finer for them—or the Lord? God has a mighty team when a family works together like this.

So now it's up to you

I hope you will **not** be interested in the corrective features of this plan only. There is a temptation to settle for disciplinary control and stop there. I trust that won't be true in your case. You'll be missing so much if you neglect to install the positive truths in your teens. Think again about the three things I've suggested:

1. Locate an "on fire" group of young people. Arrange to have your teens invited. Take them yourself if you have to.

2. Enroll in the witnessing course and acquire the thrill of Christ for yourself. It will give you a fantastic joy in common with your kids.

3. Bring the thrill of Christ to your church. Don't be content to share your testimony only. See what can be done to get a class started that will show the people how to work with the Holy Spirit outside the church.

NOTE: When your youngsters begin to glow with the Spirit, their zeal will be boundless. Their judgment may not match their enthusiasm. They will need guidance from parents who understand how they feel. That's why you should take the course. You will be able to combine what you learn with your mature judgment and guide them in the systematic building of their strengths in the Spirit. If you don't, their enthusiasm will rise and fall with the tide of FUN in the group. You want them to develop into steadfast workmen for Jesus, faithful no matter what befalls them. That can come only as you work with them to keep them close to the FIRE in Christ.

HARNESSING THE FIRE

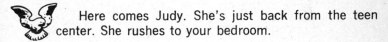 Here comes Judy. She's just back from the teen center. She rushes to your bedroom.

"Mother! Mother! Are you folks still awake!"

"Yes dear, come on in."

"Oh mom, you should have been there! You remember this Billy Jean I was telling you about? She's the girl who was so worried because she thought she was pregnant? Well, she came to the center tonight. And she sat at the same table with me. When they turned the lights down, I got a chance to present the Lord to her and she invited Him into her heart. She was so happy. We both just sat there and cried!"

"How wonderful Judy! That's your first soul, isn't it!"

"Oh mother, you can't imagine what it is like to lead a soul to Jesus. It's just . . . well it's . . . I can't describe it, it's so wonderful!"

"Indeed it is, dear. Mother knows the thrill of Christ too."

"Of course you do, mom. I thank the Lord for parents who are not ashamed of Jesus!"

Judy is red hot. She's like that molten iron we saw at Kaiser Steel. She's pliable. You should have no trouble penetrating her with the parent's package.

"Now you have some treasure laid up, Honey. Do you know what the treasure of heaven is?"

"I'm not sure."

"It's people. People are the Lord's most prized possession. That's what makes them the real treasure of heaven. Throughout all eternity you will see this girl and rejoice because you were the one who invited her to Jesus. Now that you have been faithful to do this, you can expect the Lord to trust you with something important in the next life. If you care about souls while you are on earth, you can be trusted with the most valuable thing the Lord has in heaven. The winning of this girl will count heavily toward your future job in heaven."

"Wow mom, I'm so happy. I never believed it could be so wonderful serving the Lord! I want my whole life to count for Christ!"

How does that sound? How do you feel now? That's a long way from the snippy Judy who sassed you when she couldn't invite her girl friend to stay overnight. Remember how you slapped her? Now here she is, wanting her whole life to count for Jesus. You may congratulate yourself as a successful parent. For you have now raised her—"as unto the Lord!"

You can let go of Judy now. It's all right for Jerry to leave home. You have done a good job. The Holy Spirit is ready to take over. When you see your children in heaven, you will praise God for what HE has done in them. Your soul will explode with ecstasy when Jesus says . . . "Well done, thou good and faithful servant." You see, God would not be able to polish those lives as He has . . .

WITHOUT YOU!

Appendix

TWO URGENT QUESTIONS

What's a parent to do when . . .

- Her teen-age daughter gets pregnant?
- His teen-age son gets hung up on drugs?

This book wouldn't be complete without dealing with these two situations. I will discuss them, but no extensive dialogue is needed. You can develop your own dialogue now that you have the basic principles. However, there is a specific approach to problems like these. First we'll consider . . .

THE PREGNANT GIRL

To begin with, I don't have to tell you it is foolish to argue over whose fault it is once the situation has occurred. The question is, what to do about it? The seven step approach presented here, shows how to face the matter as a Christian. Master it. It is a plan you will be able to use when other serious problems arise with your youngsters.

❶ KEEP YOUR COOL. Your girl is already suffering. Scoldings and accusations won't help a bit. Sure you're hurt. You feel better when you can blow off steam. But don't let it all out over her. Parents identify so completely with their children, that when a child has a failure, it is as though the parent failed. Nothing makes us more angry than personal failure. So watch out that you don't vent your personal rage on your already stricken daughter. Keep your cool. It will pay off if you do.

> **NOTE:** We live in a day when sex pressures on young people are awesome. We are fast coming to the day when more people will be pregnant BEFORE marriage than after. Pre-marital sex no longer has the social stigma it once carried. That doesn't justify it, of course, but with the absence of social pain, a powerful restraint is gone. There is no reason for a parent to panic. Pregnancy can be handled as calmly today as any other problem. There's a lot of help available now. With the absence of public

217

criticism, it isn't the tragedy it was once. Again, that doesn't make it right, but it does ease some of the anguish.

2 **GO TO THE LORD.** As soon as you get the news, let it trigger your spiritual instinct instead of your fears. Go at once to the Lord. Why? Prayer shifts your eyes from yourself and your hurt, to the One Who can turn the situation to profit. If you want to get the most out of any trial, involve Jesus from the first moment. The temptation is to say, "What have I done to deserve this?" If your mind goes to Christ, your attitude will be . . . "This is a testing from the Lord. He wouldn't send it if He didn't think we were ready for it."

> **NOTE:** There are no accidents for godly people. Nothing happens in the life of a Christian apart from God's plan. Depending on your maturity you will say, "Thank you Lord for this trial," or you will say, "Lord help us out of this mess." The immature Christian will see only his problem. A lot of time will pass before he gets around to considering what God's part in it might be. The more spiritual the Christian, the faster his mind flies to Jesus when a problem arrives. When you hear the first word that your daughter is pregnant—WATCH OUT! Satan will be working, trying to influence your reaction. If your first thought is "How could this have happened to us?" Satan will win. If your first thought is, "Praise the Lord. He has considered us worthy of another test," you will win. Christian maturity is rated between those two extremes.

3 **ASSUME THE GODLY ROLE.** You have been God's authority in the home all along, but in emergencies, when your child is in deep trouble, you can assume God's part more than at other times. Does not the Lord hear our cries for help? Does He not rush His comfort when we need Him? Now you have an opportunity (depending on your daughter's attitude—see below) to DEMONSTRATE the kindness of the Lord. You are now in a position to PORTRAY His compassion and mercy.

> **NOTE:** No doubt you have taught (by words) your children how merciful God is. Here's your chance to back those words with tenderness and understanding in the Lord's Name. When your weeping child is in your arms wanting your forgiveness, give it. But as you do, say, "Of course mother forgives you, just as the Lord forgives us." Bringing the Lord into your reply makes for

powerful communication by drama. You penetrate her spirit with the nutcracker technique. Only this time, you didn't apply the discipline. The pain of her pregnancy was already there. You merely add the truth of divine forgiveness from the parent's package to provide the other arm of the nutcracker. Thus she is caught between the emotion caused by her problem and your counsel about the Lord. Pregnancy can be a tenderizing experience. Wise parents will exploit it to the limit—**for the Lord!**

4 **DETERMINE YOUR DAUGHTER'S ATTITUDE.** I mean her **real** attitude. Naturally she is distressed. She wants relief from her situation. She may say all kinds of things to win your sympathy. But underneath her weeping exterior are her real feelings. You must discover them. You need to know how she really feels before you can decide what action to take. Your daughter's attitude toward your authority in the home and God's claim on her life is the KEY to this entire approach. If she is tenderly submissive you will act one way. If she is at all rebellious, you will act another.

> **NOTE:** Don't take your girl's words at face value. There might be another attitude underneath the facade. Again, there might not be. The one on the surface may be her true attitude. But you should always check. You don't know how to proceed unless her true attitude is known. Some girls, for example, unconsciously allow themselves to become pregnant as an act of rebellion. They strike back at their folks this way. Remember the boy in Chapter One who was glad to be sentenced for stealing? He was unconsciously striking back at his parents for over-protecting him and turning him into a helpless dependent. Of course, it could be your girl has consciously allowed herself to become pregnant. In that case it would be an overt act of rebellion. She wanted to hurt you with it.

Recently I counseled the parents of a pregnant daughter. She had moved away from home, wanting more freedom. In a sense, her parent's responsibility had ended inasmuch as she was no longer under their roof. Yet, she was only 16, so we might challenge her parents on that. Be that as it may, it wasn't long before the girl was pregnant. Upon learning the news, the parents wanted her to come home. The girl was willing to accept their help, but on her own terms. She still wanted her freedom. She even laid down the conditions under which she would return home.

Now these parents were born-again Christians. They were puzzled by their daughter's attitude. That's why they were sitting in my study. They wanted to know what their position should be when their girl demanded such things as no restrictions on seeing her boy friend (the one who got her pregnant); they were to accept her pregnancy as a part of her life style; they were not to try to involve her in the family's spiritual life in any way.

Her parents were shocked at my advice. Once it was clear what her attitude was, the counsel was easy.

"Don't bring her into the house. Let her go the way of the world. Let her hit bottom. Pray for her, but don't spend one cent of God's money or extend yourselves in any way to ease the situation for her. Do absolutely nothing."

I explained the "destruction of the flesh" principle to them. And how she would have to go through the tenderizer in order for God to change her attitude. That is, if it could be changed. The parents were willing to give God's way a try—although they said it seemed monstrous to them when they first heard it.

● God did put the girl through the tenderizer. She sank quite low, going into prostitution. But finally she had enough. Like the prodigal son who finally came to his senses, she also reached a point where she was fed up with the rebellious life. She rushed home to her parents. They had been waiting and praying. It paid off. It was hard for them to keep their hands off, but in the end they were glad they did. It is so much easier to rush to the aid of your distressed child. The parental love instinct almost compels you to do it. But it is better to let God handle the situation when there is work to be done on a teen's attitude. See now why ATTITUDE is the key to this approach?

HINT: Don't be fooled. Some teens are not the least bit sorry about their pregnancy, but they want you to think they are. They disguise their real feelings to win your sympathy and help. Others, of course, are genuinely repentant and deserve all the help you can give. To test your child's attitude, watch her face when you bring the Lord Jesus into the discussion. See how she reacts when you speak of the things of God. Is her heart open to what you have to say about Him or would she rather not hear about it? Children can disguise their feelings about pregnancy, but they don't tend to disguise their feeling about the Lord. Those who are rebellious just don't want you to mention Jesus. Those who are tender, graciously heed what you say about Him.

5 **ADOPT YOUR COURSE OF ACTION.** Once you determine your daughter's real attitude, you will know how far you should go in helping her. The more tender your girl toward the things of God, the greater should be your effort in standing by her. You mirror God's response to a tender heart when you do. If her attitude is hostile or defiant, you would mirror God's response in that direction too. See again how it is the child's attitude that guides your decision. A tender-hearted girl should receive all your help, a resentful and rebellious girl should get none.

Jennie's parents came to see me. She was a 17 year old who had fallen in with the hippie crowd and become pregnant in one of those bedroom vans the boys drive nowadays. The boy was 17, a high school drop out who worked in one of the local markets.

"We don't understand her," they said. "She isn't the least bit ashamed. Instead she's proud to be carrying this boy's baby. She calls it a love child. She says their baby is justified because 'God is love.'"

"Does that mean they plan to get married?" I asked.

"Oh no, they don't want to get married. They feel marriage ties people down so they can't do their own thing. She thinks we should help because she is our daughter and the baby has been conceived as a love child. She keeps saying 'God is love,' and expects us to accept that as justification for her attitude. What should we do?"

I observed for them how her attitude was actually rebellious. She wanted this baby on her own terms, contrary to the Word of God. She was correct in saying "God is love," but that doesn't mean God is blind. God expects two people to marry and provide a home for this child which is NOT theirs, but His. Consequently, this girl would have to be treated as one who was unrepentant and self-willed. She was USING God's Word, not submitting to it.

221

"She should get no help from you at all."

"Shouldn't we at least see that she gets to a decent doctor? After all she is our daughter."

"No, don't even do that. If you do, you will dilute the consequences of her rebellion. If she thinks she can USE God, by hiding behind a statement about His nature, turn her over to HIM and let Him deal with her. In no way should you ease the situation. As long as she wants to go her own way, let her and this boy see how far their 'God is love' excuse will take them. I want you to be steadfast in this position until there is a genuine change in her attitude."

"You mean, taking a strong stand for the Lord could cause her to change her mind?"

"It could, provided you warn her."

WARN HER?

Let's assume you are Jennie's parents. What I am about to suggest may seem awful to you, for it will compound your girl's difficulty. But I assure you, God can use it to deliver her from this evil, provided of course, she is one who can be delivered. Some do not want to be delivered no matter how they suffer.

Jennie hasn't been nasty to you, just stubborn. But stubbornness is also defiance. She refuses to give up her boyfriend, insisting her relationship with him is justified because "God is love." It is going to take something unusual to change her attitude. The warning technique is perfect for it. The first scene goes like this:

"If you persist in this attitude dear, we can't help you. Not only that, but you put yourself in a position where God has to discipline you."

"What do you mean?"

"One thing God is particular about, is that children obey their parents. According to His Word, if they refuse, it will go hard with them. A girl's respect for her parents can go a long way in assuring her a decent life on this earth. But if she defies them, she can expect real trouble."

HINT: Have your Bible ready. Let her read Ephesians 6:1-3. Call her attention to those words, "That it may be well with thee."

222

The implication is that it will NOT be well with the rebellious child, perhaps shortening his life on earth. That is a definite possibility. When parents deliver their sons and daughters over to Satan for his flesh-destroying work, their lives could be drastically shortened (1 Cor. 5:5). If they do not repent and return to the way of the Lord, they could be removed from this life long before they should. Showing her the verse and mentioning the consequences of rebellion in an actual situation, makes deep penetration with the Word of God. The Holy Spirit will use it again, reminding her of those words . . . "That it may be well with thee." They will haunt her as the consequences of her rebellion begin to mount up.

"We won't be able to lift a finger to help you, dear, if you persist in wanting your own way about this. You'll be entirely on your own to get help and pay for it as you can. It isn't that we don't love you, we do. But we dare not disobey God and finance your rebellion. We can't afford to do anything that makes it easy for you to resist the way of the Lord. You are rebelling against Him, you know, when you go against His Word like this. It is our painful duty to warn you and your boyfriend, that you could be in for some real trouble."

(pause)

"In fact, we'd hate to be in your shoes."

● You recognize those words, don't you? They activate the warning technique. The moment you say them, the hearer automatically suffers a strange sensation. There is a feeling of impending disaster. Invaribly the response comes back:

"Why, what's supposed to happen?"

"We don't know exactly what God will do, dear. But all sorts of things can go wrong when we're out of God's will. If I were a young girl carrying a baby, the last thing in the world I would want would be God's discipline coming down upon me. He knows where we're tender and His hand hits hard."

"You mean He'd actually strike me?"

"Not as mother and daddy have spanked you. His blows come in the form of accidents, sicknesses which strike our bodies, and usually we get hurt in the pocket book. Also honey, things could go wrong between you and your boyfriend. I don't know what He will do. I only know I'd hate to be in your shoes."

(Pause)

"Why, you've already got a problem finding a place to stay."

"You mean I can't live here at home?"

"No, not if you are going to defy us with this unholy relationship with this boy. The Lord would not want us to use our home to shelter a girl who knowingly flaunts her will in His face. We would then be out of His will and He would have to deal with us. We don't want God's chastening hand to fall on us. No dear, you and your boy friend will have to find some way to get along by yourselves. We hate to see it happen, because we love you so. It tears us apart to have our daughter leave home under these conditions."

● When you turn Jennie loose after such a warning, she will be primed to interpret the first disturbing event as coming from the hand of a displeased God. She knows she is out of His will. And she also knows what it takes to get back into His good graces again. Without your telling her, she knows you are right in standing with Him against her. That adds to her fear. And fear, as we have seen, is a powerful force which can move people to do what is right.

NOTE: Once Jennie has been warned in this fashion, the Lord Himself is in a position to send the afflictions. Until you inform her of her situation before God, any accidents which come against her would be shrugged off as "bad breaks." What's worse, God's hands are tied. He does not send afflictions for their own sake, they have to accomplish His will. It is His will that Jennie understands her hazardous situation and that HE is dealing with her. But that will not be the case unless you WARN her. It is the warning that does the job. That is your part in the process. The Spirit takes it from there. As long as Jennie continues her rebellion, the Holy Spirit will be on her trail to see that every misfortune appears as the hand of God. Even now she is aware that having to leave home is a working of God, and is but one of a series of events which might follow.

When your daughter leaves

Even as she packs, she is weighing your words. She is

asking herself, "Is it worth it?" That is what she has to decide. The price tag is going to get higher and higher and she senses it. What will help most right now is your love for her. Not one mean word has passed from your lips. You have not judged her as a bad girl, neither have you censored her for getting into this mess. You have merely stated your position before God and what is required of a mother and father who fear to be out of His will.

It's important that you see this. You have not been unkind to Jennie. Everything you have said and done has been consistent with the parent-child bond which exists between you. She senses you ache to help her. She knows it is a temptation for you to jump in with both feet and deliver her from her trial. You are in a position to do a lot to make it easy for her and her boyfriend, and she knows it. But you just can't, because you fear God more than you yearn to aid your child. You're not about to let Satan use family devotion to tempt you to defy the revealed will of God. That would merely be an added crime against heaven.

While you cannot do anything to ease the situation, you can do EVERYTHING that shows your love for Jennie. Help her pack. Let her take a suit case and anything else you may have given her, which might be useful. It's all hers, anyway. Make suggestions, if you want to, as to what things would be best for her in her condition. Make sure every act and every word reveals love and kindness toward her. She's not your enemy. She is your darling daughter and you love her.

> "Good-bye honey. We hate to see you go. It breaks our hearts to part with you like this. Please remember we love you. And above all, run home, won't you, the moment you change your mind about the way of the Lord. We'll be here ready to help you, when you do."

● Make that parting as tender as you can. You want her to remember it. Embrace her. Reassure her you love her. Sure it is an act of discipline, but underneath is that fabulous relationship of parent and child. You must preserve it. Remember, I said NO single act of discipline can separate your child from you when you are bound by a warm relationship. Not even an act as severe as this one.

NOTE: I know it sounds awful to send your child from your home like this, but it isn't as risky as it seems. The Holy Spirit is going to watch over her. You have committed her to HIM for discipline since there really isn't anything you can do about her rebellion yourself. As far as survival is concerned, she'll make out all right. What's the danger, really? She's already pregnant. About the worst that can happen is that she will be thrown in with a rough crowd which will either sicken her (as she thinks of her gentle parents at home), or appeal to her if that's what her heart really desires. If she prefers them to God's people, there's nothing you could do about it anyway, even if she stayed at home.

The one thing you must do for her is pray. Don't minimize that. Prayer is God's method for accomplishing His will. Ask the Holy Spirit to deal with her according to what HE sees in her heart, and to send whatever is necessary to secure her repentance. He'll do it. But He does wait for you to ask. He hates to be taken for granted. Then prepare yourself for some disturbing news. Jennie might absorb a few mean licks before you hear that knock at your door and hear those heart-rending words . . .

"Mama, can I come home?"

Wouldn't it be great to have that bedraggled child rush into your arms, sobbing out her sorrow? How you have prayed for that moment. As you squeeze your broken offspring to your bosom, your heart sings praises to the Lord. How you will thank Him for giving you the grace to "Be strong in the Lord!"

That's what it takes, you see, to do this—God's grace, combined with your willingness to BE strong in the Lord. It does take strength, for you will be severely criticized. If the grandparents are not born-again, they won't understand. But God understands and He's the only One you have to please. If your daughter is finally salvaged for Christ, what do you care? See this: unless you go the limit and use the warning technique in cooperation with the Holy Spirit, you have NOT done all you can. Those who pamper their children, easing the squeeze when they rebel against God, CONTRIBUTE to their downfall. The best way to ruin a child is to cooperate with her when she begins to go the way of the world.

God's way is not always easy, but it is clearly the best.

"Mamma can I come home?"

Betty's parents came to my office along with Terry's parents. A terrible secret had come out. Betty hadn't been feeling so well in the mornings and a trip to the doctor revealed she was pregnant. She had become intimate with Terry, a fine young boy in the young peoples' group at church. They had been to a youth conference at a mountain retreat and things worked out so that Betty rode home with Terry. The two of them were alone.

NOTE: It is not uncommon for young people to become sexually involved following their participation at a youth camp. In a retreat situation, where the world is shut out for a few days and there is a steady diet of spiritual things, a great deal of godly enthusiasm can be generated. Young people sometimes get high on Christ, really turned on for Jesus. Unfortunately, spiritual highs are akin to sexual highs. That is, the same feelings which accompany sexual satisfaction also accompany spiritual highs. Thus a spiritual experience can be used by Satan to trigger sexual feelings. Given the opportunity, sexual intimacy can occur. Not a few

227

young people have become his victims after a glorious youth conference. A rock conference can do the same thing, it should be noted.

Betty and Terry were ready to confess what they had done. They were so ashamed. Their hearts were extremely tender. They were normally submissive children anyway. Not only were they sorry, they were willing to do whatever was required of them. Terry, though a little young to get married, was willing to forego his college plans and become a responsible father of the child. Though the two kids had never once thought of marriage, they were willing to do what was best for the baby. In other words, their attitude was great.

Here again, the counsel is obvious.

● In this case, I advised the parents to go all out in helping their youngsters. They were not to be condemned, not even scolded. They were to be understood and loved. The parents would be out of order in saying such things as "Didn't you know better?" or, "How could you think of doing such a thing?" Of course, the kids knew better. But they were placed in a situation where they couldn't handle the drives awakened within them at the conference. Besides, Satan was on hand to exploit their aroused feelings. All that he needed was an opportunity. That came when they were allowed to drive home alone from the conference. It would not have happened had not the OPPORTUNITY been provided. The parents needed to understand that.

The children and their situation was to be totally accepted. Then I showed the parents how they could USE the situation to display God's mercy. If they would combine the pain of pregnancy with the truth of God's forgiveness, they could drive home a truth that would stay with those kids all their lives. In that way, a lot of benefit could be derived from an otherwise difficult situation. Along with that, they would also be able to demonstrate the difference between God's forgiveness and the consequences of evil. Though God forgives the guilt of our sins, we bear the consequences—always. We'll say more on that in a bit.

6 **BE READY FOR REPENTANCE.** Once you have turned your girl over to Satan (the Lord actually) for the "destruction of the flesh," you should hold yourself in readiness for the day when she has had enough of the devil's dealings and changes her mind about the way of the Lord. If at any point in the "destruction" process your girl's heart is tenderized by the blows of the world, you must be ready to receive her with open arms. After that, you should do all you can for her.

That is the way God receives us when we stop our bullheaded determination to have our own way and turn around and come running back to Him. I know it is tough to adopt God's attitude toward your own children, but it is the ONLY way to go. Will others criticize you? Indeed, especially the grandparents. They will think it is awful. Unless they themselves are deeply involved with the Lord Jesus, they will not understand your actions. They won't even try. But hold your ground. There's a good chance your daughter will be salvaged and come running back to the way of the Lord. You won't be sorry if you do things God's way, no matter what others think. His way is best, always.

> **NOTE:** I know it isn't easy for a mother to let go of her pregnant teen and see her suffer as she goes the way of the world. It's not easy to cast off a child you have borne and raised. But then neither is it easy for God to cast off those who refuse the gospel. "He would that none should perish," yet they do. And He makes no attempt to cling to them. If they want to go away from Him, He lets them, though it pains Him to do so. A lot of love and sacrifice has gone into each soul arriving on this earth. God loves all of them the same, "for there is no respect of persons with God." It is a matter of following God's example to cast off the child who refuses to walk in the counsel of godly parents. In O.T. times, God ordered that those who would not walk in His ways should be "cut off" from Israel. Yet, any time a soul repented of his evil, God provided for his full restoration.

7 **HANDLING THE CONSEQUENCES.** Unfortunately there is no way to alter the consequences of your girl's mistake. God will not remove the pregnancy. He will totally remove the guilt of her sin, if she asks Him. Christ's blood was shed for that. God forgives with total forgiveness. But forgiveness and consequences are two separate matters. Even though she is completely forgiven, the consequences remain. No matter what your daughter's attitude is, a way has to be found to handle her pregnancy. We'll assume she is tenderly submissive and you are ready to help her. You and your girl are now faced with three choices:

    a. Abortion
    b. Adoption
    c. Marriage

Abortion

For some Christians this is a bad word. A decision for abortion should not be based on public opinion, but YOUR OWN opinion as to when the fetus becomes a PERSON. Earlier in the book I said this was a question which concerned only the abortionists. But now that you have a pregnant daughter, who is not very far along, you should form an opinion. It could guide you in taking the right action. Here are the three views:

(1). God places the soul (person) in the fetus at conception. This is the Roman Catholic view.

(2). The fetus does not contain a child until the mother feels life. This is the popular view.

(3). The fetus is simply an animal until birth, at which time the soul is placed within.

If you hold the opinion that God does not place the person in the fetus until after the fourth month (or when the mother feels life), then an abortion would be no problem for you. The fetus would merely be body tissue with no independent life of its own. It would be like removing an appendix or some other mass of tissue. Certainly it could not be murder as some claim.

If you hold that there is a person inside the fetus from the moment of conception, then abortion could be out of the question for you. You would be making a decision that would deprive someone of his chance at life. And it would be pre-meditated.

If you feel there is no child present until the moment of birth, then you could also consider abortion as a possible solution.

Aside from the moral issue, it has been my experience that abortion solves the problem with the least amount of bad side effects. If the girl is very young, say 13 or 14, then it can be done and forgotten. You avoid any risk of her not being ready for pregnancy. The surgeon's scalpel removes the tissue and God's forgiveness removes the guilt feelings. In cases of rape or where the girl is an innocent victim, this is the preferable route in my opinion. But again it depends on when you think God places the person in the body. I make this comment from long counseling experience. There are no regrets or haunting questions like those which come when one goes the adoption route.

Adoption

If you find you cannot go for an abortion, the next best thing is to let the pregnancy go full term and place the baby for adoption. This assumes the father is either unknown or refuses to marry your daughter. It could also be that marriage would be inadvisable because the kids are so young, or there is simply no way for them to get married.

There are fine Christian agencies with godly couples waiting to adopt babies. These people look on their work as a ministry for Christ. They feel they do the Lord a real service by placing unwanted babies in homes where they will be raised in Christ. Usually the future parents are willing to pay all the expenses. Since most are unable to have children of their own, they are willing to assist the girl in trouble for the privilege of receiving her baby.

CAUTION: Do not try to arrange an adoption without either a lawyer or working with a licensed adoption agency. There could be legal complications later on, and those are usually a mess when the new parents have come to love the baby as their own. Also, the mother should NOT be allowed to know who has her baby or where he is. It should be forgotten. But will that young mother have regrets later on? Yes. She's bound to wonder what has become of her child. But again this is a consequence. She should NOT suffer any guilt, for God has removed that. But there is no way to keep her from wondering what happened to the child she bore. However, the passing of time eases such pain.

● It is a mistake for a young mother to keep a baby and try to raise it by herself. She may love the baby, but there is no way for her to provide the father/mother environment called for in God's plan. Usually such children end up in the hands of grandparents. Such children are far better off in homes where they are adopted by both a father and mother who will raise them in Christ.

Marriage

If your daughter and her boyfriend were already talking about marriage, then there need be no thought of adoption. They will simply have to get married sooner than they expected. It won't be easy to have their plans suffer a setback, but that is the consequence of their folly. However, if the boy is not a Christian, or is someone whom your daughter does not wish to be joined for life, it would be wrong to force the marriage upon her. If the girl is quite young, she will not be able to make such a judgment. It would be very wrong to expect her to know what was best for her life when many adults can't answer that question for themselves.

> **NOTE:** On the surface it sounds as if marriage were the ideal solution to the pregnancy problem. If the truth were known, a whopping percentage of marriages today occurs because couples have been intimate and the girl is already pregnant. It is more rare today when a child is not born in less than nine months after the wedding. Do such marriages really work out? Some do. But sadly the divorce rate among these couples is extremely high, even when they are Christians. The marriage solution isn't as idyllic as it sounds.

To be FORCED into marriage because of a pregnancy hardly makes for an ideal marriage. Marriage is tough enough when two young people have the same ambitions in Christ and are otherwise suited for each other. Take two young people who have compatible talents, long to serve the Lord, and are terribly drawn to each other—even they encounter difficulties which often seem insurmountable. But their resources are NOT drained away from the Lord through being married to the wrong person. That is one of the heartaches of a pregnancy marriage—so much energy has to go in making the marriage work, nothing is left for Christ.

ACTION

If your daughter's attitude is tenderly repentant, these are your options. One of these three—abortion, adoption, or marriage—will be best for her. The decision will be as much yours as hers if she is very young. The older she is, the more she can decide for herself. No matter which of the three you elect, give your daughter your best effort for the Lord's sake. Stand in His shoes and go all out to help her. Forgive her completely and in such a way that you act out God's forgiveness. And afterwards behave toward her as God does—**as though it never happened.** If you can do that, the whole experience will be a rich one for you and your girl. God knows how to turn tragedy into blessing. After all, He's a Genius!

Your social set (including your church) could be a little smug about this pre-marital pregnancy, but set yourself to be content with God's approval. He doesn't think as men think. He uses such things to accomplish His will. Again, depending on your maturity in Christ, you will accept the incident as coming from God's hand. Accordingly you will want to extract from it all the profit you can for your daughter and yourself. As far as testings go, a pre-marital pregnancy is no more stressful than sickness or an auto accident. It is one of a series of things God uses to strengthen a family. If you act out God's role in this trial, it will draw your family closer together.

> **NOTE:** During the pregnancy, your daughter should not go to church, unless your city has a large one where a stranger can hide. There is no way for her to remain in the family church unless she is ready to bare her sin and ask the church to understand while she displays her pregnancy. Only the rarest girl could do that. You do not want her in a position where she has to LIE about herself, i.e., saying, "My husband is overseas, etc." Satan would love that. One lie leads to another. Likely you should attend another church yourself. That would avoid your being tempted to lie about your girl's absence. During the pre-natal period she could depend on radio, TV, and family fellowship—possibly a teen group, for spiritual nourishment. Outside the church you need not be so cautious. The world is very understanding about unwed mothers, while Christians are often cruel. It is lying to the church that you must avoid, for the Lord inhabits His people. Lying to them is like lying to God (Acts 5:4).

● Of course, if your daughter is rebellious and contentious, then she should bear the consequences without your help. She can go to a county hospital or a clinic for unwed mothers. Let her work it out for herself. It is only her attitude that is denying her your assistance. There are a lot of places girls can go for help in the larger cities. If you live in a rural area it will be more difficult for her. Even so, do not step in with any help until she relents and turns to the way of the Lord.

Do not use God's resources to finance your self-willed daughter's rebellion. All that you have has come from the Lord. It should be administered in His Name. It would not be consistent with His name to use a penny of it in support of someone who rebelled against Him. Therefore, let the price tag alone. The stiffer the price, the sooner she is likely to feel her rebellion is too expensive. There are prodigal daughters you know.

THE TEEN-AGE BOY ON DRUGS

God can use this trial in your home as surely as that of the pregnant girl. It is merely another form of testing. The approach to this problem follows the same steps:

1 **KEEP YOUR COOL.** It doesn't help a bit to panic. Nothing is accomplished by letting your rage spill over. Of course, you'll be upset. More than that, you might even be scared. There's so much drug talk in the news these days, you'll be tempted to picture the worst.

Somehow parents don't discover their teen's drug habit until it causes trouble. That is, he is arrested for possession or some criminal act attempted to support his habit. With more and more information being fed to the public these days, aware parents are learning to recognize the signs of drug use. You might very well catch your boy in the experimental stage. That would be a blessing.

NOTE: Drug use is now spreading so fast it is soon expected that every teen-ager will have tried marijuana at least once. Yours could be among them. Experimentation is not addiction. It is natural for kids to experiment. Sampling marijuana is not dangerous. Using it may not be either except as it leads to stronger drugs. That's the real hazard. The percentage of those starting with marijuana (pot) and graduating to pills, and from thence to hard drugs, is about one in ten. That's too high to fool with. At least for teens who are easily influenced by other teens.

② **GO TO THE LORD.** As soon as you become aware of the problem go to Jesus first of all. As in the case of the pregnant daughter, acknowledge it as a test from God and ask Him for the wisdom to handle it. It is vital that your eyes be on the Lord BEFORE you tackle the problem. Otherwise, you will not see it as coming from His hand. You will not act like a man of God. Receiving wisdom from God is not just a Christian cliche. You do need wisdom and God gives it on request. Only then will you face the problem as a divine test and not as an "accident" of life.

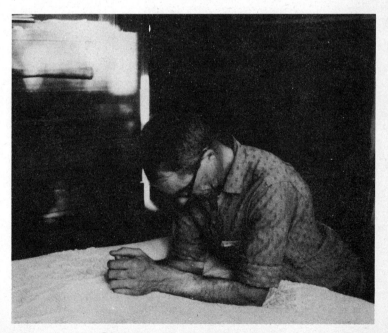

Dispose of your feelings here.

235

CAUTION: Don't let the fact that you were not prepared to learn your boy was taking drugs destroy what communication does exist between you. It is urgent that you keep any rapport which already exists. You want to build on it. So guard every word you say or plan to say to him. Don't berate yourself for failing to immunize him against the drug influence. Every parent will face this in the near future. It falls into the same category with long hair, far-out clothes, wild music, sex, dissent, and everything else young people use to challenge the life style of those over 30. The drug scene is part of every town. It is found in all levels of society and all grades from junior high on up. If, for some reason, you have failed to detect a deep need in your boy, he is almost certain to make the drug scene one way or another.

NOTE: God's wisdom will first of all prompt you to learn something about drugs. The government, as well as local police departments, produces excellent manuals on drugs and drug recognition. It would not be wise to approach your son with total ignorance on the subject. Should you behave hysterically over one experiment with marijuana, for example, that would tell your boy you have no contact with the world in which he lives. Nothing can drive an adolescent further from you than over-reacting to his situation.

3 **ASSUME THE GODLY ROLE.** Drug use is serious. Prepare yourself for the serious role of standing in God's place. You are God's agent and have been all along. But now you will have to play your part with more seriousness. The situation calls for it. The point now is to ACT as He would. Again, it will be your son's attitude that will govern your action. If he is willing to heed your counsel and is responsive when you speak of God's way, then you can be generous. The Holy Spirit will help you uncover the real need in his life. Then you can see about filling it.

NOTE: If your boy has been using drugs for some time, he may be ready to give them up. That is, he might simply be looking for a good reason to kick the drug scene. With divine wisdom you will be able to give him a satisfactory reason. Therefore, it is obvious you should approach him with so much sympathy and understanding he will feel as though another teen were talking to him. A dad who wants to help his boy over the drug bump, has to get down on a level that makes it seem as if he too is interested in drugs. He could ask his boy such questions as, "What's it really like, son?" Then show a genuine interest in his replys. Get him to describe his feelings when he is high. The boy will be shocked, "Wow, dad, are you thinking about using?" Get that attitude over to your boy and the two of you will be able to communicate. You can see it is the opposite of judging him. Do as I suggest and he will start spilling all he knows about drugs—and himself.

● Once your boy starts talking about his habit (or experiments), listen intently to everything he says—as though you were thrilled to learn about it. Give him a few, "Really?" replys. He may act sheepishly at first, but he will open up more and more when he finds you are not critical. He does want to talk to you. You'll discover that after he gets started. No matter WHAT he says, don't react with the slightest sign of disapproval. Then, as he talks, you will pick up clues as to WHY he takes drugs. Kids don't go on drugs without a reason. Sure, some try them out of curiosity, but there has to be a powerful reason before a kid gets hooked. Drugs are not all that great.

> HINT: At no time ask WHY he takes drugs. It will come out. He really wants to talk about it. It will thrill him to find he can talk to you—man to man. If he is doing it as an act of rebellion, he won't say so directly. It will come out as a complaint about something at home or school. If it is simply because other kids are doing it, he'll say so. The way to find out the CAUSE is to get him to tell you HOW he got started. Show a warm interest (not concern) in that part of his story and he'll respond like magic. Kids long for such interest from their folks.

Ask your boy what marijuana tastes like. Tell him you always wondered what it would be like, because you have heard so much about it. If you really wanted to give him a "shock treatment" you could tell him you'd like to try a puff to see what it was like. That kind of a shock would open him up. It's the last thing in the world he expects. It's so non-censorious, he almost feels as if you are with him. Of course, you're not about to approve what he is doing. At this point you are establishing communication to find out WHY he is on the stuff.

You need to know why. Once you have that information, you can come up with a replacement. Your teen will not WANT to go off drugs until he is offered something better to take their place. This is why so many Christian teen centers are successful with kids on drugs. They offer them the thrill of a new life in Jesus. A lot of them quickly abandon drugs to give Christ a chance, especially when other teens testify to the "highs" they have in the Lord. Kids who have been on drugs for any length of time know they lose their ability to lift a person.

> **NOTE:** The TV singer, Johnny Cash, admitted to taking over 100 pills a day when he was at the peak of his drug habit. Finally it got to the place where drugs did nothing for him. Then he traded them for the life in Christ. He testified that he found in the Lord what he had been seeking all along and didn't know it. Many kids are bored today. They wander about looking for kicks. They try drugs. If your boy is looking for a kick, you can give it to him. There's one he will like a lot better than drugs. It is the thrill of witnessing for Christ in the power of the Holy Spirit as outlined in Chapter Twelve. That thrill gets better and better as one moves ahead in the Lord. Pills, on the other hand, get weaker and weaker as one builds his immunity to their kick.

4 **DETERMINE YOUR SON'S ATTITUDE.** Your graciousness keeps the channel of communications open between you and your boy. Hopefully you will get close enough to him to uncover his real feelings. Your objective is to discover his attitude toward you and the way of the Lord. If he proves to be rebellious, then you must be ready to demonstrate the Lord's firmness. If he turns out to be warmly submissive, then you should stand ready with the Lord's help. His attitude determines the course you will follow.

> **NOTE:** Kids say all kinds of things when they are in trouble and want a way out. Therefore, you must look beneath your boy's words to discover his true attitude. Teens can act as though they are truly sorry, when down inside they are as rebellious as ever. When the crisis has passed and they are off the hook, their rebelliousness surfaces again. Repentance on the part of a teen can best be measured by his attitude toward the things of the Lord. Again this must be demonstrated repentance, not the verbal kind. You must be able to see a genuine interest in your boy

when you speak to him of life in the Lord. If your boy is not interested in God's help, he does not merit yours.

If your boy proves to be hostile to your authority, or the things of the Lord, then he has to be treated as was the pregnant, but defiant daughter. If he is merely caught in a vicious habit and really wants God's help, then you can go all out giving him the Savior's sympathy and supply. But unless you are wholly satisfied that he really wants to put away his drugs and go the way of the Lord, you should do nothing to ease the squeeze. God has him in the nutcracker and you must supply the tenderizing truth. Don't allow yourself to be fooled by a superficial attitude.

5 **ADOPT YOUR COURSE OF ACTION.** Once you know how your boy feels about putting away his habit and looking to Christ for help, your course of action is clear. Don't be wishy washy about it. You are a man of God. Stand firm in God's place to administer deliverance or discipline. If your boy is repentant and wants the Lord to deliver him, your course of action will be based on the reason for his involvement. He is likely to be in one of three categories:

a. **An experimenter.** The same compulsion which led us to sneak off and try cigarettes and liquor, when we were kids, leads this newer generation to try drugs, particularly marijuana. The fact that it is illicit, makes it more exciting. A few experiments with "pot" or "grass" are harmless. The discovery of it in your boy's life shouldn't send you into hysterics. That would make it impossible for you to help him. The experimenter is easily reached by parents whose actions indicate they understand it is natural for young people to experiment with such things.

b. **An insecure boy.** Drugs make the insecure lad feel as if he is somebody. For a brief period he thinks he is important. Young people in the poverty groups suffer from insecure feelings continually. Any insecure lad will try drugs if others tell him they make him feel like a big shot. Peer groups easily pressure such kids to "find" themselves this way. It's a small price, they think, to pay for the illusion of being someone. Over-protective parents who dominate their youngsters and suffocate their personalities, practically force them to try drugs. The same could be said of those parents who demand perfection from their child.

c. **A lad seeking oblivion.** He is the most frightening, because he takes drugs to escape the reality of life. He wants to blot it out. To him the world is a mess. He doesn't want to live in it any longer. Using drugs, he withdraws into an isolated sphere where everything is beautiful and peaceful, for a time. Parents who continually wail over conditions today infect their youngsters with a morbid view of life. When they hear that drugs are a "happy" escape, they are ready to try them. The boy hungry for oblivion is often the hardest to reach, for he takes constantly harder drugs seeking a way out.

● Depending on the degree of your son's involvement, there are four ways to help him:

(1) Face to face counsel as his father.

(2) Teach him the art of self-defense through the anti-satan skill.

(3) Obtain professional help for him.

(4) Get him involved with a Christian teen center specializing in drug victims.

I cannot offer exhaustive counsel in the space of an article. But I can present enough to get you started. What is given should remove some of the terror that can strike when drugs turn up in your home.

● Let's consider help for your boy at each of the three levels mentioned above:

a. **When he is just an experimenter.** If you approach him as a parent who understands how natural it is for a boy to experiment, you can reach him easily. Arm yourself with literature that shatters the myths surrounding drug use. They really don't do for people what they claim. The point to make with an experimenter is that drugs destroy energy, ambition and the creative drive of the victim. For the privilege of a few momentary sensations, a boy risks trading off the best of his own abilities to make something of his life.

Contrary to what users teach, drugs do not lead to self-expansion, but self-isolation. The user tends to withdraw from others, gravitating to a small sick society of fellow users. All your boy need do is look around his own peer group to see that this is true. Sure enough, there are the users collected into closed, withdrawn cells. He would be hard pressed to find

240

a single addict doing anything significant about the world in which he lives. The young experimenter will shy away from drugs if he can see what it might do to his body and the isolation of his life.

b. **When he is insecure.** When a boy lays hold of the news that God loves him so much He sent His Son to die for him, it lifts him out of the ordinary at once. It is no small thing to find the Maker of heaven and earth that wild about you. Then to learn that you are made in His image, designed to spend eternity with Him, raises one to a position of remarkable importance. When such knowledge glows in a lad, it cancels a lot of insecurity. Therefore, the first step in building self-assurance is learning WHO he is in Christ. When a youth discovers he is important to Jesus, it does something to his spirit. After that, if he can learn he is also USEFUL to God, it adds to his feelings of self-importance. It becomes a practical matter when the Holy Spirit begins to use him as a witness to reach others around him.

> **HINT:** On the surface one might think that witnessing was not for the insecure lad at all. That it was a work reserved for those who are bold in the Lord. That just isn't so. When Jesus gave the Great Commission He knew what it would do for a person's ego. Even the shyest, most timid Christian boy can get started witnessing, for there are very simple steps to follow in the beginning. The first one, for example, consists of an experiment with the Holy Spirit which shows the young Christian how God's power works to overcome his fears. I've been training young witnesses for years. I have seen the miracle which occurs when they discover, by EXPERIENCE, the Spirit of God using them. Once your boy finds the Holy Spirit working with him intimately, his self-estimation rises sharply. Let him taste God's anointing in that first step, and he'll want to try the next step up the witnessing ladder.

Along with the excitement of witnessing for Christ, let your boy get involved with the work at a Christian teen center. At first, the association will be useful to him in putting away his habit. There is some therapy in being with others who are also kicking the habit. As soon as he starts winning for himself, he can help other kids get off drugs. That, too, is satisfying. It gives a lad a lot of assurance fast.

c. **When he is seeking oblivion.** If your boy has reached the place where he is saying, "Stop world, I want to get off," he is in a bad way. Likely he is a heavy user. It takes real doses to secure the blackout. What's worse he has undoubtedly opened himself to demonic penetration. But now you have determined that he wants to kick the habit and is ready for God's help.

Those using hallucigents to get "beyond themselves," open the door for satanic influence. In their desire for "mind expanding" experiences, they abandon the divinely installed controls and make themselves susceptible to demonic penetration. The devil, through the weakness of the flesh, has no trouble manipulating drug victims. It is easy for him to intensify the desire and deepen the entrapment. The sad thing is, as the drugs lose their power to relieve, Satan's power increases.

> **NOTE:** The person desiring to kick a deep seated habit on hard drugs is in for a battle. The family doctor should be consulted. Clinical help may be needed. If your boy has to go through withdrawal, you'll want professionals on hand. Even so, if he is born-again, he can call upon the Lord and the Holy Spirit will give him a mighty assist. There's a world of difference between the way a Christian goes off drugs and the route a pagan youth must take.

But how do YOU help your boy? By equipping him with the anti-satan skill. This assumes, of course, that you have not already taught him to deal with the devil. If you had, likely he would not be on drugs now. Therefore, he needs to know the techniques for delivering himself from Satan's grasp. It may shock him to learn how drugs open a boy's mind to the devil's work. But he won't resist the truth. No one has to tell him there is a compelling force at work within him. It should be easy to sell him on the idea of defending himself against Satan.

> **HINT:** As soon as your boy understands that satanic influence compounds his problem, give him a copy of DEALING WITH THE DEVIL. He'll read it hungrily, wanting the deliverance it promises. After he has read the book, demonstrate for him how you speak directly to Satan to exercise authority over him in Jesus' Name. Then ask him to try it while you watch. He'll feel a little foolish, but this is serious and he must do it. Shortly he'll have the feel

of the words on his lips. The strangeness will be gone. Then give him a verse to use when Satan tries to sell him on the idea of another "fix." A good one is, "Delight thyself in the Lord and He will give thee the desires of thine heart." Have him use it aloud once in your presence. Only then will you be sure that he is equipped to defend himself against the next attack of Satan.

● I said it would be a battle. He may have to deal with Satan as many as 30 times in the first hour. Satan doesn't want to let go of him. But he only has to break Satan's hold once. If he tastes the flight of Satan one time, the experience will be so exhilarating and encouraging, he'll be ready for the next round. The kick of putting Satan to flight per James 4:7 . . . "Resist the devil and he will flee from you," exceeds that from drugs. If you are faithful to teach your boy to FIGHT in this fashion, you will see him delivered. After all, what power can stand against the blood of Christ?

Then—as soon as he has tasted the Lord's victory over Satan—he should get started witnessing. His next taste should be a sample of the Spirit's power to use him in reaching others. Let him taste that a few times and he won't want oblivion. The kick of moving in the power of the Holy Spirit is so great, one can't let it alone. He gets hooked on it. That's the genuine experience people seek, but Satan offers a counterfeit experience, through drugs. The rapture that people find in drugs is exceeded by that in the Holy Spirit—and it lasts.

> **NOTE:** The kick from drugs is not unlike the thrill of Christ. Drugs, in fact, encroach the realm of spiritual experience. When users talk about "discovering themselves," and getting "beyond themselves," they are using religious terms. They are substituting drug highs for the spiritual high. Getting to "know yourself" has always been a part of vital Christianity. Until a man sees himself as a sinner, he doesn't want a Savior. Until a man sees himself as a "citizen of heaven," he has no desire to live there. Until a man learns how to amass a fortune in Christ, which he can enjoy forever, he will continue seeking wealth in this life. Christianity, not drugs, is the way for people to discover themselves. Wise parents will find a way to present the Christ life as it really is. Then when their youngsters sample its convulsing thrills, the drug world will have nothing to offer them. It is obvious, however, that a parent must also know the thrill of Christ or it would be impossible for him to tell it like it is.

● It won't be easy for you to take a godly stand against an unrepentant son. There will be lots of pleading from different ones for you to relax your position and rescue the lad, even though he persists in his rebellion. Mothers especially can hardly stand to see their children suffer, even when it is of their own making. But hold your ground. You won't be sorry. A firm stand is the best hope of salvaging the boy. Yes, he will have to go through the tenderizer. He may taste the bitter dregs of defiance. But it is necessary. If the seed of repentance is in his heart, suffering will bring it out. If you relax, diluting the consequences of his rebellion, it may delay or even frustrate his repentance.

6 **BE READY FOR REPENTANCE.** While you must stand as firm as God in the matter of discipline, you must also be like God in your readiness to receive a repentant sinner. Somewhere along the downhill road your boy is traveling, he may come to his senses. Finding the price tag too high, he could say . . . "I will return to the house of my father." He knows that means a return to the way of the Lord. When that day comes, you must be ready with God's forgiveness and help. In that moment you can lavish your love on him and do your best to see him delivered from his affliction.

7 **HANDLING THE CONSEQUENCES.** Let's suppose you have been successful in getting down to your boy's level and have determined his real attitude. He is not interested in giving up drugs. Neither does he care about God's will in the matter. Since that is the case, you cannot help him. He must now face the consequences—alone. He is in the same boat as the pregnant daughter who defied her parent's wishes to cling to a boy who scoffed at marriage. When young people rebel against their parents, and the way of the Lord, their parents are NOT to coddle them. They must be allowed to suffer the consequences of their folly. It takes a real man of God to let his son "go to the devil," but it has to be done. That's the way God deals with His erring sons.

Use the warning technique

First make sure your son understands his rebellion is not only against you, but also against God. God has no lips but yours to say this to him. Once he understands this, you are in a position to warn him that God will deal with him severely. The key words, as you recall, are . . .

"I'd hate to be in your shoes."

That puts the technique into operation. After that, your son may reply:

"Yeah, what's going to happen?"

Your answer comes from the Word of God:

"If any man defile the temple of God, him shall God destroy; for the temple of God is holy, which temple ye are" (1 Cor. 3:17).

Then you continue . . .

"You are that temple son. God says so. He says He will destroy anyone who defiles the sanctuary. You may not be aware of it, but your mind is the sanctuary of God. That's where Christians meet with God. In their imaginations they fellowship with Him. And here you are using mind destroying drugs to desecrate God's sanctuary. That puts you in danger of God's discipline. Here, read it for yourself. . ."

> **HINT:** Have your Bible ready. Open to the verse and let your son see those terrifying lines. Likely most Christians gloss over those verses, not knowing what to make of them. The meaning is clear just the same. As your son reads, the Holy Spirit will clinch the truth in his heart. He will sense by the Spirit that he is in danger of God's destroying power. As soon as that truth reaches your son, the Spirit will be in a position to let afflictions come against him. Brace yourself for the worst kind of news. It could come soon, particularly if you ask God to send tragedy into his life. When it comes, thank God immediately. Don't be found expressing anxiety when God deals out discipline. If your boy continues his rebellion, do not be exercised should God take him home. That word destroy means exactly that. Physical death could come to him, though his soul will be saved if he is born-again.

"You mean God would really destroy a person just for using drugs?"

245

"Those are His words, son, not mine. It's been my experience that God does exactly as He says. For that reason, I'd hate to be in your shoes. I'd think twice about this matter, if I were you. I think you'll find it less painful to surrender to the Lord now and let HIM help you kick the habit. If you don't, there's no telling what will become of your life."

NOTE: It should be observed that God Himself does not send the afflictions. He doesn't have to. He merely removes some restraint from Satan and permits him to go to work on the defiant Christian. Normally the blows come gradually, increasing in intensity. As soon as you sound the warning, the Lord is ready to act. There's no point in explaining to your son how God uses Satan to deliver the blows. That would be meaningless at the moment. If and when he comes to his senses, he will then be glad for the explanation. At that time you will be able to explain Satan's part in inspiring his rebellion and triggering his appetite for drugs. He will need the information to understand the fight he has on his hands when he tries to kick the habit.

Will your boy be salvaged? Possibly. But God has no control over it. Your boy has a free will. God allows no one to tamper with it—even Himself. The Lord knows what it will take to bring forth his repentance, if he is inclined that way. But you can be hopeful. Above all you must pray for him. Ask the Holy Spirit to bring to his mind all the Christian training you were able to plant in him before he became involved with drugs.

The time may come—and he could be anywhere, any city, any slum—when he will say to himself, "Living for Christ couldn't be any worse than what I am going through now." The moment his mind makes that turn, the Holy Spirit will be able to draw him back to the Lord. So keep yourself ready to receive him. Should he truly repent, desiring to return to the way of the Lord, he will need the benefit of those things I set forth in the steps above.

Now then, can I count on you to gather up the knowledge of the preceding chapters in this book and bring them to bear on these two questions? I hope so. If you can combine that information with what I have presented here, you will have plenty of know-how for handling two of the worst problems parents have to face. You may not have to deal with a pregnant daughter or addicted son of your own. But you could have a friend or relative who does. Should they come to you for help,

YOU NOW KNOW WHAT TO DO!

YOUR TEEN-AGER UNSAVED?

 A short distance from New York City is a small cemetery. It contains a grave marked by a headstone with only one word written upon it . . .

FORGIVEN!

Apparently the wonder of God's forgiveness meant more to this person than the time he spent on earth. Where there is consciousness of sin, the human soul aches to be forgiven. The same is true of your teen-ager. When he is conscious of sinning against you, he wants you to forgive him. When he is conscious of sinning against God, he wants God to forgive him. God is eager to forgive your teen-age sons and daughters, but someone has to bring His forgiveness to them. Who?

GOD WANTS YOU TO DO IT?

Throughout the book we have assumed your children to be safe in Christ. But that may not be the case at all. We are going to consider that possibility. Were your children already teen-agers when you came to Christ? Then it is possible they have not yet received Christ as Savior. If they do not know the forgiveness of God it is up to you to see that they do.

Does that frighten you? It could. Some parents are afraid to speak to their teens about Christ. They fear they will laugh at them or say "no." Rejection, or even the possibility of it, is terribly threatening. It is powerful enough to silence many parents. Of course, the task would have been very simple had you dealt with your children when they were pre-teens, but you goofed. Now it has to be done during the crisis years. That makes it harder, to be sure. However, once I lay out the steps, you may not consider the task so formidable after all.

But why me?

That's what you want to know, isn't it? Well, dear parent, you are the best person to deal with your youngster. Why? For several reasons:

1. Better than anyone else, you know your boy's thoughts. You know him so well, you can almost tell what he is thinking. You know when he is serious about something and when he isn't. You can read him like a book.

2. To a certain extent you can control the moment he will come to the Lord. Better than anyone else you can pick the right time for him to consider Christ as his Savior. How? By coordinating the soul-winning scene with a time of discipline. You'll see how as we proceed.

3. You are in a position to check his life for evidence that the experience was genuine. Lots of people go through the motions of accepting Jesus as Savior, but many of them are not really saved. There are signs of life which must appear when someone has eternal life. You are in the best place to watch for them. You are the one person who can judge whether his experience was REAL or not.

4. If for some reason you suspect his experience was NOT real, or that he has failed to make a commitment to Christ, you can persue the matter until satisfied he has received the Lord. Inasmuch as the salvation experience can be related to times of forgiveness, you can bring it up as often as discipline is necessary.

PREPARING FOR THE INTERVIEW

Here are some things to consider before we come to the soul-winning interview:

1 The interview should be an EMOTIONAL time. There is no way for you to say to your boy . . .

"Now son, I want to talk to you about the Lord, so let's sit down here together. You need to hear what I have to say."

Why won't that work? It's too academic. It creates a sterile situation with the THEORY of the Christian experience offered in an unemotional scene. People are emotional creatures. Unless their emotions are involved, their whole person is not involved. The result would be an intellectual decision only. Discussions that are purely intellectual, merely tell a lad what he OUGHT to be. Not until his emotions are stirred is it something he WANTS to be. In order for the salvation experience to be genuine, an emotional stirring is necessary.

How do we get it? By adding the presentation of Christ to a forgiveness scene. That is, a child is disciplined, forgiven, and then confronted with the opportunity to receive God's forgiveness. You'll see how that works. We're coming to a scene. We have already seen how discipline provides an emotional experience. Kids are aroused when punished. The forgiveness which follows is also emotional. When we harness all that emotion to the salvation interview, we have great forces at work to secure a genuine decision for Christ.

Recall how I mentioned that preachers and evangelists tell tear jerking stories to provoke response to their messages? You need the same thing to make your salvation interview effective. You've got it when you couple the presentation of Christ with the forgiveness that follows discipline. Where there is no emotion, you end up with a sterile teaching situation— and that is NOT an experience.

2 Be prepared to use a tool. Take up the booklet . . . "Your Biggest Decision" . . . it is a presentation of Christ. See — in the back of this book. — This little tool will do a great deal of the work for you. It will save your having to think of what to say or memorizing a complicated presentation. Most parents are not equipped for that anyway. For the most part you will be reading this booklet to your teen. Then, as you come to the moment of decision, he will participate in the dialogue with you.

> **HINT:** Should the Holy Spirit providentially arrange for a soul-winning class to be conducted at your church about the time this book falls into your hands, be sure to get in on it. Such training would not only enhance you with the skill, your confidence would be greatly intensified. In no way do I count on such a thing happening, but I mention it in case it turns out to be God's plan. The action described in this book assumes you are NOT a trained soul-winner.

3 It will be your custom to be alone with the Lord before a time of discipline. Now that we are adding some soul-winning technique to the program, you could ask the Lord to go before you and prepare your son's heart. Ask Him to bear witness to your words as you speak. Trust Him for it. You don't have to be skilled or polished when you really trust the Holy

Spirit to bear witness to the truth. All that is needed is a way to get the truth into your teen's understanding—with emotion. Once it is there, **no matter how clumsily you have presented it,** the Holy Spirit will do His part.

THE SOUL-WINNING SCENE

Now let's go back to a tender moment in chapter seven. Remember how you had to discipline Jerry when he refused to clean up his room? He went storming out of the house after you slapped him for his impudence. After staying away all day, he returned home to find the family had eaten dinner without him. He was ashamed of himself, but you didn't rush to coddle him. He had to fix his own meal from the refrigerator.

Then, as he was sitting alone at the kitchen table, you joined him. You wanted to forgive him, but as yet he hadn't asked you to. Your hand reached across the table for his.

"Son, do you understand that mother had to discipline you because she loves you? I do you know, very much. And I'm ready to forgive you if you want me to."

"Of course I do, Mom. I really do."

Then came those precious seconds when you forgave your boy. If he was like many boys, he may have gone to your arms and told you he loved you. Such a scene brings us to the right moment for presenting Christ to your son.

> **NOTE:** Can you imagine the emotion present in this scene? This is very necessary. There is nothing artificial about it. His feelings are genuine—and they can be harnessed to your soul-winning plan. Such a moment is more powerful than any generated by an evangelist's story, for it is tied to the dearest of human relationships, i.e., father-son, or mother-son. Is it clearer now what I mean about using the discipline scene for winning your child to Christ? You would be able to use ANY situation where your child needed forgiveness from you, and relate it to the forgiveness of God. Once you have forgiven your boy or girl, you are in a position to speak of God's forgiveness.

"Jerry, do you know why mother was so eager to forgive you?"

"Because you love me?"

"Yes, I do. But it goes beyond that. It feels good to be forgiven when you have done something wrong. I know how you feel at this moment, because I feel the same way when God forgives me. We all want to be forgiven when we've sinned.

You know honey, when you defied mother, you not only sinned against me, you sinned against God. It's not your first sin either, you've sinned against Him many times. We all do. I can't forgive your sins against God. He has to do that. Just as nobody can forgive a debt owed to someone else, neither can I forgive your sins against God. If you want His forgiveness, you have to ask Him just as you asked me."

"Weren't you relieved to have mother forgive you?"

"Yes."

"Wouldn't you like God's forgiveness as well?"

> **HINT:** At this point, look your son squarely in the eye. If he's still in your arms, hold him away from you so that you can look at him face to face. As you say those words . . . "Wouldn't you like God's forgiveness . . . ?" nod your head affirmatively. This will help him to respond. He could be struggling with the answer, but your nodding head will encourage his reply. If your son is not in your arms, make sure you are in front of him, holding both his hands as you ask the question. Even the touch of a mother's

252

hands (or his father's) is something the Spirit can use. If you want to practice this little scene in front of a mirror before trying it with your son, don't be embarrassed to do so. It can help a lot.

"Sure, I guess I would."

He will be a bit cautious. Don't let it alarm you. Satan knows what is coming. He has already started his hindering work. There will be some apprehension on your boy's part, possibly some hesitancy. Don't let it throw you. The Holy Spirit is ready to back you to the limit. Besides, the moves I am giving you are calculated to cancel the devil's effectiveness.

ACTION

From your purse (pocket) or some other convenient place of concealment bring forth the copy of YOUR BIGGEST DECISION. As you do, say to him:

"Here son, sit down beside me. I want to show you something."

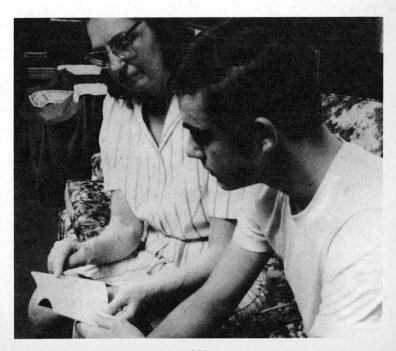

Go ahead and take a seat where he can sit beside you. Be prepared to move right along once you start the plan. If your husband is wise to what is happening, he can answer the phone should it ring. If he is not in on the action, take the phone off the hook before you speak to your boy about forgiveness. If you take what precautions are within your power, the Holy Spirit will take care of those that are not.

"This booklet tells how a person goes about receiving God's forgiveness. It's not very long. I'd like for us to read it together."

NOTE: "Your Biggest Decision" is a 10¢ booklet. It sets forth the mechanics of receiving Christ step by step. The plan is identical to the one found in the author's book, SOUL-WINNING MADE EASY. The difference here is, the one using the plan is NOT a trained soul-winner. It is designed so that a man can lead himself to Christ simply by reading it. Of course, that means, someone else could read it to an unsaved person to bring him to the Lord. This makes it ideal for parents who do not have the soul-winning skill. The decision it secures is just as valid as any secured by a pastor or personal worker in a church situation. Those desiring to acquire the soul-winning skill should order a copy of SOUL-WINNING MADE EASY.

"I'm going to read the words aloud, Jerry, but I want you to read along too."

HINT: Don't wait for Jerry's OK to begin reading. Just start in. You can use your finger to point to the lines where you are reading. Your moving finger keeps his eyes fixed on the place. Thus, he will hear the words in his ears and see them with his eyes. If he stops you for a question, answer it as briefly as possible and then continue. Satan will be working on Jerry's thought processes. Non-related questions could be raised. Defer them by saying, "I'll answer that in a bit," and then move on. Deal with important questions, but with Satan on your trail, you dare not tarry for any long discussions which might move Jerry's mind from the target.

● You continue reading the material until you come to page 21. There you reach the place where Jerry is to participate. About the middle of the page you will find the words . . .

254

"If I came over to your house and knocked at the door and wanted to come in, what would you say?" At this point, ask Jerry to read.

"Jerry will you read the answer, please?" He gets ready to reply:

"I'd say come in."

NOTE: Just that much action helps to prepare Jerry. He has already said, "come in," with his lips. This conditions him to say the same thing to the Lord. Now read the next lines as though you were speaking directly to Jerry. You could even say to him something like this: "You know dear, even though we are reading a booklet, what it is saying is true for you right now. I'll read the statement and you read the answer."

"All right then, the Lord Jesus is waiting to come into your heart right now. Will you open the door? Will you let Him in?" Your finger goes to the next line to guide Jerry to the reply:

"Yes, I will."

NOTE: At this point he is more apt to be reading words than indicating a willingness to open his heart to Jesus. As his mother, you might be able to sense what he is feeling. In any event, the saying of those words conditions him to speak to Jesus. He will be doing that shortly. Now I want you to look at the page again. Find where it says, "Get to a place where you can be alone." See it? Good. Here you substitute the word "we" for "you" so that it now reads . . . "Get to a place where WE can be alone." Do the same thing in the lines below so that it reads . . . "We're alone now." Then you continue reading aloud until you come to the prayer of the open heart. Jerry should read that aloud. Ask him to.

"Honey, we've come to the very words a person says to Jesus in prayer when he is ready to become a Christian and receive God's forgiveness. It is saying such words to the Lord—and meaning them—that brings His forgiveness. That's what the man is doing in the picture there. He is saying these very words to the Lord.

"A second ago you read the words . . . 'Yes, I will.' Do you think those are words you could say to the Lord—and mean them?"

"Yes."

"All right then, I want you to read the prayer out loud if you will."

● Jerry reads the prayer. But of course he is not actually praying. He has yet to speak to the Lord directly. To get him to do that, I now ask you to say something to him that is not written on the pages of your booklet. This is the only part with which you need to familiarize yourself.

"Now dear, I want you to bow your head with me. We're going to talk to the Lord. I am going to pray first. I will use the same words you just read. But I will say them in short phrases. As soon as I finish a phrase you say it after me. But don't say it to me. I want you to picture the Lord as standing before you, waiting for you to say those things to Him. Speak directly to Him. He will hear you."

HINT: Do not wait for Jerry's reply. Let your hand go to his shoulder. Rest it there firmly. That touch will be used by the Spirit to help Him act. Then bow your head without looking at him. Ignore anything he might do. He'll see your bowed head. Ah . . . feel that? The movement of his shoulder tells you his head has dropped in surrender. This is the place he will balk if he is going to. But his head dropped. That tells you his surrender is taking place. He's ready to speak to the Lord. You begin . . .

"Dear Lord Jesus . . . I'm sorry for sinning against You . . . I want Your forgiveness . . . and I want Your life for my own. I give You mine for what it is worth. I here and now . . . open my heart to You. I now put my trust in You . . . as my personal Savior. Amen."

"Oh Jerry, that's wonderful!" (Control your feelings. Be ready to move on.) "But let's read the rest before we stop."

Continue reading until the booklet is finished. A little over a page is left. Then close it. Look Jerry squarely in the eye once more.

"Did you really mean that dear? (Yes.) As far as you are concerned, did you open your heart to Christ? (Yes.) If you honestly and truly invited the Lord into your heart, would you give mother a kiss?"

He does! The joy of the Lord floods your being! It's over.

NOW THEN . . .

Have I answered the question . . . "What's a parent to do?"

If so, all that remains is for you to make sure the Lord's witness accompanies my words. That is vital. I'm satisfied the Holy Spirit has had His way in the preparation of this manual. I KNOW it is His work. But you must also be satisfied it is His work.

> **NOTE:** Nothing is true because I say so. The Word instructs God's people to discern for themselves what is truth and what is error. They are instructed to test EVERY spirit, regardless of how big his name might be in the religious world. No Christian should trust ANY work unless it carries the Spirit's witness to his heart. If the Lord bears witness to what is written here, you may safely receive it. If you do not find His witness in my words, then by all means set the book aside. I depend on the Holy Spirit to keep me from error. But you are obliged to satisfy yourself about the REAL Author of this book.

The Spirit may have witnessed to your heart as you began reading this book. I expect Him to. If He has not yet sealed it, don't lose any time asking Him about it. As you come to the last pages, close your eyes and lift your spirit to the Lord Jesus . . .

"Master, is this plan for me? If so, will you please show me how to apply the truths to my own situation?"

Within seconds—if you are a sensitive Christian—you will have God's indication. A positive witness will come in the form of happy expectation. You will feel grateful to the Lord for answering a need in your home. Your pulse will quicken a bit as you see yourself doing these things with His help. A negative witness from God would take the form of discomfort. You would experience a fearful anxiety about everything you have read. In fact, it might bother you so seriously, you could toss and turn at night.

Of course, there is always some anxiety. That's normal. I am referring to the kind that gives you cold chills. Not the kind that everyone feels when faced with something new and important. A date with the dentist can give you squeamish feelings and be fully in the plan of God. However, if fearful-

257

ness grips your heart, it means God does not want you to use the plan. Do not attempt to use it until such time as you are able to experience peace when you see yourself trying the steps.

WHEN YOU RECEIVE HIS WITNESS

Give praise to the Lord! You can expect your home to be different. You will be different, too. There is no way to install such a program without changes occurring in you, too. You will not be the same person for long. Fathers become more godly as they set the example for their sons. Mothers become sweeter and firmer at the same time. The entire household is affected as the parent's package takes root in lives.

Once you have God's approval, make your commitment quickly. Satan will be watching. As you close the book, say . . . **"Lord, if you'll help me, I'll do it."** That is important. Be sure you mean it. God means it when He gives His witness. Without the Spirit's cooperation, this plan is useless. This is NOT a worldly method for dealing with teens—it is **God's Method.** With any program we undertake in His Name, He says to us . . .

"Without Me ye can do nothing" (John 15:5).

● The Lord is ready to move! You should be too. If the father is truly God's man in the home, then mother and dad should consult together. If he isn't, then mother need only secure the father's permission. Don't wait for your husband to get on the ball. Satan will prod you to procrastinate. That could make you lose years. The kids could be raised and gone by then.

He's sly, that devil. As soon as you have God's approval and are ready to begin, he will send dampening notions to your mind. Usually they begin like this: "Perhaps it would be better to wait until . . . ?" It doesn't matter what is tacked onto the end of that phrase. If it keeps you from getting the plan into operation, it originates with the devil. All he wants is to keep you from installing discipline and truth in your home. He will fight hard to prevent it.

NOTE: Ignore Satan's suggestion and trust the Lord's witness instead. It's much safer. Inasmuch as this book has arrived in your hands at this particular time (that's the way God works), it is better to assume the Master is ready to start the plan now. It is wiser to trust the timing of God than heed the devil's suggestions. If you find yourself procrastinating, it means you have to deal with the devil. There is a special technique for handling this procrastination wile. You'll be amazed at its effectiveness when you read DEALING WITH THE DEVIL. I told you about this skill earlier. You'll find it listed in the back pages.

Satan will also suggest this plan is hard to use. He's right. At no point have I said it would be easy. But then is it easy to watch your children go down the devil's drain? Certainly not. It is agonizing to see them drift from the Lord to the ways of the world. What you are going through now is not exactly painless. Lots of mothers have tear-soaked pillows. They are broken-hearted over the way their kids are turning out. So don't let Satan scare you off with the idea this is going to be tough. You already know that. The Lord asks many things of us which are not easy. But they are surely worth the trouble.

Think back to when you gave birth to your children. Was that so easy? There was pain then, lots of it. But did that keep you from having your babies? Indeed not. You wanted them, pain or no pain. As soon as a mother has her new baby nestled in her bosom, her delight is so great she quickly forgets the pangs of birth. Yet, she could never know such joy, without the agony of travail. So it is with the installation of the nutcracker. It may hurt to squeeze your kids for Christ, but when you see them blossom in His likeness, you are never sorry. When they finally go from your home with the package installed, your soul will be satisfied. You know they are ready for the long haul with the Holy Spirit. You'll be glad you didn't wait a second longer to get started.

SATAN WANTS THOSE CHILDREN

The devil is after your girl. He wants your boy. He has desired them ever since they were born. He was successful in getting you to ignore their spiritual coaching in the pre-teen years. Knowing it is easier to train twigs than straighten trees, he persuaded you to neglect their little spirits during the tender years. Isn't that true? We talked about that early in the book. We used a drawing to set forth the stages of their development.

259

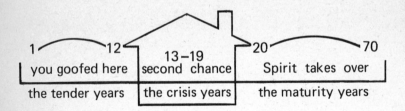

1 12 13-19 20 70
you goofed here | second chance | Spirit takes over
the tender years | the crisis years | the maturity years

So you goofed during the tender years. Now you have a "second chance" during the CRISIS YEARS (13-19). Satan will do his utmost to see that they are not equipped for the years of maturity. He knows what the Holy Spirit can do with a young man or woman who leaves home with the parent's package installed. Such lives are easily molded after the likeness of the Lord. Neither does Satan want your children "laying up treasure in heaven." He wants them to be ashamed at the judgment. Nothing would please him more than to have them enter eternity "flat broke," taking their places with the paupers of paradise.

> **NOTE:** There is not room here to develop the biblical evidence for the fact that we have but one life to live for Christ—and when it is over, only that which is done for Christ will last. Many of God's people are going to be shocked at the judgment. They will say, **"If only we had known it was going to be like this. How differently we would have applied ourselves. We would have served the Lord more faithfully if we knew our futures were being determined by the way we served Him on earth!"** But you know that God has packed His Word with warnings about this very thing. If you are not alert to this truth, order a copy of WHY DIE AS YOU ARE! It will change your outlook on heaven and get you ready to live with Christ in eternity.

JUST ONE LIFE

Christianity is a life. God puts us through one life on earth to get us ready for another—WITH HIM. Haven't you wondered why we were born on earth instead of heaven? If heaven is where God really intends for us to live, why not start us off there? Our time on earth is probationary—a conditioning which gets us ready to live with God. But how can a man get ready for eternity unless he knows what the Lord expects of him? And who will teach him but his parents? This is what God means by raising children . . . "as unto the Lord."

Those fathers and mothers refusing to SHIFT the emphasis from this life to the next one, do terrible damage to their children. Why? It is ETERNAL damage. There is no way to make up for lost opportunities on earth. There are no makeup classes in Christianity, no way to care for failures after we leave this life. We have but one opportunity on earth and that's it.

If your children fail to live for Christ because you neglected to teach them the URGENCY of getting ready for heaven, they will suffer LOSS at the judgment (2 Cor. 5:10). So will you. You will live with your neglect. You will see your children. Your failure will be before your eyes, forever. It will not be easy to look upon a son or daughter who could have blazed brightly for Jesus, but was denied the privilege. How tragic for folks to feel it is more important for their children to succeed in this life rather than the next.

Misplaced ambition

"No George, you can't go over to Billy's house. You haven't finished your homework. Your education has to come first if you expect to get ahead in the world. You don't want to grow up to be a nobody, do you?"

Maybe you didn't use those exact words, but surely you've said something like that. It's a matter of personal pride to want your children to get ahead in this life. We want them to achieve, to excell. What father is proud of a lazy son? What mother delights in an indifferent daughter? Parents harbor expectations for their teens. But honestly, now, isn't that yearning for THIS LIFE only?

Wouldn't you say most fathers and mothers are happy to have their children marry well, adjust to society, and raise nice families—and let it go at that? Most congratulate themselves as successful when they raise children who stay out of trouble, secure good jobs, and make a place for themselves in society. You know they do. Most feel success in the world's eyes is equivalent to success in God's eyes. But is that really the case? Not as far as God is concerned.

A young friend of mine attends a large fundamental Bible College here in Southern California. He recently polled the 1300 or so students to determine their appreciation of heaven. He wanted to know how they weighed life on earth against the next one in heaven. He reported his shocking discovery to me:

> "Doctor Lovett, you wouldn't believe the attitude of these kids. Out of the entire student body I found only two who had any interest in how they might fare in heaven. The rest were interested in dating, getting on with their careers, and how they could make out in this life. After interviewing them all, I got the feeling heaven didn't exist, except as a Bible doctrine. They weren't aware of the Judgment Seat of Christ. It meant nothing to them. Everyone seemed to think we were all equal in Christ and that the judgment was some sort of a celebration banquet!"

Isn't that amazing? Perhaps you're wondering, "Were all of those kids really born again?" As far as we can tell they were. It's that kind of a school. They accept only the cream of evangelical churches. My friend couldn't believe such indifference could exist on this conservative campus. But it does. The devil had done a masterful job in blinding the parents of those kids. Obviously those fathers and mothers never got around to teaching them of the Christian's judgment and how to prepare for it. Of the two who did have some awareness, only one was working to advance himself in the next life.

● Can you guess what my young friend is doing this very day? He's going about that campus challenging every student with this shaking truth . . .

> "The Lord said, 'lay up for yourselves treasures in heaven. . .' Did you know that if you don't, you won't have any when you get there? No one else is going to lay it up for you. Everyone has to earn his own eternal fortune. If he doesn't, he'll enter heaven flat broke and stay that way forever. We have only this one life to accumulate our wealth in the next life."

This young man tours that great campus warning the saints. The Holy Spirit is backing his words. As of now, one professor and more than two dozen students have been awakened and are challenging others. The Lord may use him to bring revival to the whole school. He has taken the main truth from my book WHY DIE AS YOU ARE and printed little charts to show the shortness of this one life compared with the endlessness of eternity. It looks like this:

A CHRISTIAN IS A FOOL TO INVEST HIMSELF IN THIS LIFE WHEN HE IS GOING TO SPEND ETERNITY SOMEPLACE ELSE.

(See time comparisons below.)

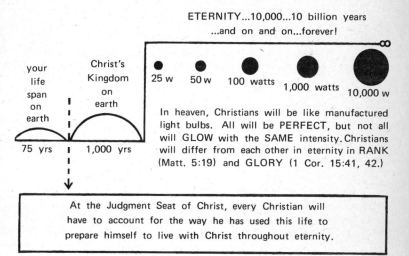

ETERNITY...10,000...10 billion years ...and on and on...forever!

25 w   50 w   100 watts   1,000 watts   10,000 w

your life span on earth

Christ's Kingdom on earth

75 yrs   1,000 yrs

In heaven, Christians will be like manufactured light bulbs. All will be PERFECT, but not all will GLOW with the SAME intensity. Christians will differ from each other in eternity in RANK (Matt. 5:19) and GLORY (1 Cor. 15:41, 42.)

At the Judgment Seat of Christ, every Christian will have to account for the way he has used this life to prepare himself to live with Christ throughout eternity.

NOTE: When we speak of laying up treasures in heaven, we do not mean the accumulation of riches, such as we know on earth. The wealth of heaven is that which means the most to the Lord Jesus —PEOPLE. How do we know? He loved them to the "uttermost," sacrificing His life for them. There is no greater love (John 15:13). People are the wealth of eternity. Therefore, to grow rich in Christ, one must invest himself in others, in Jesus' Name. Witnessing, coaching Christians in godly living, and helping the unfortunate for Jesus' sake, are among the ways to wealth in heaven. The joy of eternity will be the thrill of being surrounded by those you have enriched in the Lord. Poverty in heaven, then, will be the absence of people you have reached or strengthened in Christ.

Remember the Christian mother who was so worried when her son was arrested? He had been riding in a car in which the police found liquor. She protested that a day or so in jail would mar his record. She thought such a black mark would keep him from getting ahead. Where? In this life. She was not thinking of his HEAVENLY record. It meant nothing to her that God could use the experience as divine discipline. His social record meant more to her.

But is she so different from those mothers and fathers who push their youngsters to "get ahead," and "be somebody" in this life. She was a Christian, yet her thinking was the same as all others with worldly ambition. How differently she would have acted had she wanted him to "be somebody" in the NEXT life. A flawless social record won't count for much at the Judgment, but the man who is willing to be a NOBODY for Christ will reign with Him. Here's how Jesus feels about it:

> **"Whosover will come after Me, let him DENY HIMSELF, and take up his cross and follow Me"** (Matt. 16:24).

The life that counts

The Lord does not want your children to leave home without the package installed and working. If they do, His hands are tied. He will not be able to send the pressures and stresses into their lives needed to shape them in His likeness. If they go from your control ignorant of God's way, they will not be able to respond as they should to heaven sent circumstances. It takes a working knowledge of the parent's package to extract the spiritual profit from a trying situation. What a waste if God can't use those next 50 years to fashion your children as He wants.

Have you considered what this failure really means? Your children will spend their next 50 years EXISTING rather than getting ready for heaven. Oh sure, they might end up as statesmen, famed scientists, even wealthy industrialists—but what is that if they are not ready to die? Worldly success for 50 years is not even a flicker when compared with eternity. It would be better for your children to beg in the streets, if that's what it takes to make them a success in God's eyes, than to win the plaudits of the world. Parents who exalt worldly success above eternal success are the blindest of fools.

Before I came to Jesus I lived by the slogan, "time is money." That was because I was desperate to be a millionaire. In reaching for riches, I became a slave to the god, "mammon." I served him faithfully. Money was on my mind continually. I thought of schemes when I went to bed. They were on my mind in the morning. Everything I read or saw related to money. I never did anything or went anywhere that didn't help to advance my financial position.

In those days I was building hotels and motels, selling them as fast as I could get them up. In something like eighteen months my personal fortune reached $868,000.00. I was approaching the million I wanted so badly. But then came Jesus. I was saved by "accident" as some of you know from reading DEALING WITH THE DEVIL. Overnight my desire shifted. I turned from earthly wealth to heavenly treasure. The Lord shifted my ambitions. I still wanted to be a millionaire, but in heaven only. That's why my life is devoted to winning souls and helping people live for Christ. Now you know why I am interested in you.

If your boy is salvaged for Jesus because God put this book in your hands, I will see him in eternity. My reward will be looking upon what God has done through me. However, it won't be as great as yours, for you are the one who must sacrifice to make the plan work. There are many things parents would rather do than take the trouble to install such a plan as this. But I doubt if there is anything that can make them as rich in Christ. Wait until you reach heaven and see what your investment produces in Jerry or Judy. Won't you rejoice to see those children rich in Christ? That will also be my reward. I want to see you there, exultant and beaming over the way your children turned out for Jesus. If enough families make the same sacrifice you do, I could still be a millionaire— in heaven!

THE DIGNITY OF DISCIPLINE

We tend to regard the discipline of our children as a routine matter. But the punishment of a youth is far from routine.

It is one of the noblest things a father or mother can do. But how do you get this across to parents?

One day I dared to do something unusual before my congregation. I whipped a 16 year old girl right there in front of my people. I did it to dramatize the dignity of discipline. It was pre-arranged, of course, for the girl had done nothing wrong. She had agreed to accept the blows for the sake of the lesson I wanted to bring. It came off in a startling way.

I asked the girl to leave her seat in the auditorium and step up to the platform. She stood beside the pulpit. The audience gasped when I brought out a green garden stick and swished it through the air a couple of times. They guessed what was coming, for I had just finished teaching on discipline in the home. I called the stick a "magic wand" for that's how it worked on my two daughters—like magic. Then, with the girl beside me, I took out my black WEDDING MANUAL and began to read aloud. The audience was mystified:

> "Dearly beloved, we are gathered here in the sight of God to administer holy discipline, which is honorable among all men, and therefore, not to be entered into unadvisedly or lightly; but reverently, discreetly, and in the FEAR OF GOD. Into this holy estate, Elaine (the girl's name) comes now to be disciplined."

Mouths fell open all over the auditorium. I closed my black book, asking the audience to bow in prayer.

> "Father, wilt Thou bear witness to the truth that You Yourself punish with pain as I apply the rod to Elaine. Amen."

Then as the audience watched, I had Elaine bend slightly as I prepared to bring the switch down with a few well placed swats. They were not to be painful, for this was a ceremony only. You could have heard a pin drop. People seemed afraid to breathe. They knew the blows were coming, but they weren't prepared for my next words:

> "Elaine, I now punish you in the name of the Father, the Son, and the Holy Spirit. Amen."

266

Then I delivered the lashes. The audience felt them, I'm sure, even though they were mock blows.

● I took that means to demonstrate the dignity of discipline. The punishing of a boy or girl by Christian parents is as solemn as a marriage ceremony. If a preacher can say, "I now baptize you in the name of the Father, Son, and Holy Spirit," a Christian mother or father can do the same when they apply the rod in Jesus' Name. Both events can have a dramatic effect on a person's life. To raise a child in the "discipline of the Lord," is no less sacred than winning a soul, preaching a sermon, or taking communion.

To spank a teen—in the Lord—is a holy event. It would not be out of order for a mother or father to say, **"I now spank you in the Name of the Lord Jesus."** You can see at once what that would do for the parent. There could be no anger, certainly. I recommend that this phrase actually be used when you start the program. That is, when first installing the nutcracker, you should tell the teen he is being chastened in the Lord's Name. After that, do so only as it seems warranted.

● Well, we've come to the end of the book. I'm hoping you have already sensed the Spirit's witness. The plan is God's, not mine. That's why it works. The truths and principles aren't new, they're as old as the Bible itself. The Holy Spirit has merely arranged them to fit our situation today. I trust my part has been clear enough so that you understand how the plan works. If you do, won't you give it a try?

Will you make mistakes? Sure. But the Holy Spirit is ready to use even those, when you are ready to do God's will. There will be times when you think you are not making any progress, but don't give up. The Lord will let you see the harvest if you are faithful.

> "Therefore, my beloved brethren, be ye steadfast, unmoveable, always abounding in the work of the Lord, for as much as ye know that your labor is not in vain, in the Lord" (1 Cor. 15:58).

Now then, instead of letting your trials with your children drive you to your wits end, let them bring you into a new relationship with the Holy Spirit. You will find yourself on a higher spiritual plane the first time you try the plan. Start with the simplest things. Get a few successes under your belt. In time you will have complete victory no matter how tough your children may seem at the start. Finally, when they leave your home with the package installed, you'll hear God's "well done!" in your soul.

When youthful troubles strike your home again, you will not be saying . . . "What's a parent to do?"

NOW YOU KNOW!

OTHER TITLES

mentioned in this book

by C. S. Lovett

PERSONAL

CHRISTIANITY

P. O. Box 157

Baldwin Park, California

91706

(213)   338-7333

WITNESSING COURSE. . .by correspondence

Dr. Lovett serves as your personal coach.

As a man cannot go from the ground to the roof of his house without a ladder, neither can a Christian go from silence to active witnessing without a plan which breaks up the distance into easy steps.

If your children are excited about the witness-life and you want to keep pace, you'll be thrilled with this course. If you are disturbed by their lack of spiritual enthusiasm, here is the know-how that can involve them with the Holy Spirit and set them on fire for Christ! Drop a note to PC saying:

"I've been reading WHAT'S A PARENT TO DO? Please send me the free packet that explains the course and tells how to get started."

PERSONAL CHRISTIANITY IS ..

A local church with a literature ministry.

We are incorporated under the Laws of the State of California as a local church.

We not only provide a worship center for the residents of the area, but exist as a "ministry of helps" [1 Cor 12:28] toward the "Body of Christ."

PC is not affiliated with any denomination, organization or council of churches.

God has given PC the task of producing the spiritual mechanics for personal obedience to the Great Commission and maturity in the Christian life. Unique, know-how tools are developed within the church and made available to God's people everywhere. Our outreach is by means of the U.S. Postal system which makes possible *personal contact* with individuals and churches across the land and throughout the world.

We bear the name PERSONAL CHRISTIANITY because we seek to involve people personally with the Lord Jesus, the Holy Spirit and the Great Commission.

All who care about Christ are welcome to worship with us. Those further interested in "equipping Christians for action," are invited to invest their talents and strengths with ours. We are interested in every Christian and church willing to take a vigorous stand for Christ in these gloomy days.

Brother Lovett was saved through his "accidental" attendance at a minister's conference where he eavesdropped the conversation of a group of nationally known Christian leaders. There he overheard a discussion on the mechanics of salvation. For years he had been under conviction, yet no one troubled to introduce him to Christ. Armed with the necessary insight for the salvation experience, he hurried home to share it with his wife, Marjorie.

Together they knelt and invited Christ to come into their hearts. This delayed salvation experience accounts for his burden to do away with the vague and shadowy notions of Christianity and present the truths of God's Word man to man.

A graduate of California Baptist Theological Seminary, he holds the M.A. and B.D. degrees conferred Magna Cum Laude. He has completed graduate work in Psychology at Los Angeles State College and holds an honorary doctorate from the Protestant Episcopal University in London. He is a retired Air Force Chaplain with the rank of Lt. Colonel.

Pastor Lovett is the author of the books and tools produced by Personal Christianity. Able to express the profound things of God in simple, practical language, his writings strengthen Christians the world over. The advent of his "Soul-Winning Made Easy," has drastically changed evangelism methods in America, while the anti-satan skill offered in his "Dealing with the Devil," has alerted multitudes to their authority over our enemy through Christ. Dr. Lovett's experience as an editor of the Amplified New Testament and a director of the foundation which produced it, prompted him to begin work on the Personal New Testament.